How you could build a

$10 Million

PROPERTY
PORTFOLIO

in just

10 Years

How you could build a
$10 Million
PROPERTY
PORTFOLIO
in just
10 Years

PETER SPANN

HarperCollins*Publishers*

NOTE

All investments carry risks. The views in this book are of a general nature only. You should always seek appropriate professional advice from qualified and licensed advisers before considering borrowing and investing in property.

Please also note: Government requirements concerning borrowing and property investment vary from state to state. Governments may also change these requirements from time to time.

HarperCollins*Publishers*

First published in Australia in 2004
by HarperCollins*Publishers*Australia Pty Limited
ABN 36 009 913 517
A member of the HarperCollins*Publishers* (Australia) Pty Limited Group
www.harpercollins.com.au

Copyright © Peter Spann 2004

The right of Peter Spann to be identified as the moral rights
author of this work has been asserted by him in accordance
with the *Copyright Amendment (Moral Rights) Act 2000* (Cth).

HarperCollins*Publishers*
25 Ryde Road, Pymble, Sydney, NSW 2073, Australia
31 View Road, Glenfield, Auckland 10, New Zealand
77–85 Fulham Palace Road, London, W6 8JB, United Kingdom
2 Bloor St East, 20th floor, Toronto, Ontario M4W 1A8, Canada
10 East 53rd Street, New York NY 10022, USA

ISBN 0 7322 7429 X.

Back cover photos of author by Scott Cameron
Cover design by Louise McGeachie
Typeset by HarperCollins in 11/14 Sabon
Printed and bound in Australia by Griffin Press on 79gsm Bulky Paperback White

5 4   05 06 07 08

Dedicated to dreams — may they come true.
Most of all, though, this book is dedicated to Roy
Spann, my father, who always held the dream that
one day he would own his own home but proved to
me that respect earned is more valuable than any
form of money, and to my mother, Margaret Spann,
who worked tirelessly to give me everything I
needed, wanted and desired in the world.

Contents

Preface

$10 million … Sort of rolls off the tongue well doesn't it?

And for most people it would make a *big* difference to their lives. And for many of you acquiring $10,000,000 in prime property over 10 years is entirely possible. I know, I did it in less time, and I know others who have achieved it and literally hundreds of people who are on their way to achieving it using the strategies you are about to learn in this book.

Depending on how much time, effort, energy and money your are prepared to put into your strategy you could do it in less than 10 years or it might take you longer, but it is an exciting journey to financial freedom, and it is one that is worthwhile starting sooner rather than later. The sooner you start, the sooner you'll get there no matter how long it takes.

No matter where you are now, no matter how much or how little you have, investing in property can be a path to financial freedom for you.

It can produce income, growth in your asset base, and tax breaks unparalleled in any other form of investment. And, if you are smart (the type of 'smart' I intend to give you in this book), and persistent, it can lead you to great wealth.

Take a minute to dream. Go on, right now. Think of something you want that would make your life a little better, easier, more fun but which, for some economic reason, you don't have. Important or frivolous. Doesn't matter. Just one thing.

Property has the potential to deliver it. Not only that, if you were to fill a page of those things — a page of dreams, a page of desires, wants, needs — property has the potential to provide you with all of it.

Take a look at any 'rich list' (often published by *BRW* here in Australia or in the *Forbes*' Rich List in the US) and you will see an extraordinary number of people appear on the list courtesy of their property investments. All are multi-millionaires. Some are billionaires, and some are multi-billionaires.

And in a recent *BRW* survey I read, 74% of them were self-made. They didn't inherit it (so you can stop your search for rich parents who are suddenly inspired to adopt you). They didn't win it (so you can stop hoping for that big Lotto win). And they didn't take forever to get it.

Over 60% got on the list after their 60th birthday, 2% after their 80th (so it's never too late). Over 30% were women and this figure is rapidly climbing. Amazingly, immigrants were four times more likely to make it onto the list than people born here. I presume they came searching for a dream and found it here. Most people were just ordinary people like you and me.

You need a plan, a strategy of investment, some determination, a bit of resilience, a pinch of creative flair, and a tad of luck, and you will be successful with property investment. And not only successful, you could become rich.

Property can bring all the things you want. It can also be the biggest pain in the butt, wearisome, soul-destroying and potentially bankrupting activity that you may ever experience in your life.

What's the difference? Skill. And the belief that you *can* be successful, you *can* do it, and you *can* find financial freedom. And more than anything that's what I wish to impart to you in this book.

The book is in three streams — first, my story on how to be successful at property investment; secondly, tips and traps with investing in property; and thirdly, a whole heap of stories from my clients who have ventured into the ever exciting and mostly profitable area of property investing. They have taken the time to write stories of successful and not so successful forays to encourage you and also to help you avoid their mistakes (most of which they wouldn't have made if they had just stuck to the right strategy in the first place).

Like all my books, this one is not a cover-all, detailed analysis of everything to do with property investing. Other people's books have well and truly dealt with all that and I encourage you to read them (there's a list of good books at the end). What I have found is that most people don't lack detail. In fact, most people have too much — they over-analyse and that prevents them from having a go. Most people lack the motivation and strategy to be successful.

My strategy is a simple one: that there is money to be made by combining natural growth in the market, adding value and taking advantage of the tax environment which encourages investors to be successful.

By reading the stories in this book, you will discover that many people have made fortunes in property by just giving it a go and not being discouraged when they made mistakes.

For some strange reason, adults think that they have to get everything right first go (which is impossible), and either don't start because they keep discovering something else that could go wrong or give up after their first go because they made a few mistakes.

We forget that the process of learning and progressing is by trying something, getting it as close to right as we can in our circumstances and improving our performance next time.

Just because investing involves money, people panic over even minor mistakes. I can't tell you the number of mistakes I have made over the years. And yet, I have made millions in property.

The important thing is that you get in the game. Develop a strategy or just use mine — it seems to have worked for literally thousands of people. Get in the game and keep on playing.

Most people really enjoy property. While some things are tedious, like dealing with bank managers and the occasional tenant who goes psycho, the fun of owning, rejuvenating, earning money from, and generating wealth through property is uniquely suited to most people. It is accessible and exciting in its implications for your future.

I wish you well in your investing and hope one day soon to add you to my success stories!

ENTERING THE GAME

'Daring ideas are like chessmen moved forward; they may be beaten, but they may start a winning game.'

JOHANN WOLFGANG VON GOETHE, 1749–1832

CHAPTER 1

There You'll See It

Climb to the top of a hill overlooking any city in the world and there you'll see it …

Property!

Dusk is my favourite time.

The lights twinkle and the sunset bathes everything in magnificent colours.

Property …

More than anything else, ever, it holds a power over people beyond its mere value in dollars and cents.

Wars have been fought over it.

Empires made and ruined because of it.

People have lived, loved and died for it.

It was there before we existed and will exist long after we have gone.

People have left their countries of birth and travelled long perilous journeys to seek more of it.

Dynasties have been built on it.

Fortunes have been made.

They call it 'the Australian dream' to own a small (or large) piece of it.

They're not making any more of it.

And just about everybody wants a part of it.

That's why it has value, and that's why its value is ever increasing.

We're even buried in it. Ashes to ashes dust to dust.

And all those reasons and more are why you should have some of it too.

And most importantly of all, you can have it.

AND YOU SHOULD.

CHAPTER 2

A Glorious Summer's Day

There it was, gleaming in the sun. Perhaps the most magnificent piece of plastic I had ever seen. I caressed it affectionately in my hand. It was cool to the touch.

I couldn't believe how excited I was to have that 'Sold' sticker in my hand, and, as I walked to the sign to apply it, I was almost overflowing with emotion. Pride, satisfaction, relief, and a twinge of regret were all there, but most of all amazement. In selling this property I had cleared more than $8,000 profit. In just nine weeks!

Now, that may not seem all that amazing to you, but for me, working for $4.72 an hour as a part-time check-out operator, it was more than I had earned in nine months. And more than that, it had been so easy.

My mind was going crazy. Based on this success, I imagined I could repeat the process six times a year — that would be $48,000! At that point in my life, this seemed an extraordinary amount of money. Of course, now I know that it is possible to earn this on one decent deal on one small property. But then ... oh, the riches of it all.

I had visions of a 'luxury' lifestyle already streaming through my mind. Maybe I could afford to rent somewhere half-way decent instead of the condemned house I was sharing with 18 other people. Maybe I could buy a new car instead of the $400 Leyland Marina I was driving. Maybe I could even eat out once in a while, which would make a change from the canned tuna I was currently eating. Oh yes, all these amazing things were filling my mind.

Little did I know that these simple dreams were but a tiny prelude to the lifestyle property would bring me and so many of my friends in just a few short years. But I get ahead of myself.

Encouraged by a Wealthy Friend, who had taken me on as a

kind of mentoring project, I had managed to save up the preposterous sum of $9,000 in just over a year. He had suggested that I start my investing in property because I had shown an interest in it and it was where he had started, but on my budget I couldn't afford much.

The bank, God bless its loving heart, had offered to loan me the princely sum of $20,000, so I had to find a house that had potential and cost less than $30,000 at a time when the average house price where I was living had just exceeded $100,000.

In an early piece of advice, my Wealthy Friend had said, 'Look for new developments, new infrastructure, and lots of "For Sale" signs with "Sold" stickers on them.' So I got in my little $400 car and went for long weekend drives with my Beautiful Friend, looking for this mythical suburb with the 'Sold' stickers and prices I could afford.

Our drives got longer and longer as we went further and further from our home base, but they were lovely afternoons in the beautiful, fine Queensland weather — good company and lots of fun looking inside the houses of people we would never know.

Some suburbs had lots of the 'Sold' stickers but prices were way too high. Other suburbs where I could afford to buy had lots of sad-looking and faded 'For Sale' signs but none of those magical 'Sold' stickers were anywhere to be found.

Every week we would get out the map, find somewhere we hadn't been, and look in the real-estate section of the newspaper to find houses we could look at. And off we'd go.

Of course all the real-estate agents I spoke to thought I was crazy (most still do!). 'You will never find anything for that price around here!' they scoffed. More than one was rude to me. Some were nicer but all a bit condescending.

Week after week it was the same story. Either the suburb was going nowhere or I couldn't afford it. Then one glorious summer's day, my Beautiful Friend suggested we go on a picnic. She made up some sandwiches and a flask of cordial (oh yes, we were living the good life!) and we wandered down to the train station to head off to the only beach we could get to for a $1 train fare — Sandgate, near Brisbane.

For those of you who don't know it, back then it was a rather sleepy little hollow, which, while you could hardly say progress had completely missed it, had hardly been 'discovered' either. And the people who lived there liked it that way. And so did we.

In air-conditioned luxury and in less than half an hour (the trains in Brisbane were superb), we were whisked off to a beach where we were almost alone. There were picnic grounds, safe swimming and young families all enjoying the same simple pleasures my Beautiful Friend and I came to experience.

I would read (usually books on investing that my Wealthy Friend had set for me as tasks) and my Beautiful Friend would paint. When we got hot we'd go for a swim. When we got hungry we'd eat her sandwiches and save up for a big treat — an ice-cream that would run down your hand and give you marvellously sticky fingers.

My Beautiful Friend said the magic words, 'Gee it would be nice to live here.' And all of a sudden I wondered what was happening here with real estate. I wandered off in the direction of town and found a quaint little real-estate office in a cottage at the end of a quiet street.

When I walked in, they looked almost amazed to see me, as if I were the only customer they had seen in a while. I introduced myself and told them that I was looking to invest. The agent, a full-faced and bespectacled but gentle-looking woman, probably in her early sixties, smiled warmly and asked me what I knew about the area.

She explained that house prices in the area had just started taking off, as people in Brisbane realised it was a such short drive away (made easier by the opening of a brand new multi-lane bridge into the town), it was near the beach and had everything you could need or want within a five-minute drive of home. And prices were low.

She flicked through a big, heavy folder with well-worn pages which were obviously the properties she had for sale. She mumbled and occasionally ripped out a page, crushed it with a violence unexpected from somebody who looked like my grandmother, and threw it in her rubbish bin. After what seemed like an eternity she finally stopped.

'Mmm,' she murmured. 'Now, this could be interesting. Would you consider a little rundown two-bedroom cottage in Redcliffe? They're selling it for land value only, but it's on a tiny block, just barely big enough for the house, and of no value to most people. The good news is the price — only $30,000!'

'Would I?' I practically leaped out of the orange vinyl chair. 'When can I see it?'

'OK, let me look in my diary.' The agent made a big show of opening her diary. The dust storm that was created would have impressed some Arabs! She thumbed through a number of pages before obviously coming to the conclusion that she really didn't have anything on at all and said, 'How about right now?' She had a big smile on her face in a way that told me she knew that I knew that she knew she had nothing on.

Minutes later we were in her car on our way to the house. She certainly hadn't oversold it! Rundown was an understatement. Barely uncondemned would be a better description.

The front yard was like a junkyard with 'stock' that consisted of two car wrecks, one with evidence of recent occupation, two or three bed frames, a fridge and an old TV cabinet. The house itself was barely visible above the jungle-like grass. The veranda was closed in with fibro, the roof was crooked and the walls had strange gaps in them. It had a wooden kitchen with a wood-burning stove and lino on the floor, but the strangest thing about it all was the smell. Something between dead cat and three-day old prawn shells!

The agent must have thought the look on my face was dejection, because she said, in a rather Southern Texan style drawl (odd because we were nowhere near Texas and she had not had an accent two minutes ago), 'Well hunny, whada cha all expect?'

However, what was actually showing on my face was determination. 'If this is all I can afford, this will have to do,' I thought. 'Can you offer them $25,000?' I said.

She glared at me with a look that small-minded people give somebody they deem to be less fortunate than them — something between pity and revulsion. 'Are you sure?'

'Oh, I'm quite sure.'

Two days later I was the proud owner of a two-bedroom cottage, just five blocks from the sea, and I had paid the princely sum of just $26,000.

Lesson

Make looking for property a journey of discovery — of new places and lives — and a fun part of your life.

CHAPTER 3

Why Property?

Six months earlier ...

'What do you mean you don't own any property?' questioned my Wealthy Friend, with a tone that implied I was a complete waste of his time.

'But ...' I started, only to be cut off immediately.

'I told you to get a job, and buy a house and *then* check in with me.'

'Well, I got a job and I've managed to save some money, but you've got to remember I'm only a check-out operator!' I replied indignantly.

'Humph,' was the only sound I heard in reply.

Some time ago I had sought the advice of my Wealthy Friend. I was broke; flat, cold motherless broke. I was so broke I couldn't get enough to pay bus fares and had to walk everywhere. Nobody would employ me and I had real trouble making ends meet. Heck. I had real trouble even finding my ends!

The only person I knew who had any money was the father of a girl I had once dated. He was a multi-millionaire many times over and self-made. I had convinced him to take me on as a mentor. He agreed on the one condition: basically, that I would do whatever he said. And it was becoming obvious that already I might have failed.

'Look, I'm sorry,' I began, only to be cut off again.

'Don't be sorry, I'm not angry at you. I'm more angry at myself. It's obvious that I did not give you enough instruction. You seemed to understand, so where did I slip up?'

'I don't think you did.' I said, convinced it had to be me, not my Wealthy Friend.

'OK, let's start at the beginning, did we go through the obvious reasons to buy investment property?'

'Yes, but run them by me again, will you?' I asked, just in case I'd forgotten anything but trying not to sound stupid.

'Well,' my Wealthy Friend started, 'the primary benefit of owning property as an investment is that most people are familiar with it. This means they are starting with something they don't have to learn a whole new language for. They understand how property "works". They know how to buy a house, get finance for the purchase, that you can rent it and get income from it, that houses generally grow in value, and there are some tax benefits. This means they don't struggle with the basics and can get on with refining their techniques.

'Of course, herein lies a problem too ... Because most people are familiar with property, they can also lull themselves into a false sense of security thinking they actually *know* everything they should, that they are some sort of Monday morning expert or something.

'The most important thing when contemplating any investment is to have a strategy, and I am going to give you a sure-fire property strategy that has made me millions.

'Did you know that over half of all property owners earn less than the average wage (about $35,000), and that over the last 140 years property prices have doubled on average every seven to 10 years?'

I shook my head.

'What do you think that means?' quizzed my Wealthy Friend.

'Well, obviously owning a house isn't as hard as I thought.'

'Yes, property investment is *very* accessible. What else?'

'If houses double every 10 years or so, then you've got built-in growth.'

'Yes, well-selected, quality property is growing for you. It earns you money through rent and builds equity that makes you rich. And because everybody needs somewhere to live, property is not subject to the same rapid price fluctuations that shares are. What do you think that means Peter?'

'Lower risk?' I answered tentatively.

'Absolutely. Well, at least compared to other investments like some shares, options, futures and so on. All investments carry risk, some more than others, and of course there can be very risky property investments as well. Or if you acted stupidly or with greed in property, you could add considerable risk, but generally residential property is at the lower end of the risk scale. Does any of this sound familiar to you?'

'Yes it does. I remember that you explained to me that all investments have three essential ingredients that have to be weighed up: Growth — in other words the investment goes up in value over time. Income — in other words the investment produces a cash return in the form of rents, dividends, or interest. And risk — in other words your potential to lose money.

'I also remember that you said it was impossible to get high growth, high income *and* low risk in any one investment.'

'That's right. If you want high growth and high income you will have to accept higher risk. If you want low risk you will have to sacrifice some growth or some income on that investment. These are immutable and unchangeable laws of investing. If you *ever* think you have all three look again. You are missing something.'

'So what approach should I take with property?' I asked.

'Well, that of course depends on your strategy. My strategy is to go for high growth, and low risk, which means that, to a certain degree, I sacrifice income. In Australia, this seems to me to be the obvious strategy because you can claim a tax deduction on any shortfall between income and expenses. It means that I can build my asset base, and therefore my wealth, quickly. And I can always turn those assets into cash later. It is much harder to turn cash into assets.'

'So, you say go for high growth and low risk?'

'Yes. Of course, you do not have to sacrifice too much income to get reasonable growth. It is possible to buy property that will get OK growth and still break even or even make a positive cash return.

'Some people prefer to get a high income from their property and I can understand the attraction — cash flow is always popular — but I think I can make an argument that over the long term growth is better. The average person, using my property investment strategy of "Leapfrogging" can acquire 10 or 12 quality properties over the period of a decade that could be worth about $2 million. Can you remember the average growth rate on residential property?'

'You said is was about 8% per year.'

'That's right, property in Australia, on average since the 1950s has grown about 8% every year.

'That means the growth on our imaginary investor's property portfolio in year 11, would be about $160,000. And all of it belongs to them. If they were to cash that in by selling some property every now and again, or better still, drawing down on that equity, they could live off that growth for the rest of their lives. Only 2% of Australians earn more than $150,000 a year, so that would put our investors in the top 2% of earners in this country.

'To earn $160,000 a year through cash-flow positive property, you'd have to own 61 properties each returning $50 a week! Sure it might be possible to acquire 61 properties in 10 years, I certainly did it, but that took a *lot* of work. Rents will also go up a bit but I am sure you'd agree it is much more plausible that an average person could acquire 10 properties in 10 years than 61?

'And we haven't even taken into consideration that rents double on average over nine years as well, so our investors would probably be earning $100 to $200 a week in net rents as well. That's why I prefer to go for growth, rather than income. I am not saying that going for high income doesn't work — with the right strategy it can, but just that my growth strategy has made me millions of dollars and so that's the strategy I prefer.'

'So why not go for growth *and* income?'

'You're forgetting risk.'

'Yeah, but if you really went for broke and took some high risks you could get rich real quick and then you'd be home free.'

'I understand your impatience, but impatience leads to greed and greed leads to mistakes. My strategy is not a get-rich-quick scheme — it's a get-rich-slow-and-safe strategy. While all wealthy people have taken a big risk at some stage in their lives, a wealthy person would never build in risk to their investment strategy. And you used the words that describe it properly — "going for broke".

Problem is, when most people "go for broke" they end up that way, and you know enough about that for us not to be bothered discussing it.'

I sure did. By this stage I was sick of canned tuna and had well and truly run out of ways to serve it creatively.

'Anyway, it doesn't make sense to be greedy. You can become very wealthy in a relatively short space of time. For most people 10 to 12 years is reasonable enough time in which to become a multi-millionaire. And have fun along the way.

'So have I convinced you of the benefits of owning property yet?'

'Yes.'

'So?'

Lesson

If you want high growth and high income, you have to accept high risk. If you want low risk, you have to sacrifice growth or income on your investment. Investing in residential property in Australia can bring high growth and low risk, and sacrifices to income are compensated by taxation benefits.

NOT VERY TAXING

I am a surgeon in rural Victoria and have been living here for 15 years, now aged 48. My interest in real estate began when we bought the place next door in East Geelong, mainly to control and ultimately evict the tenants. My wife and I spent about $15,000 painting and cleaning it up and rented it out to a vastly improved set of clients. That was about 1998.

Realising that after tax it only cost me about $20 per week it seemed logical to buy some more.

I thought about it, did some research and decided that Brisbane, being the fastest growing major Australian city, provided the best prospects. We booked out three days and flew to Queensland, saw many agents in inner Brisbane and bought a house in Ascot with sensational river/city views for $430,000. I then went to Darwin and bought a townhouse in the inner city for $420,000.

Enter Peter Spann. I did Peter's Melbourne four day course in about October 1999 and started buying everything I could get money for. I now have 21 properties in Melbourne, Sydney, Brisbane, Darwin, Geelong.

My sensational wife is as enthusiastic as me and in her own fantastic detailed way renovates them very well, usually with upmarket appliances and landscaping and we employ gardeners to maintain them.

We usually spend $70,000–$110,000 on the jobs, and have always found that not only does the increased rent more than offset the additional interest, but that we seem to have a zero vacancy rate, and no hassles from the tenants.

I feel that we are poised to buy another five to 10 places in the next 18 months, the limitation now relates to serviceability on my fixed interest-only loans. Most are negative geared. We keep drawing out equity and have a relationship with valuers in all cities. Basically I am paying interest but absolutely no tax.

Brisbane has been our goldmine, and we intend to keep going there in the next 12 months. Our capital gain over the first two to three years has been approximately $2 million.

RUSSELL & MICHELLE

CHAPTER 4

What to Buy, What to Buy?

'But what type of property should I buy?' I asked, wanting to stall and find an excuse for not buying a property that I thought would be good enough for my Wealthy Friend.

'Well, let's give that some thought. What type of property is available apart from houses?'

I gave it some thought ... 'Shops.'

'Right, that's called commercial. Commercial also includes things like offices and warehouses and parking spaces. The upside of commercial is it can get much higher returns then residential property, sometimes two or three times the amount. Plus the tenant is often required to pay all the expenses of owning the property like rates and taxes and so on, which makes the return higher still.'

'What about growth?' I asked.

'The right commercial property can grow very well. Premium commercial property can go through bursts of very high growth, and assets like shopping centres can grow very well too. But you've probably guessed by now what you have to sacrifice if you want to own commercial property ...'

'Low risk?'

'Exactly. During downturns in the business cycle, commercial property, even good commercial property, can be vacant for extended periods of time. And, you're competing with the "big boys". Those big players often offer huge incentives like extended rent-free periods and fit-out allowances, as much as 40% to 50% of the rent. And these incentives are often paid out up front. That means that if you owned an office you wouldn't get any rent for months or years, plus you would have to pay for the tenant's fit-out costs, which can be huge.

'And,' my Wealthy Friend went on, 'these incentives are paid out during the down times to get tenants, just when it's the worst possible environment for business, so you have the double-edged sword of watching your tenant go broke just as they were about to start paying the rent. Remember 80% of businesses go broke in their first five years. You don't have nearly that same risk with somebody renting a house.

'On top of that, in order to rent commercial property it has to be refurbished regularly. Good for the depreciation allowances, not so good for the cash flow.'

'So do you own any commercial property?' I asked.

'Yes, but not before I built up a multi-million-dollar residential property portfolio and had substantial income. Really successful commercial property investment is beyond most people until they have substantial income. You might be lucky and do well, but personally I have never left my wealth up to luck.

I would much prefer to be investing with the professionals than competing with them. If I want commercial property, I put my funds in well-managed commercial property trusts.'

COMMERCIAL PROPERTY TRUSTS

Most large-scale commercial property is managed through trusts. Money is raised by selling units in the trust to investors. A management company is appointed, and they get a cut of the action, usually a percentage of the returns plus a percentage of the capital growth. The unit holders in the trust get all of the rental return after expenses and any of the capital growth in the assets. Even after all the costs and expenses are taken out (not usually many because with commercial property the tenants pay for most of these) and the manager takes their cut, the returns can range between 8% and 18% per annum, with an average of about 12%. And because of the trust structure those returns often come fully tax-paid. So both the trust and the management company can be worthwhile investing in.

It's important if you are going to invest in property trusts that you go big and look for diversity — that way any cash flow hiccups brought on by vacancy are smoothed out. Look for quality of asset and manager.

A well-run commercial property trust can generate a positive cash flow, but more exciting, it can fund any cash-flow negative amounts from investing in prime property. For example, if you were to purchase a $200,000 investment property for the cost of $35 per week (a prospect we will explore in chapter 21), it would take an additional investment of just $15,000 in a diversified range of commercial property trusts averaging 12% yield per annum to fully fund that negative cash flow.

And the capital growth can be quite good as well. When I first bought into a trust at the beginning of 1997 shares were $4 each. Now (at the time of writing) they are about $15. That's a 375% increase in just six years. Pretty exciting!

'OK, that's put me off commercial property for a while. Um, what about a factory or warehouse? I heard they could be good.'

'Industrial property — very similar to commercial in a way. The good thing with industrial property is that it is usually cheap because that is the only way the land can be used. That's why the return is high. Less maintenance than commercial but industrial property can still be vacant for extended periods of time and so there's the risk. Because it is low-grade land, there is very little opportunity for growth unless zoning changes and little opportunity to value add. So, personally, I stay away from it.'

'OK, well how about a nice beach house? Wealthy people always seem to have holiday homes,' I piped up, imagining sunning myself on the balcony.

'Good for recreation, not so good for investment. Prices fluctuate widely in holiday areas, so do rentals. When you do rent the property during peak times the prices are high, but generally the properties can remain vacant for long periods during the quiet times. And who wants to own a holiday home when the only time you can use it is when nobody wants to? So you have a choice of either renting the property when you can for the high rents and not using it yourself, or taking the peak periods and losing your shirt during the other times.

'Also because of the high wear and tear, you are constantly replacing the furniture and fittings. Again, good for the depreciation, lousy for the cash flow.'

'But,' I replied quickly, thinking I had caught him this time, 'I know *you* own a beach house. I've been there with your daughter.'

He gave me a look that reminded me a young man should never bring up things he does with another man's daughter. 'Yes, that's true, but I see it as an indulgence, not an investment, so another thing that comes after you're rich, not before. There are lots of very nice hotels in the world for holidays and they will cost you a *lot* less than a holiday home.'

'Well, you own a farm too, so what about farms?'

'Ah, yes, I am a Queen St farmer. But again, just a place to put my horses. People own rural properties for the love of it, because it's in their blood. Only the biggest and the best can make money out of rural pursuits these days. I do it as a hobby. You've got to admire farmers in this country; after all, their efforts built this nation, but in terms of investment, farms are bull! And they cost a fortune — owning a farm is a good way to get poor — not a good way to get rich!'

'So that counts out farms, but what about "normal" land. I was told that only land goes up in value, so doesn't it make sense to buy land and not bother with tenants?'

'Maybe, but it's those tenants who pay your bills. Land doesn't earn anything. Which means no income and no tax deductions. You could own two or three houses for the same repayments on land.'

'OK, so that leaves houses and flats.'

'Yes, for most people residential property offers the best mix of return, growth and low risk. That's how I built my fortune and if you look at my wealthy colleagues, most of them have substantial portfolios of residential property.'

'Right, so commercial has high returns but is too risky, industrial doesn't offer much scope to value add, hotels are better than holiday homes until you are rich, and farms make you poor. So residential offers the best bet.'

'Spot on — you learn quickly.'

'But should I buy houses or apartments?'

'Good question. Well, remember we said that it is the land that goes up in value? Well, that would indicate that houses and townhouses would have the best growth and this is true. But there are other factors that can come into it as well.

'Firstly, many people starting off can't afford to buy a house, especially in the major capitals where it is best to buy, so their only option is to buy an apartment.'

'And,' I quickly butted in trying to score some points, 'I've heard you say many times that you've gotta be in it to win it. So that would mean you're better off buying something you can afford now that waiting around for the perfect house that you might be able to afford later?'

'Exactly. Better to be in the game than out of it. That way you are at least making money. Statistics are on the side of owners of apartments as well, because about 70% of all renters rent apartments. And rental returns can be high for a good-quality apartment in the right area. In areas where land is very scarce, for example on Sydney Harbour, apartments can grow at the same rate as houses.'

'So, if you can afford a good house buy a good house; otherwise get into the game and buy the best apartment you can afford?'

'Right. More important than any of that, though, is to remember the primary rule of buying investment property, and that is to buy what is going to suit the tenants in the area. This is *so* obvious that many people overlook it. They are searching for a property and suddenly they find a "bargain". Casting aside all common sense they buy it to find it's not what the tenants who want to live in that area want to live in and they can't rent it. They have to lower and lower the rent to get a tenant, and so eventually it's not looking like much of a bargain after all, and then when they come to sell it, they find there's little capital growth.'

'I once had a somebody come to ask me my advice on why they were unable to rent a house they owned in Paddington, Sydney. Now, you know Paddington, what type of tenant rents in that area?'

'Trendy types, yuppies and dinks, the "pink" market.'

'So what do you think they would want to rent?'

'Well, some would want those terrace houses, but probably done up so they could show them off. My guess is something straight out of the pages of *Belle* magazine or something cutesy wootsy.'

'Yes, they are prepared to sacrifice size for style. This person said they had bought a great place and fully renovated it, but couldn't get a tenant even though they had dropped the rent by half. "But it was such a bargain," they said! Turns out they had, indeed, bought the red-brick modern house and renovated it suburban style. Nobody wanted it. And there was nothing I could suggest. That house would have rented for a tidy sum in a family suburb, but in this suburb it was a dog.

'If you were to buy such a house in a young, trendy inner-city area, you probably wouldn't be able to rent it out. If you were to buy a flat in a family suburb, same deal. The top rule of buying investment property is buy what suits the tenant. If you can't afford that, find another suburb.'

'OK, so residential it is, and look for what the tenants want to rent.'

'So, what's holding you back now?'

Lesson

Investment in residential property offers an attractive combination of lower risk, higher growth and higher income than other sorts of property.

RETIREES MAKE GOOD

We are retired, living in Perth, and were looking at our life savings dwindling rapidly as the bills kept coming in. The big fund managers had all lost money for us, so I said one day 'I can lose money by myself without paying someone else to do it for me', then proceeded to do just that, by building home units to sell to other people. As Peter correctly stated at the 'Money Magic' seminar, the only people who make money on that are the builders.

In May–June 2000, we attended 'Welcome to Wealth', and 'Money Magic'. Before the seminar was over, we were looking for suitable properties, and bought three small apartments in the first week, using our remaining cash. Within two months, we had bought eight apartments, followed later by another three. One was bought effectively for nothing by selling our unproductive beach house and turning the proceeds into a productive apartment. We chose the inner Perth suburb of Maylands for our investment, with 11 units spread over four buildings. They are all managed by our agents. Vacancy is very low — about 5%, as we chose moderate rentals to achieve customer satisfaction.

There was an unexpected problem early in the exercise when we found that the banks would not lend on units below 50 square metres in area, but our mortgage broker overcame this by lumping five units into one proposal, and now we have all 11 units financed this way. In all we outlaid about $170,000 to buy units worth about $480,000, plus our home at $160,000, for a personal net worth of $420,000. Two years later, we have property worth $1,040,000, for a personal net worth of $740,000.

Our units are only slightly cash-flow positive, meaning that we still have to watch our expenses. I have learned to do monthly budgets, quarterly GST returns, and annual summaries using a spreadsheet. Everything taught by Peter has worked out as advertised or better. Our original prognosis was to take about six years to reach our first million, but it will be more like three to four years at the present rate.

ERIC & VAL, PERTH, WA

CHAPTER 5

Where I Discover You <u>Can</u> Make a Mountain from a Molehill

I had wanted to say, 'Sure, I get the benefits but I just don't get how they apply to me,' but I didn't want to sound negative. Instead I said, 'Well, I have been taking all the work the supermarket will give me, I've been living for free in a friend's house which has been condemned, and I have only eaten canned tuna for months. I've put every spare cent I could into a savings account but I've only managed to save $9,671.12 exactly and that includes interest.'

'OK, that's great, so why don't you own a house?'

'Um,' I started hesitantly, beginning to wonder whether it was me or my Wealthy Friend who was obviously missing the point big time, 'Nobody is going to sell me a house for $10,000!'

'Ahh, now I see,' retorted my Wealthy Friend. 'You've got Small Man's Syndrome.'

'What?!?' I said, now quite offended.

'You're thinking small. People with a limited mindset always believe that what they have is never enough to start. You can become rich in property for just $35 a week, but most people think small, so they don't think it's possible. Therefore they never start.'

'I see ...' I said, hoping this would get better.

'I call it Small Man's Syndrome. It's why people buy lottery tickets. They think that the only way to "make it" is to win a million dollars, but how many people win the lottery? And the ironic thing is that most people who do win the lottery end up worse than before they won. Some even end up bankrupt. And you know what excuse they give?'

'No.'

'A million wasn't enough! Can you imagine that? Somebody drops a million dollars or more in their lap and they think they don't have enough to be rich. Funny thing is, most of these people were earning less than the interest on their winnings would have brought them if they'd just deposited them into a normal savings account in a bank. They could retire forever on their winnings but because of small-minded thinking they blow it all.'

'Right, but what's that got to do with me buying a house?'

'You think $10,000 is not enough. $10,000 is *more* than enough. You can buy a whole house for that in some parts of the country.'

Even though I didn't believe him at the time, many years later I read a newspaper article about a government first-home owners' grant of $7,000. Most people used it as a small part or all of their deposit, but more than two dozen people had used it to purchase a house outright! And judging by the photos, those places weren't dumps either.

He was right of course, I had been thinking small. It's an easy enough trap to fall into. Surrounded by negativity I found it hard to believe I could do anything at all let alone become a property millionaire.

People laughed at me when I told them about my efforts to save money. Mocked me for living in the rundown house where there was no electricity. Jested when they opened my cupboards and all they saw was tuna, and my car, oh, what a bomb it was! People I didn't even know laughed when they saw that car. How could I ever succeed when I had all this working against me?

'You need to meet my friend Glenda,' said my Wealthy Friend. 'She works at the local pharmacy. She'll have the right prescription to cure you of Small Man's Disease. Come on, it's almost lunchtime. I'll drop you off.'

Lesson

Don't let your destiny reside in things outside yourself. Stop waiting for something to happen; just do it.

BETTER THAN EXAMS

I attended your property seminar when I was 17 and half-way through my VCE. I had always been good with money and had saved up a decent amount by this time, as well as having some in shares from when I was 14, and working at the local supermarket earning a whopping $8 per hour.

Two and a half weeks after my 18th birthday I bought my first property for $70,000 in Brooklyn, Melbourne. I was able to do this by having a good deposit in cash. To help with the income, my mother went as a joint borrower, so on paper it looked as if mum was helping to pay for the loan, however, I was doing it all on my own.

Before settlement a unit in the same block sold for $85,000. So the next day I made some calls and arranged for a valuation. The valuation came back at $80,000 unrenovated. In the next few days after I had received the valuation another unit in the same block came up for sale. Three weeks after my first property had settled I purchased this second property which I got for $85,000 at 90% finance. So while all my friends were preparing for exams during lunch breaks and free periods I was off on appointments with my lending manager and conveyancer, dressed in my school clothes, getting strange looks from other workers, asking me if I was lost. Six months down the track, after the second property had settled and the tenant moved out, I was able to get in there and renovate, which I did for around $3,500. I received a valuation for $100,000. I couldn't believe it. I tell my friends that it is printing money the legal way. Both properties were bought while I was still in year 12 (which I completed) and working only part-time. My goal is to be a millionaire by my 23rd birthday and financially independent/retired by 25.

MICHAEL, SUNBURY, VIC

CHAPTER 6

A Trip to the Pharmacy

I felt quite odd riding in my Wealthy Friend's Rolls-Royce. It was a metallic gold colour, and these were the times when a Rolls-Royce commanded respect, a *lot* of respect. People looked at the car.

It was a busy time of day so my Wealthy Friend didn't park, he just dropped me at the kerb and pointed me in the direction of the pharmacy.

I walked in unannounced. I identified Glenda, a pleasant woman about mid-forties and asked one of the staff if I could speak with her. They were a bit busy so I just stood and waited.

My Wealthy Friend insisted that I visit him wearing a suit and a new tie every time — I wondered how I was supposed to save when I was spending all this money on clothing, but he just repeated, 'The clothes are the mark of a man — you can never hope to be successful if you don't at least look the part.' I must have looked very official in my suit because a woman approached me with a concerned look on her face, grabbed me by the arm, and dragged me behind a shelf of products.

Just as it became apparent she was about to actually *show* me the rash she was muttering about, but before I had the chance to explain to her that I wasn't a pharmacist, I was rescued by Glenda. After swiftly attending to the customer's needs she returned. 'Now, how can I help you?' she asked with a smile on her face.

'My friend told me you could help me with property?'

'Shh,' she hushed, holding a finger to her lips. 'Somebody might hear you.' She pushed me even further into the shelf. 'We can't talk here,' she said, looking around quickly to check that nobody was within earshot and lowering her voice to a whisper. 'I'll meet you in the cafe opposite in 10 minutes.' And then she walked away quickly to serve another customer with a loud, 'Thanks, and have a great day!'

This struck me as seriously odd behaviour. Suddenly I thought I might be in the middle of a conspiracy. Maybe she had some property that had fallen off the back of a truck she could sell me cheap. Maybe that was my Wealthy Friend's secret? I felt as though I should be wearing a cap and carnation, smoking a cigar (or a least sucking a lolly), and talking in a drawn-out accent, it was all so clandestine.

Glenda finally walked into the cafe, ordered a sandwich at the counter, and sat down in the booth opposite me. 'Sorry about all that,' she said, now obviously relieved to be away from work. 'Nobody in there knows about my little property dealings, and I'd prefer to keep it that way. I'd hate them to think I was rich or something!'

I felt like asking, 'So are you rich?' but thought discretion might be better. 'So, you know my Wealthy Friend?' I asked instead.

'Oh yes, he's my Wealthy Friend too.'

I must have looked shocked. 'Surely you didn't think you were his only little project did you?' she asked with a little laugh that made me feel more like I was in a special club than I was being chastised.

'Well,' I said, 'actually I did.'

'You've got a lot to learn then! You must be at the very beginning. Am I the first you've talked to?'

I nodded.

'Well, let me start at my beginning then. I met our Wealthy Friend when he came into the pharmacy to get some medicine for his wife. She had an ongoing illness and he would personally come in about once a fortnight to have a prescription filled. "Far too important to leave to an assistant," he would say. But I secretly suspect he liked getting out of the office.

'We got to talking. Of course, I couldn't help but notice the Rolls-Royce and complimented him on it. Then I somehow let it slip that, while I liked working in the pharmacy, I never felt financially secure. I had worked for quite some time and I was doing well, but I knew that I'd not have enough to live from if ever

I had to quit work, and I felt I had to go back to work far too soon after having my son. I wanted to spend more time with him growing up but we needed the money.

'He asked me if I would be interested in investing. At first I thought he had something to sell or had a hot tip, but I was intrigued and he seemed a nice enough fellow so I agreed to meet him here and have some lunch together. I remember it distinctly. We sat in this very booth and I had to pay!'

We both laughed because I had become quite accustomed to 'shouting' my Wealthy Friend lunch. They were always modest bills, but I had begun to wonder if that's how he became rich, by never having to pay for anything!

'I'm sure you know what we talked about,' she went on. 'The Key to Wealth, The Key to Success, the Secrets of Money Magnetism. I was determined to apply them but wasn't really sure of how they applied to me. I tried to discuss them with my husband and the people at work, but they were all either not interested, thought it was a hoax, or just plain discouraging. But something told me that our Wealthy Friend was for real, so I persisted.'

I knew what Glenda meant. I was amazed at people's attitude to wealth. Before I started with the projects my Wealthy Friend had set me I had thought everybody wanted to be rich. But I had soon discovered that most people weren't prepared to make the (small) effort necessary to become rich and quickly dismissed those who tried to so as not to prove themselves wrong.

Glenda resumed, 'Something held me back though. It was obvious to me that what our Wealthy Friend was saying made sense, but somehow I just couldn't get over the mental barrier of starting. I had managed to save up about $9,000 from my pay and put it aside in a term deposit in the bank as my little nest egg for a rainy day. I couldn't see how it would get me far, but at least I *knew* I had some money if I ever needed it.

'Then one Saturday I got a call from our Wealthy Friend. He wanted to know if I had anything on and if I didn't would I like to go to an auction with him? If nothing else I thought I'd at least get my first ride in a Rolls-Royce. Imagine my disappointment when he pulled up in a daggy old ute!'

Now, there was something I didn't know. I had only ever seen the Rolls-Royce.

'When we got to the house I was horrified. Really, fixer-upper was too nice a description, but our Wealthy Friend was fascinated and went over everything with me saying repeatedly how much money could be made on the house. Personally, I couldn't see it. All I could see was mess and peeling paint and smelly old carpet, but he seemed so intent I listened anyway.

'Well, the auctioneer started and when the bidding was done our Wealthy Friend had bought the house for just under $80,000. I had no idea if he had bought well or had been ripped off but he was obviously pleased with himself.

'He drove me home and asked what I thought of the house and I didn't know what to say, so I just said, "It seemed nice."

'"It could have been yours," he said, "The money you have saved would have been more than enough as the deposit and any bank would have been happy to loan you the rest." I tried not to look horrified. He just smiled and said nothing else.

'Well, I didn't see him for about three months and I thought I had done something wrong at the auction, so when he called and invited me to another auction I was quite surprised and accepted the invitation straight away.

'"I don't usually do this" he said, as soon as I got in the car, "But I thought it might be the easiest way to illustrate my point." Well, imagine my surprise when we pulled up in front of the same house that he had bought three months before, except it wasn't the same house, well not exactly … It had been transformed!

'Gone was the forest of weeds and noxious plants at the front — replaced by fresh turf and some bark-surrounded trees. A fresh coat of paint inside and out had the place sparkling. The smelly old green shag pile was now gleaming polished wooden floors, and the kitchen and bathroom looked totally new but somehow looked familiar, but I didn't have time to suss out why before our Wealthy Friend dragged me out the front to where the auction was about to begin.

'There were about 20 people gathered on the lawn, and as the auctioneer took his first bid everybody must have heard me gasp, as they all turned around and looked at me. Embarrassed, I covered my mouth but was still amazed that the *first* bid was over $100,000.

'Of course, our Wealthy Friend just stood there and smiled and hardly seemed impressed when the house finally sold for $127,000. "Thought I'd get more," was all he had to say. "That's why I never do this normally."

'"Do what?" I had to ask.

'"Sell," he said. "Anyway, I hope it proves my point: that you can make money with even $9,000. Hard to believe we're in the middle of a recession isn't it?" I didn't even know what the word recession meant!

'Well, did he prove his point! I was so excited I immediately made up my mind to buy my first property. It was not quite as tatty as the house our Wealthy Friend had bought but still needed some work, and I could buy it for $75,000. When I had finished fixing it up, I asked the bank to revalue it. They said it would be worth $110,000. $35,000 less expenses in three months! Well, I almost couldn't believe it.

'After that, property buying became like an addiction. Eight years later I own nine properties, and after paying all the bills each month, I make three times more from the net rents than I do by working in the pharmacy — even since my promotion to manager! And the most exciting thing is that while they have been paying for themselves they have also been growing in value.

'If I take off my loans from what the properties are worth, I'd have to be at least $900,000 in the clear. I might even just be a millionaire. *And*, nobody apart from my husband and son know! After all the negativity, I decided I'd only tell people like you — people who have already decided they genuinely want to know.'

'Wow,' I said, obviously impressed, 'All that with just $9,000 to start?'

'Yep. I can't believe more people aren't doing it. Sure I had some ups and downs, but now I know that I am financially secure, and today I'm working because I want to, not because I have to.'

'Gee, but how did you buy all those houses?'

'Ah, well I'd love to answer that but I have to get back to work. You've heard enough from me anyway. I think you'd better talk to our Wealthy Friend again! Good to talk with you. Oh, and it's your shout for lunch! Good luck.'

Lesson

Don't be discouraged by people who don't want to know about wealth. Learn from those who are wealthy.

NEVER GOING TO LOSE

I bought a four-bedroom postwar home in Oxley, Queensland in November 2000 for $148,500. We live in that house and have spent about $30,000 on renovations. The property is now valued at around $275,000 — so I am very happy with the equity I have gained in it.

My partner and I have both purchased units in the same block in Auchenflower. The block is about 40 years old and not much from the outside, but it has large bedrooms, is close to the railway station and to Milton Rd (without the noise), and is only 3 kilometres from the city. We each paid $125,000 and get $190 per week rent. On our interest-only loans the repayments total only $660 per month, rates are around $1,300 a year, so it is completely cash-flow positive. This is brilliant for me as I am about to have my first child and will not have an income for some time. I don't know that I am going to get a huge amount of capital growth quickly on the property, but Auchenflower is a good area, so I'm never going to lose.

JANET, OXLEY, QLD

CHAPTER 7

The Three Benefits of the Key to Wealth

'So, did you enjoy your meeting with Glenda?' asked my Wealthy Friend.

'I sure did. Imagine becoming a millionaire with just $9,000 to start with. I'm now so excited about beginning I could hardly wait to see you again.'

'Ah, I can tell the benefits of The Key to Wealth are starting to kick in with you.'

'What benefits?' I asked, still thinking about the million dollars.

'Well, do you remember the Key to Wealth?'[1]

I had to think. Even though my Wealthy Friend had fully explained all the mindset concepts in his tutoring, they were still only new to me. 'The Key to Wealth is knowledge applied.'

'And what does that mean?' he asked.

'The way I understand it is people are paid for what they know. The more you know the more you can earn. But not in a theoretical sense, because lots of people who know lots aren't paid much or at least they don't fulfil their potential. If you gain knowledge and have something to apply it to, and then actually apply it, you can become wealthy.'

'Good. That's a principle that has been talked about by successful and wealthy people since the beginning of time — the power of ideas. But there's more to it than that isn't there?'

'Yes. You told me that knowledge will protect me from being ripped off and that every problem that I have can be solved by gaining knowledge. I found a quote from Albert Einstein that illustrates what you were saying. He said, "The significant problems that we have today cannot be solved at the same level of thinking we had when we created them."'

'Great, and what do you think he meant by that?'

'Well, I think he meant that all our problems are self-created. That somehow we either made them up or at least contributed to them because of the way we think. I know that before I met you I had a lot of negativity. I still do I guess, but I know that negativity clouded my mind and limited my options. I thought I couldn't achieve much. Even though I have managed to save money, I didn't think I could start investing because I didn't know that I had enough. The new knowledge that Glenda gave me has actually solved my problem. I thought I didn't have enough to start so I did nothing. Now that I know I can start, I will.'

'Excellent, now you're cottoning on. Once you understand the Key to Wealth you start to experience its benefits. The first benefit is that knowledge applied solves problems.'

'So you mean every time I have a problem I just have to get more knowledge?'

'Yes, but remember knowledge itself is only partially useful. It is always better to find somebody who has already solved the problem you have or a similar one and seek their knowledge. Remember even though society is changing rapidly, the same issues and problems we face have been faced by many others, and some of these people have found their own solutions to them.

'People think they are alone. People think that they are the only person with a particular problem. This is why support groups are so popular. People are relieved to find others who share the same issue to overcome. The problem with support groups is when nobody there has actually solved the problem shared by everybody.

'If you look at wealth creation, there have been hundreds of books written on the topic. The more you read, the more discerning you will become and the less likely you are to be ripped off by the unscrupulous, unreliable or just plain incompetent. And there's the second benefit of the Key to Wealth: applied knowledge creates wisdom. And when you are wise you can become self-guided.

'Many people are trapped because they think they don't know enough to get started so they seek out advisers. While some may be worthwhile, many of these advisers have not actually done what is needed to become successful. I'm sure you've heard the stories of financial advisers who are having trouble making ends meet.

'While all successful people have advisers, each individual is finally responsible for their actions, and the only way they can judge what is good for them is through self-guidance. Self-guidance through wisdom creates a sense of security and self-esteem. And when you have high self-esteem you make good decisions and feel good about them.

'Can you guess what the third benefit of the Key to Wealth is?'

'I'm not sure, but since I met you and I have been reading, and certainly since I met Glenda, I am feeling much happier and more positive.'

'Excellent! And that's the third benefit — applied knowledge acts as a motivator. And unlike most motivation these days which is just hype, this motivation lasts. Applied knowledge opens up a new future for you. And that future can be anything you want. I have found in my life that when I lack motivation I seek knowledge. Every time I learn something new that I can apply to my life, I get a boost in motivation. This allows me to do more. When I actually apply that knowledge, I get skill. This allows me to be more consistent. The more consistent I am, the more successful I become. Real internal motivation leads to success.'

'So let me check if I've got this right. The Key to Wealth is knowledge applied, and there are three benefits to this key:

- Knowledge applied solves all problems.
- Knowledge applied creates wisdom, which leads to self-guidance.
- Knowledge applied motivates.

'Wow, I'm starting to understand how powerful the Key to Wealth is. That means that as long as I can identify what's wrong I can solve all my problems myself *and* build my self-esteem *and* motivate myself.

'Absolutely, so are you ready to go and buy that house?'

'No.'

'OK, so what's missing?'

'Where do I buy? What do I buy? How much do I pay? Just trivial things like that!' I replied.

'Time to go back to school I think,' he said with a smile.

Lesson

Knowledge applied is the key to wealth. It also creates wisdom and motivates. Remember you are not the first person to face your problem. Use other people's solutions and become discerning and motivated by your own experience.

MUM'S THE WORD

I am a mum at home with two kids and I was really looking for another opportunity in my life. Your seminars really grabbed me, so I got started straight away. I had no business sense whatsoever so the learning curve was very steep, but I thought I had enough equity to allow for some errors so I pressed on. I revalued our home and drew down $140,000 from a line of credit. I purchased my first property in August 2001 at a cost of $276,000, spent $25,000 on the renovation and had it revalued at $335,000 four weeks later. Property number two was purchased in December 2001 and cost $265,000 plus a renovation of $25,000, revalued at $360,000 four weeks later. Wow! It was working. Property three I purchased in February 2002 for $310,000, spent $12,000 on the renovation, and had it revalued at $390,000.

All were rented easily because I decided not to be greedy with the rent, just get them rented. I had many hiccups, such as builders that were crap, builders that left half-way through jobs, builders having affairs with bimbos on the job — actually builders, far more than any other trade, were the major hassle. I found the bank hard too. At first I told them too much and generally wasn't sure what I was doing. Some of the loans are principal and interest and I want to change them to interest-only, but that will come.

Everyday when I turn on my mobile phone I see the message 'One foot in front of the other' and I smile because I am beginning to realise that all of this business stuff that I knew so little about is just basically silly words that sound hard. And you know, I sit back and think, 'Hey, I now have four houses, that was certainly worth any of the hassles I incurred.'

CAROLINE, QLD

CHAPTER 8

The Old School Yard

When my Wealthy Friend said time to go back to school I didn't think he meant literally, but a few days later I found myself at his youngest daughter's school.

Once a week one of the children in her class invited a parent or guardian to come into the class and explain what they did. He carried with him a big green bag, which seemed to rattle as he walked. This could be funny, I thought.

The school was a public school in the obviously affluent suburb where my Wealthy Friend lived. When I quizzed him on why he sent his children to a public school when he could obviously afford a private school, his response was simply, 'Some public schools are better than many private schools. I pay taxes, so my children can learn for free. I'll send them to a private school for the last few years so they can make good contacts, but my children will learn 90% of what they need to know in the School of Life.'

Made sense to me. My parents had both struggled enormously to get me to a private school, even though I had won a partial scholarship, and here I was working as a check-out operator.

'Hello everybody,' said my Wealthy Friend, by way of introduction. 'Would you like to play Lego?'

This question was met with cheers. My Wealthy Friend opened his big green bag and inside were a number of smaller bags in different colours. Moving around the class, he paused in front of each child, whispered something I could not hear, listened diligently to their reply, and then selected which colour bag he would give them. The bags contained Lego, an instruction sheet and some Monopoly money.

Some of the children sat waiting for permission to open the bags. Some dumped the contents on their desks and started building immediately without looking at the instructions. Others opened the bags, read the instructions and started from there. One child meticulously sorted the blocks by shape and colour and then started. And two fought over the bags. 'Please build the item I have allocated you,' was the only instruction my Wealthy Friend gave.

As they put block to block, different things appeared. Shops, houses, cars, planes all began to take shape. I found it curious that nobody had all the blocks they needed and all had a number of blocks that they did not need.

My Wealthy Friend needed to give no instructions to the children to begin using their Monopoly money to buy and sell, or simply use nous to trade blocks. A couple bullied others into giving them the blocks they needed to complete their pieces; some willingly gave away their pieces; and others would not give away the pieces no matter what they were offered, asked for or threatened with.

Some couldn't finish the project and asked others for help. Some finished quickly and set about building other things. Some lost interest when they couldn't do the project and left it for somebody else to do.

When finished, some children used their extra blocks to add 'special features' to their completed works. Others just kept the spare blocks aside. And some set about selling their spare blocks to others. Some traded their finished pieces and a couple even 'bought' finished pieces with their spare blocks or Monopoly money.

My Wealthy Friend went amongst the children checking their progress, giving suggestions, intervening in arguments when necessary and helping those who needed it to complete their projects. Every now and again he would take out more Monopoly money from his pocket and give it to somebody to facilitate a negotiation or help them finish their project. By the end it was obvious that the class had 'built' an entire town.

My Wealthy Friend then asked for attention and asked a series of questions: 'Who has more or less Lego than when they started? Who has more or less Monopoly money? Who has more than one completed item?' And so on. Then he led them in a discussion on how it all occurred.

The 12-year-olds were remarkably astute in their observations about how closely the game resembled what their parents did all day: working, building, trading, outsmarting or being outsmarted, making and losing money, negotiating or being bullied. Eventually, one of the children thought to ask the question, 'So if this is what our parents do all day, what do you do?'

Without answering, my Wealthy Friend sat down at the teacher's desk and cleared a big space on it. He then asked the question, 'Who owns the Lego?'

The children, by now well into the spirit of discussion, held a short debate on this but it was eventually agreed (bar one dissenter) that it was indeed my Wealthy Friend who owned the Lego. So he asked them to bring the Lego to the front of the room and assemble the town for him.

It was impressive, shops, and houses, and factories, and cars and an airport with planes, and even what appeared to be a junkyard with all the left-over pieces, now all assembled on the teacher's desk.

'When I came in here, all I had were some pieces of Lego, a little bit of Monopoly money and you. Now you have Monopoly money and I have a whole town. That's what I do.'

When the children realised what had happened, some laughed, most applauded, and a couple even cried. One glance at the teacher assured me she was horrified.

'Who agrees,' went on my Wealthy Friend regardless, 'that owning the town, or even a small part of it is more important than the Monopoly money you have?'

All the hands went up.

'What if I came there now and exchanged the Monopoly money for real money? What then?' Some thought that was a terrific idea, but most still agreed that it wouldn't be long before they spent the money but owning the little town would be real neat.

'Every day I exchange money for labour. I pay people to build things for me. I buy property, shares in companies, businesses and so on. You can make the decision today about which side of this desk you'd rather be on. Either on that side where you trade your labour for money, or on this side where you get to own the town.'

I was amazed that some of the children literally and immediately got up and moved to the other side of the desk.

'Listen to your teacher. She can teach you some important things, but always remember which side of the desk you end up on has got nothing to do with what you learn at school and everything to do with where you decide to be in life. I'll leave the Lego town as a reminder to you of that, but always remember it belongs to me and you never know when I might turn up to collect the rent.'

And with that my Wealthy Friend got up and walked out.

As I left I noticed the teacher was still aghast, some of the children were bewildered, but many, with firm resolution, had very much decided which side of the desk they would end up on.

When I finally caught up with my Wealthy Friend, he was sitting on a bench under a huge Jacaranda tree in the playground eating a sandwich.

'Lunch?' he asked, offering a sandwich to me as I approached. Knowing this would probably be the only free lunch I would get out of him, I accepted.

'That was a bit harsh wasn't it?'

'Better now than at your age,' he replied. 'Those kids are fed crap every day. I just wanted to give them the truth. Their parents are living in a self-created nightmare of untruths about the way things are in the world. Look at you. Your parents struggled to get you through school and where did it get them or you?'

He had a point. My father had worked all his life and had retired with a small payout, a smaller still pension, and had earned hardly enough to buy his first house, which both my parents were struggling, even now in retirement, to pay off. And me, well, here I was scabbing a sandwich lunch from a rich dude!

'The truth is this: *you* and only you decide which side of the desk you end up on. You can believe the lies about getting a good education, a good job and working hard, but all you'll end up with is a tiny slice of welfare, if there's even any of that left. *Or*, you can decide to accumulate quality assets and eventually work only if you choose to.

'Build Lego and work for peanuts for other people all your life or understand that the reason the rich get richer and the poor get poorer is simply because many people don't choose to ever do what Glenda did and have a go at accumulating something of real value. Something that people want, will pay to live in and eventually buy at a profit to her.

'It's no conspiracy. The rich don't care how many people become rich. In fact they don't understand why *everybody* doesn't take the opportunity to become rich. After all, it's available to everybody and just under their noses.

'If just one of those 12-year-olds gets that message, by the time they are your age they'd be rich and they could choose to do anything they liked with their life. They could truly live a dream.'

Lesson

You and only you decide whether you gain financial freedom or remain a tool of someone else's dream.

FREE TO BE AN ARTIST

I always wanted to study fine arts. I knew my income-earning potential was limited with this, so I asked Mum and Dad about investing. They had been to a 'Wealth Magic' seminar and had sent my older sister and my younger sister, Stephanie, who was 14 at the time, to the seminar. She had started using the share strategies Peter Spann taught to buy some shares. She had done quite well. So my parents agreed to send me and my brother along.

We got very excited about buying a property together but, as we weren't yet 18, our parents had to go guarantors on our loans, which they agreed to do, but they wouldn't lend us the money themselves.

We found a fabulous little apartment for $120,000. My brother had enough for his half of the deposit but I didn't have enough. It was obvious that I would have to borrow the money from Stephanie. She had turned her starting capital of $200 plus savings into $7,000, enough to pay my half of the deposit.

She charged me interest, of course, but I was on my way. We did a small renovation to the apartment and rented it straight away for $150 a week. Each of us only had to put in $6 a week as the difference between the rent and the costs. We had it revalued at $170,000. A $50,000 profit in just six months *and* I had borrowed the money from my 14-year-old sister.

Now I knew I could be financially free and be an artist, or whatever else I wanted to do.

PHOEBE, VIC

CHAPTER 9

Leapfrogging off the Three Secrets of Money Magnetism

I was getting to appreciate his point. All around me people worked hard all their lives and didn't seem to make much progress.

My Wealthy Friend was certainly a nice person but he was no better than many of my friends who were struggling financially. And although I knew some scumbags who were rich, I also knew a lot of scumbags who didn't have any money either.

My Wealthy Friend was certainly smart but it was more 'street wise', and I don't think anybody would describe him as an intellectual genius and yet those of my friends who were really smart didn't seem to get ahead either.

And even those, like doctors and pilots, who had well paying jobs, only seemed to have bigger bills than everybody else to go with their big houses and nice cars. They didn't actually seem to be any more financially free than I was.

So I had already concluded that becoming rich had nothing to do with what quality of person you were, what your job was, or how smart you were, and now my Wealthy Friend's demonstration to the schoolchildren confirmed it. Obviously, you needed to make the decision to be rich, and then follow the right strategy.

I had definitely made the decision to be rich, but bar the Lotto truck backing up and dumping a million or two into my loungeroom, I had to admit that at this stage I hadn't done anything different or special to actually become rich.

I knew I needed to take action. I knew I wanted to be on the right side of the desk but I was still lacking the strategy to do so.

My Wealthy Friend must have sensed what I was thinking because he motioned me to look at some children playing in the schoolyard.

'Ah,' he said, '*This* is what I brought you to see.' I looked to where he was motioning and saw the children playing leapfrog. 'My daughter told me they played this game. Watch.'

Sure enough, the game played out exactly as it has for hundreds of years. One of the children bent over and my Wealthy Friend's daughter used their back to leap over them.

'See how much further she can travel using the leverage of the other person's back? She goes much further, much faster, and with less effort. That's the principle that successful property investors use to get ahead fast.'

I must have looked mystified.

'How do most people buy a house?'

'Save up a deposit, borrow the rest.'

'And then what?'

'I guess they pay off the first one and save a deposit for the second one.'

'And how long would that take?'

'A few years, I guess.'

'And the rest. The average person takes 17 years to pay off a home loan. Then probably five or more years to save the next deposit. Even though you're investing and keeping the risk low, the average person would be dead before they could make enough money to live from *that* strategy. Too little leverage.'

'So how do you speed it up?' I asked.

'Leapfrogging.'

The strange look I had on my face said it all. I obviously still had a way to go to understand my Wealthy Friend's quirky sayings.

'Leapfrogging is simple:

- use equity or cash as first deposit;
- rejuvenate the property to add value;
- increase rental;
- wait for the equity and income to grow;
- have the property revalued;

- refinance to draw down new 'free' equity for your next deposit;
- continue to buy property without deposits as long as you can continue to service your debt.

'It takes advantage of the Three Secrets of Money Magnetism. You remember those don't you?'

'Um, yes.'

Lesson

Leapfrogging allows you to continuously buy properties using increased value and therefore increased equity as deposit for the next property.

FROM BROKE TO LOOKING GOOD IN THREE YEARS

In 1996 I was running a computer wholesale business which went under and I went into bankruptcy. I lost my house, everything. Discharged from bankruptcy in 1999 I 'discovered' Peter's seminars in 2000 and spent the next six months learning the strategies. I also realised that property and finance go together, so I changed my career in 1999 to become a finance broker. In December 2000, I bought my first investment property — an old dog but massive potential for rejuvenation. Property prices soared in early 2001. The property was purchased for $116,000 in December 2000 and by March 2001, was worth $185,000 (it's now worth $340,000 with reno). I drew down on the equity and purchased another property in similar condition. Again, equity was drawn down and two blocks of prime land purchased ready to build holiday homes on them. I purchased another property in 2002 and another in 2003. I now have six investment properties with over $300,000 in equity. All rented (except for land being built on), all with renos being performed to release more equity for further purchases.

CHRIS, NSW

The Three Secrets of Money Magnetism Revisited

I was beginning to think I was a five-year-old learning my 'times tables' or some hapless new recruit in the military being drilled by a sergeant.

'What are the Three Secrets of Money Magnetism?' demanded my Wealthy Friend.

'Uniqueness, value adding, and leverage.'

'And again, this time with definitions ...'

'*Uniqueness* is the quality that makes something stand out, be desirable, have a skill or ability, a feature or attribute that people are prepared to pay a premium for.

'*Value adding* is taking a thing that is worth something and making it worth more ...

'*Leverage* is finding a way to do something quicker, faster, better, more efficiently, with less effort or money.'

'Good, now which is the most misunderstood?'

'Uniqueness, because people think that just because something is different it must be special. The key to uniqueness is desirability — having something that people want and will pay for.'

'Excellent. Which is the most poorly applied?'

'Value adding, because people forget what is important to their target market.'

'And, what is the most powerful?'

'Leverage, because it accelerates returns when applied to something worthwhile.'

'And?'

'Leverage is also the most dangerous because it can accelerate losses too.'

'Excellent. You can now begin your research.'

Lesson

The Three Secrets of Money Magnetism — Uniqueness, Value Adding and Leverage — when used properly can significantly add to your wealth.

USING THE THREE SECRETS

Eighteen months ago, we bought a one-bedroom unit in Neutral Bay. Following Peter's seminar we looked for the wow factor — this had it — brilliant views over North Sydney from the top floor, and only two minutes from Coles supermarket, the Oaks Hotel and transport. Also a garage, which is a must for us for all our properties.

It was really tired and needed a good make-over. We found a tradesman and for $20,000 we:

- Put in a new kitchen and flooring.
- Sanded and varnished window frames, and hung bright new curtains.
- Painted throughout and fixed new door handles.
- Installed modern new light fittings and dimmer switches.
- Put in a shower curtain and mirror cabinet in the bathroom.

We paid $280,000 (so plus the $20,000, it cost us $300,000) and it was rented for $270 a week when we bought. No money down, as we had enough equity from other properties.

When we finished the upgrade, we rented within a week for $305 per week, and it was valued two months ago at $360,000.

PAUL & KATHRYN, FRENCHS FOREST, NSW

CHAPTER 11

Opportunity Knocks with the First Secret of Money Magnetism

'So, how do you think you would apply the Three Secrets in using property to make you rich?' my Wealthy Friend asked.

'Let me think ... If a property possessed uniqueness it would have features and attributes that people wanted in a home. That would make it more attractive to them, which would mean that they would be prepared to pay more to buy it or to rent it from you, which would increase your profits.'

'That's a very good description of uniqueness applied to property — features and attributes that people *want* in a home.'

'But if I was buying a property with uniqueness, that would make it more expensive to buy, wouldn't it? And wouldn't that decrease my profits?'

'Well, that depends on what you are aiming for. If you are aiming for growth, a property with uniqueness will always grow faster than a bland property. If you are aiming for return, a property with uniqueness will always rent well.

'And if you are aiming for low risk, a property with the types of attributes people want will always be easier to sell, which lowers your risk. Your profits will come from value adding, but we'll get to that later. What type of uniqueness do you think would *not* be useful to you as an investor?'

Of course, now I remembered that there were potential downsides to uniqueness as well.

'I guess things like quirky or different design, strange colours or just plain weirdness would be things that are unique about a property that would actually make it less desirable.'

'Good, you are starting to get the hang of this. Uniqueness comes from having things that people want and admire. The more things that a property has that people want, the more valuable it will be.

'Time to go for a drive,' said my Wealthy Friend.

'Right,' I said, already concerned about this task. My car, Saddam (so named because it used so much oil you needed Kuwait to run it), was flat out getting me to work at the supermarket and back, let alone go on an extended drive. 'Don't you remember my car only runs on three cylinders?'

'You can use my car,' my Wealthy Friend replied quickly, obviously having thought out that objection. My eyes lit up at this suggestion, imagining trotting around town in a Rolls-Royce. 'The ute,' said my Wealthy Friend, obviously irritated that I had lost focus on the task at hand, again.

'What am I looking for?' I asked.

'What I want you to do is drive around as many suburbs as you can in a weekend and make a list of all the things that make different suburbs, districts or even streets desirable or undesirable to live in. Let's find out if we can discover anything that adds to uniqueness.'

The drive was really pleasant. I found streets and whole suburbs I didn't even know existed. As I drove around, I not only noted down things that were obviously unique about properties, but also things that were unique about suburbs, streets and areas and, of course, I also took note of all the phone numbers on the 'For Sale' signs I saw planted around.

I knew how pedantic my Wealthy Friend was about things, so I made detailed lists and comparisons of everything I saw. I noticed, just by driving around, some very obvious things: that people who lived in a suburb all tended to be the same. The houses, although they had variations were all similar, and the people drove a similar type of car and dressed the same. Houses that were different really stood out. This fascinated me.

I noticed whole suburbs of flats and apartment buildings mostly filled with young people, and then some mostly filled with older people. I noticed some suburbs with modern houses mostly filled with young couples pushing strollers and stopping to talk with other mums and dads along the way. I saw suburbs of older houses with teenagers playing in their pools or hanging out with other teenagers.

I saw suburbs that were exceptionally well kept, with neat lawns, neat footpaths and trees lining the streets, and I saw some that were messes, with junk everywhere and no attention to the properties. I saw some suburbs full of just white faces and some where every colour known was represented.

I saw suburbs that were half full of rundown old houses and half full of shiny, immaculate, freshly renovated properties full of 20 and 30 somethings with their gleaming new cars full of stuff from decorator and hardware shops.

And I started to realise that people lived in little enclaves that were demarcated by lifestyle, income, family or work, and that while each different area was unique, the properties within each area largely reflected the similar taste of the people who chose to live there.

I was very excited when I got to present my 'findings' to my Wealthy Friend.

'Ah, you have just observed one of the most powerful concepts of business — the Cycle of Life,' nodded my Wealthy Friend sagely, when I told him how people seemed to stick together and had similar taste.

'Like people like to be with like people,' he said reinforcing his point. 'We humans like to think we are unique but really we aren't. Most people are terrified of being truly unique, of standing out, and so we congregate with our peers: people who have approximately the same level of income as us, approximately the same interests, and approximately the same lifestyle. You could set your watch in some areas by the regularity with which all the people do the same thing.

'So, because people tend to like to be around other people similar to them, whole suburbs and areas take on the characteristics of the lifestyles and desires of those people.

'And this is an evolving phenomenon. Once people start congregating in an area, they then start building around them the things they need to be happy in that area. Businesses start "popping up" to cater to their needs, which attracts more and more of the same type of people, which moves those who aren't interested in those things to seek out other areas that have them or other people of the same ilk.

'Take the case of a rundown suburb. Young people are attracted to the suburb because it is cheap and they don't have much money. But everybody wants to live in the best house they can afford, so they start renovating. Eventually renovator stores start opening to cater for all that timber and paint, then other younger people start noticing the renovating and renovator stores and start being attracted to the area.

'But rundown suburbs also have things that those people don't want — ugly streetscapes, crime, and so on, so the "new" people start petitioning council to clean things up, start setting up neighbourhood watch schemes and ringing their local member for more police. Disgruntled with the yuppies invading their area, the earlier residents start moving out.

The new police station reduces crime, making the area even more attractive for more young renovators to move in. Then those who have finished renovating need something else to do and spend their money on, so coffee shops and boutiques start edging out older-style businesses — delis replace corner stores and art galleries spring up in disused buildings. Eventually the young renovators start having children and run out of space, so they move onto another area and sell their properties to newer people who like the suburb and the people who live there and are now attracted by the lifestyle without the hassle of renovating, and so the stage becomes entrenched and will last for some generations, with new renovations in the passing years.

'If you were in one of those areas, what type of property would you be buying?'

'I guess I would want to buy either a property that needed renovating or one that had already been done rather than new property.'

'Spot on,' he said smiling. 'Did you happen to drive through any areas that were obviously very well established and had been that way for many years?'

'Yes, I went through one area that was obviously very affluent. Big houses with expensive cars.'

'Were those cars all new or were they older models?'

I had to give that question some thought. At this time, a Mercedes Benz of any era was a very expensive car to me and I hadn't thought to discern between the ages, but I was a car fan and knew the latest models of everything so I could answer the question once I had thought about it ... 'They were older models. Mostly just superseded but in very good condition.'

'Excellent, good noticing. And what about the ages of the drivers?'

'Well, they were all a bit silver-haired, but looking fit!'

He ignored my last comment and went straight to the first point. 'And what was happening, property-wise in the suburbs where all these silver-haired, older model expensive car-driving people were living?'

'I noticed a lot of new building. People seemed to be building townhouses where tennis courts once were.'

'Yes!' exclaimed my Wealthy Friend, obviously excited by the changes going on which I had noticed. 'Opportunity knocks boy! Opportunity knocks. This suburb, too, is undergoing a transformation. It was once a very affluent suburb full of professionals and successful business people who built big houses on big blocks of land. Now their children have grown up and moved on.

'They are no longer taking advantage of, or even needing their big houses and their big blocks. They don't need to show off any more — they have long ago proven themselves, and because their children have moved on, they are thinking about their "golden years".

'Most of their wealth has been accumulated in quality assets over the years and they would like to turn those assets into cash. But the owners of these properties are too young to be moving out; they now want to relax in their homes.

'The solution is obvious. Divide the larger block, get rid of the pool and the tennis court that is now unused, take advantage of high property prices, and sell off or develop the land. A new generation of affluent younger people move in to take advantage of everything such a suburb offers but, remarkably, in making the houses and blocks smaller, the suburb loses some of its gloss and gradually becomes a "less affluent" area. If it retains its strengths what do you think will happen eventually?'

'I am not sure.'

'Eventually, as those new residents build their wealth, they will start to buy up the property around them, demolish the smaller houses to add extensions or build new bigger houses, and eventually accumulate enough land to build tennis courts and pools again! And so the cycle will have been completed.'

'Wow, I had never thought of it that way. The whole cycle must take some time.'

'Years, often decades, but the cycle always rolls on. Young people are always looking for value. Families are always looking for space. The successful are always looking for size and leisure space (which, ironically they rarely actually use), and older people are always looking to convert assets to cash, with the elderly always looking for security and convenience. The cycle goes on and the buying and selling of property is driven by it.'

'I understand now, but what has that got to do with uniqueness?'

'Your opportunity to profit from uniqueness has to do with two factors. Firstly, people's desire to be seen as unique while actually not wanting to stand out. That is, in property terms, they want features and attributes in their properties and decoration that their friends will "ohh" and "ahh" about, but they don't want to stand out so much that their friends will think they are weird.

'You see, people generally make themselves "feel" unique by comparing themselves to other groups of people who are different from them. That way they can be the "same" as all their friends, while at the same time being able to convince themselves they are unique. So when you are buying property it is critical to buy property in an area that most people in the area would want to live in. This makes the property unique and similar at the same time. It is unique because it is distinct from other suburbs, but it is similar because it has all the features and attributes that somebody wanting to live in that area desires.

'Secondly, people's desire to get into or out of a suburb. When you notice a suburb or area changing you can take advantage of that by buying properties that cater to the people moving into the area. People moving out of the area will be motivated to sell, so you may be able to buy the properties cheaper, then you create uniqueness by adding the features and attributes that the "new" residents want. You will be able to profit because those moving in will be motivated to buy (or rent), so you can sell (or rent) them what they want at a premium.

'If you do so the law of uniqueness will work for you.'

Lesson

The First Law of Money Magnetism — Uniqueness.
The Cycle of Life provides opportunities for applying the secret of uniqueness. Buyers are looking for features unique to their stage in the Cycle of Life. They will pay for them if you can provide them. Sellers have often outgrown their property or their area and may be well motivated to sell.

$300,000 'PROFIT' IN A DAY

On the weekend, utilising some of the auction techniques learned from Peter Spann, I achieved a $300,000 gain in one day.

Since selling our own house nearly two years ago, we have been looking for property or land for ourselves (hubby is a builder!) and have been concerned about the market getting away from us. In the meantime, I have bought two investment properties.

A week ago, we found a block of land that knocked our socks off — views of the city, 20 metres to parkland which leads down to the Yarra River, and five minutes to the CBD. A subdivision had been completed on an existing house and land — dividing it into three lots — house and two vacant blocks.

We were interested in 'the tennis court'. Our valuation came in at a top level of $780,000, so we were already thinking we may be able to capitalise if we could buy for a good price at the auction.

On Saturday we attended the auction. The other vacant block set a record for the suburb of Kew — $1,305,000. I started to feel a little disillusioned about whether we would be able to afford our block!

I had reviewed all Peter's auction techniques and ultimately applied the strategy of rapid bidding and a little intimidation to knock out some competition and successfully bought the block for $690k.

I rang my valuer as soon as possible, and based on the size of the blocks and the record price set by the other block, he is going to prepare a revised valuation at around $1 million!

GAIL, MONT ALBERT NORTH, VIC

Chapter 12

The First Law of Property Investment

'This is the first rule of property: *always* buy what people moving into the area would want to buy or rent.

'This rule is so simple it is usually overlooked by investors. And yet it is critical to your success. Buy what people want to buy. Rent out what people want to rent. Whenever anybody comes to me with a problem in a property they bought, it almost always comes down to a violation of this one basic law.

'If you were looking at investing in a suburb where everybody is renovating, what type of property do you think you would be looking for?'

'Something characteristic of the suburb? A period house or townhouse or apartment with character, or maybe an apartment in a trendy area that was rundown.'

'Great, let's use your period house as an example. Maybe a little worker's cottage, or Federation house, or colonial, with all the details that are so expensive to reproduce these days but critical to the "authentic" look that people want. If you found a property like that in one of these suburbs do you think it would be a bargain or would you have to pay good money for it?'

'The basic laws of supply and demand say that I would probably have to pay good money.'

'Yes, but what else do you know based on the Cycle of Life?'

'Well, if that property was in demand when I bought it, one would think that it would continue to be in demand, as it still has all the attributes that people want in a property in that area. So that would mean it would grow in value and if I wanted to rent it, then I would get a good rent and the rent would keep going up as well. And because it takes many decades for a suburb to change in the cycle, growth and rent increases would be "locked in" for quite some time.'

'That's it. Now, as obvious as it sounds, people forget this all the time, and do you know what usually tempts them to violate this law of property success? Greed. Somewhere along the line they come across a property that seems to be priced far below the other properties they are looking at. What would you think if you found a house that was much cheaper than everything else in the area?'

'I'd think there was something wrong with it. It's probably falling down!'

'Yes, funnily, that is one of the things people are most paranoid about when it comes to buying property — that the house they buy will be riddled with creepy crawlies or the builder who put it up was a shonk and it is going to fall down as soon as the paint that has been slapped on to cover up all the cracks peels. But it's really very easy to get around that — a quality building inspection will tell you if the property is sound. And funnily enough they usually are, but there *is* something wrong with it. Have you guessed?'

'Wrong *type* of property for the people moving into the area.'

'Right — say a modern brick house in a colonial cottage area. People moving into the area want to rent or buy a cute little renovated cottage and live with all the others who like cute little renovated cottages and swap renovation and decorating tips and strategies over their lattes. They don't want to live in a modern house, no matter how well it is built or how "nice" it is. If they wanted to live in a modern house they would be looking in a suburb with modern houses. And people who want to live in modern houses do not look in the suburb with the cute cottages.'

'I get it,' I said. 'So, because "nobody" wants to live in it, either renting or buying it, there is no demand. So if the current owner needs to sell and there is no demand, the only way they can stimulate demand is to lower the price to a point where it is perceived to be a bargain.'

'But what happens if you were to buy it and wanted to rent it?'

'Well, I presume "nobody" who wanted to live in the area would want to rent it either, so you'd also have to lower the rent.'

'And when you come to sell it?'

'You'd sell it for much less than the other houses in the area?'

'So what does that do to your growth/income/risk equation?'

'Lower growth, low income and higher risk.'

'So, even though it appears like a bargain, is it a good buy?'

'I guess not.'

'No way! But people get sucked in all the time. Instead of buying a property that is in demand in the area. Something that people want to buy now and will want to buy well into the future — that has as many of the features and attributes as possible that people who want to live in that area want — they buy the bargain. Then they wonder why they can't rent it, and in desperation, when they have to sell, nobody wants to buy it.'

'So the first law of property investment is to always buy what people want to rent and buy in the area.'

'Exactly. Of course, the first thing you have to know is, *what* people who want to live in the area you have picked want to live in. And that's easy to discover ...'

'Of course. *That's* why you sent me on my drive; to find out what people in the areas that I look at want to live in. But if I am always buying property that is in demand does that mean I am always paying a premium?'

'Yes, and no,' my Wealthy Friend answered.

I knew there was another complicated reply coming up.

'Let's go and meet Jack, my town planner friend. I am sure you will find him enlightening. I have some forms to lodge with council anyway.'

Lesson

The First Law of Property Investment: *always* buy what people moving *into* an area want to buy or rent.

THE RIGHT RENOVATIONS

We moved out here from Scotland seven years ago. We didn't have enough for a deposit, so we chipped in with my brother and his wife to buy a classic Balmain dump between the four of us for $277,000 in December 1997.

We were young and enthusiastic and spent a year putting on a second storey. We had a bedroom per couple, we had the fridge and a telly in ours, and my brother had the microwave in theirs. Talk about cosy living! We were using the original outdoor toilet, and rented a green plastic shower for the back garden. Our friends and neighbours thought we were mad: taking a torch out to the garden in the winter to have a shower, while negotiating your way over trenches, carrying a bucket of water to flush the toilet!

However it all paid off as we sold a year and a half later for $565,000. The renovations cost $50,000. We split our profit, and payed for a great wedding in a castle in Scotland (we thought of it before Madonna!).

Grant and I then went on to buy a place of our own, and had a baby which slowed us down a bit.

We bought another Balmain terrace but by then we had attended our first seminar and realised we didn't have to do as much work, so we went for the spruce up. Bought it for $419,000 in December 1999, spent $20,000 on renovations and sold it two years later for $555,000. The midwife gave a strange look when she came to visit our new baby and the back of the house was basically a tarpaulin.

GAYLE & CRAIG, EDINBURGH, SCOTLAND

CHAPTER 13

The Second Law of Property Investment

Jack's office was a modest suburban town-planning practice, but it seemed to be a hive of activity.

When we walked in, my Wealthy Friend was immediately recognised by Jack and greeted like a long lost companion. I noticed Jack walked with a limp, but he had a warm face and a friendly demeanour and as soon as we were 'formally' introduced I took an instant liking to him.

My Wealthy Friend had business to do and they had quite a lengthy conversation about a property development the two of them seemed to be involved in, using terms I wasn't familiar with, but once they were done my Wealthy Friend whispered something to Jack which made him laugh and they came over to where I was sitting nearby.

'Come on,' said Jack. 'Let's go learn the Second Law of Property Investment.' It was an offer I found hard to refuse. Soon we were sitting in Jack's rather oddly coloured but gleaming new purple BMW. He selected an address out of the memory in the satellite navigation and we found ourselves rapidly motoring along with the pleasant but mechanical voice guiding us to our destination.

Anticipating the obvious question, Jack said, 'It's my wife's pick — she always wanted a purple car. I never wanted to buy one because I thought nobody would ever buy it from us when we came to trade it in. But our Wealthy Friend convinced me. He mentioned how well our property was doing and he reminded me of the Second Law of Property Investment: follow the money. I knew how it applied to property but wasn't sure how it applied to cars — you know how cryptic he can be.'

I nodded with a smile on my face while he continued, 'Of course, our Wealthy Friend had the answer. He convinced me that not only should I buy the BMW, but that it was totally necessary for my business because he was sure that more people would deal with me if I owned it. Like that suit you are wearing — my bet is you bought it after you met our Wealthy Friend.'

'Sure did, but purple?'

'Well, the final straw was when he asked me why I wanted all the money that we had accumulated through property if I didn't occasionally buy something of an indulgence with it. That seemed to make sense. No reason to gather riches if you're not going to spend them every now and again. So a purple BMW it was. My other BMW, the new one I just bought, is being serviced so I had to borrow my wife's car!'

I was beginning to think Jack was no ordinary town planner. Here was a man who, using simple techniques and a bit of effort, had amassed what most people would consider to be a fortune, and even though he started out earning more than I was as a check-out operator, it inspired me once again.

'So what does the Second Law of Property Investment — follow the money — mean?' I asked.

'Hmm,' said Jack, pausing to gather his thoughts, 'by now you will know that money has a flow to it. It "sticks" to people who are following the Laws of Money Magnetism and bounces off people who are not. That's why the rich get richer and the poor get poorer. There's no conspiracy, just people following a set of universal principles or not. So if money flows from people who are not following the Laws of Money Magnetism to people who are, it stands to reason that if you follow the flow of money it will lead you to wealth.'

'Yeah, I agree in theory, but ...' I trailed off not wanting to offend Jack or be overly negative about my Wealthy Friend's theories, which seemed very strange but which, I was learning fast, were amazingly accurate.

'Well, money leaves a trail, and here we are about to discover the signs,' Jack said cryptically, just as the computer said ... 'You have arrived!'

And we had indeed. As Jack backed the car into the car space which had conveniently become vacant as we arrived, using the BMW's 'park distance control' to assist with a perfect park, I looked up at the rather nondescript building we had arrived at and read the sign above the door: 'Valuer-General's Office'.

Jack led me through security, occasionally saying hello to people we walked past on our way through a seemingly endless labyrinth of grey-green painted, fluorescent-lit halls, until we came to a small counter where a bored-looking person was stamping papers with red ink.

'Hello Charlene,' Jack said cheerily. 'Can we have the median price growth records please?'

'Sure Jack, help yourself,' she said placing a small closely printed report listing suburbs and a whole series of figures next to them on the desk before going back to her stamping.

'This is the money trail. It shows you where the money is flowing in property. Have you learned about the Cycle of Life?'

'Yes. Suburbs change their character based on the needs and wants of the people moving into the area. They grow and decline over a period of decades so that they are always either attracting people or having people move out. New residents, attracted by the features of the suburb move in and start the renewal of it. Old residents are displaced. The suburb grows until the new group is entrenched and then it stabilises. After a period of time the people who live in the suburb can change their needs and the cycle moves on.'

'And what would you say about property values in those suburbs?'

'My guess is that the suburbs that were attracting new residents would see property values grow, while those suburbs that were losing residents or losing the features and attributes that appealed to new residents would be declining in value.'

'Precisely. The money is flowing from suburbs that are not aligned with the Laws of Money Magnetism to the suburbs that are. Suburbs that offer uniqueness attract residents away from suburbs that don't, and the money flows with the flow of people. So if you follow the flow of money you'll follow the flow of people.

'Novice investors take guesses as to where the money is flowing. They look at expensive suburbs or trendy suburbs and think that because the people there have money that's where the money is flowing. And while this sometimes is true, there are often many suburbs that the novice overlooks which provide the professional with better growth, return and lower risk. Sometimes some of the cheapest suburbs have some of the best growth rates.'

'That makes sense. People would be moving there because of affordability and the money would flow there with them.'

'Yes. And some of the most expensive suburbs can have some of the lowest growth because fewer people can afford to live there so there is less demand. The key to all this is understanding median price.

'Median price is simply the middle point of prices in a suburb. It is the price point at which half of the houses sold for more and half of the houses sold for less. It is not the average. The average price can be skewed by a very expensive or a very cheap sale in the suburb or even one large development being sold at an unusually high or low price, whereas the median price would be little affected by such random variations from the norm.

'Different bodies in different states track median prices in slightly different ways[2] making it a little bit confusing, but basically the figures all measure the same thing — the change of median price in a given area — say a suburb or postcode — from one time period, say a year or decade, to another. From this we can determine the current and historical growth rates for each suburb and determine where the money is flowing.

'Because we only want to be buying where the money is flowing it stands to reason if we buy in high-growth suburbs we have a good chance of success. Let's have a look at these figures.' Jack opened the report at a section headed 'Median Price Growth — 10 Years'. 'These are the figures for suburbs' growth rates on average over the last 10 years ranked in order of growth. Why do you think we would look at that?'

'Well, I would think that if a suburb had been growing well over the last 10 years, it would probably continue growing over the next few years. So what growth rate are we looking for?'

'As you know, the average annual growth rate of property in Australia over a decade is about 8%. But we don't want to be buying average property do we? Nooooo! So let's use as a starting point suburbs that have grown at above 8% per year on average over the last 10 years.'

He drew a line in pencil on the report. There were about 30 suburbs out of the 200 or so listed that fitted this criterion.

'Gee, that's not many to choose from,' I said, sounding dismayed. 'I thought there'd be more?'

'How many do you want?' asked Jack with only a tinge of sarcasm in his voice. 'Wouldn't the idea be to find one or two *top* suburbs so you could concentrate your search?'

'Mmm, that does make sense now that you say it.'

'So let's cut it down even further, by looking at the actual growth rates over the last 10 years and plot them on a graph to see if there is any obvious pattern,' said Jack, handing me some graph paper, a pen and a ruler. 'You do 15 and I'll do 15.'[3]

While not all suburbs followed the pattern all of the time it soon became obvious that most followed a similar path to growth.

'You'll see,' said Jack, as we compared our charts, 'that property growth comes in spurts. The actual growth every year varies considerably from virtually flat to very high. This, of course, averages out to be about 8% every year but you can make more money if you follow the money flow in the suburb more closely.

'You will notice that many suburbs follow this pattern: two years flat, one year up, two years jump, followed by a repeat — two years flat, one year up, two years jump. While it never does this perfectly, it is approximately right. You have to use a bit of "fuzzy logic".

'Let's take a look at this suburb's growth and plot it.'

Year	Actual Growth %	Cumulative Growth
1	2	2
2	7	9
3	16	25
4	20	45
5	8	53
6	2	55
7	2	57
8	8	65
9	14	79
10	21	100

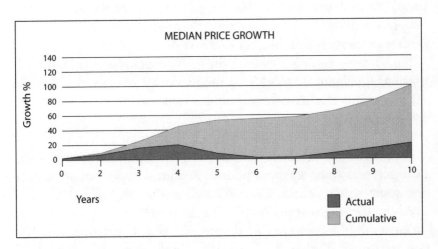

'The first year it is coming off a flat period. Very frequently a big growth spurt will follow a flat period like this. Then the growth rate kicks up to 7% in year 2. This is our warning of the growth spurt to follow. If we had bought then we would have picked up the natural growth of the next couple of years.

'Year 3 the growth is 16% and year 4 the growth is 20%. If we had bought a $100,000 property at the end of the second year in the cycle, it would be worth $139,200 at the end of year 4, or a growth of just over 39% in 2 years. And this is all pure profit to us.

'The growth rate then stagnates for a couple of years — no problem, we just sit and wait — and then it moves up to 8% for year 8. This is our warning of the next big jump, and we see 14% and 21% over the next 2 years. That would mean our $100,000 property would now be worth $233,000. Pretty exciting!

'While you don't have to be this precise in timing property to make money over the long term, it will shorten the time it takes for your property to double in value and it saves you buying before the stagnant years.

'Many people buy property in a suburb just as it has stagnated, hold onto it for a couple of years and see little growth, and then sell it as a bad investment — just as it was about to pay off for them! And worse still, those people are probably lost to the property market forever, convinced they were either no good at it or that property is just another bad investment.'

'So,' I said, getting a handle on it, 'I want to buy in a suburb that has had better than average median price growth over the last 10 years and is currently growing based on the two last years' growth rate.'

'That's it — you've got it.'

'But if the growth rates are not perfectly regimented, like in the example, and some stagnant periods and growth periods are longer and shorter than others, how do I know when the growth spurt is over and the stagnant period is about to start?'

'Generally I use the rule of thumb that if a suburb's growth rate has exceeded double it's normal growth then that suburb is overheated and it's time to move on. Where do you think you'd look next?'

'May be the suburbs around that one?'

'Good on you — yes. Often the suburbs around an overheated suburb are the next to grow and are mostly more affordable because they have not received the same sort of attention from buyers as the suburb that is overheated.'

'To use an example,' I went on to make sure I had it 100%, 'if a suburb normally grows at 8% and its growth rate hits 17%, which is more than double it's normal rate, I can consider that suburb overheated for the time being and come back in a couple of years time?'

'Yes. Just do your sums on the suburbs around it and see if they show some growth — then you are following the money!'

We turned to the page in the report that said 'Median Price Growth — 1 Year' and cross-referenced them against the three-year growth to determine the suburbs that had started growing above their normal rates. We then compared them with the list of suburbs that had shown excellent growth rates over the last 10 years to eliminate the 'overheated' ones, and I was now down to a list of 12. I looked at Jack for what to do next.

'Now, we look at rents,' he said authoritatively, turning the pages to the report titled 'Average Rental Returns'. 'Rental yield is very important to the investor. Rents help pay your costs, and the only way to make a profit is when your income exceeds your costs. The higher the rent, the better chance you have of making money. Now, what can you say about the growth/income/risk equation here?'

'Well, if I am looking for a suburb with high growth, then to get high income I might have to take a higher risk, or if I want low risk I might have to sacrifice income. So if rental income is important, why do we go for growth?'

'We follow the money! Look at the example above — we started with a property worth $100,000 and after less than a decade it was worth $233,000 or a growth of $133,000. That's high growth. If we chase high rents we will probably have to sacrifice growth, as we may be getting into a risk area that is unacceptable.

'Let's say we could get 4% rental return or $4,000 a year in a high-growth area, or increase it to 7% in a low-growth area. Follow the money. If we spread our growth over 10 years (instead of eight) for simplicity, the average growth rate in our high-growth example is 9%. The capital gain is $133,000. Rental income over 10 years is $40,000 (not allowing for inflation). So our total income plus capital gain is $173,000.

'In our second high-rent, low-growth scenario, let's say average growth is 5%. That makes capital growth $63,000 — still great but not as good as $133,000. Rental income is $70,000, which seems more attractive than $40,000. But our total capital gain plus income over 10 years is just $133,000, which is $40,000 less than in the high-growth example.

Lots of people favour cash-flow investing, which is fine and has it merits, but that's why generally I chase high growth. Over the years it adds up to better overall return.

'That doesn't mean rent isn't important! I like collecting it as much as anybody, it's just that our Wealthy Friend taught me that, in the long term, growth generally is a better approach.

'Let's apply our "higher than average" approach to rents to our Median Price Growth list and see what we get. About 4% is the average rental yield in Australia.'

I looked at the tables. Amazingly, there were quite a few suburbs that exceeded the 4% average, and some were very high — as high as 11% — but the list of suburbs less than the 4% average was much longer. I thought how easy the temptation would be to go for the high rents, especially as some of the high rental yield properties corresponded with the suburbs on my high-growth list. But I remembered the advice of Jack and my Wealthy Friend to concentrate on one strategy.

To my delight there were seven suburbs that had grown over 8% on average per annum for the last 10 years, that were growing now and that had rental yields of above 4%. One even had a rental yield of 9%. I looked at the median prices of all the suburbs on my now considerably shorter list and realised that four of them were too expensive for me.

I pointed this out to Jack, but his response was the opposite to my thinking. 'Excellent!' he said. 'Now, not only have you followed the money by going for high-growth suburbs and higher than average rental yield, you now have a focused list of just three suburbs to concentrate on. I am sure you will be able to do fantastic research and come up with a brilliant shortlist of properties to buy after that.'

I couldn't help but think, as I watched his bright purple BMW disappear down my street, how 'sparky' all the people my Wealthy Friend had introduced me to were. Obviously one of the Benefits of the Key to Wealth — confidence from knowledge — was kicking in for them! I certainly felt more excited by the second. But for now I decided to follow the water and have a long bath while thinking of everything I had learned.

Lesson

The Second Law of Property Investment — follow the money and therefore the people.

Use available statistical information to identify high-growth suburbs and higher than average rental yield in the price range you can afford.

For the quickest results, aim to buy in that part of the growth cycle when the suburb is growing but has not overheated by checking the previous two years' growth rates.

KEEP LOOKING

I have bought three investment properties so far this year (2002).

I have lived in Lane Cove for many years and decided to look and probably buy there first. I wanted to buy a unit at or under the median price which, at the beginning of the year, was $340,000. I looked for many weeks each Saturday and sometimes through the week for a two-bedroom apartment/unit of apparent good construction which would probably need refurbishment. Most such units were in the price range of $320,000 to $420,000. I looked at about 25 and started to get a reasonable idea of comparable value. I felt I needed to look at more than that but was becoming tired of waiting and wanted to 'get into the market' somehow. It had been three or four months since I first attended a Peter Spann course on buy-and-hold real estate and I wanted to get going.

One Saturday morning I came across a unit in a block of six only one or two minutes' walk from the shopping village. The block was about 30 years old and the unit was at the top at the back and had a great outlook onto tall trees. It needed refurbishment and had been rented for $250 per week and was presently vacant. The asking price was $350,000 and seemed like quite good value compared to other units I had looked at. I nevertheless hesitated and someone else bought it for $345,000 within days.

Over the next month or so I looked at more two-bedroom units in Lane Cove and attended a number of auctions. Most of the units were about 30 years old and were in the 70 to 90 square metre sizes. One of the auctions I attended for a unit once again very close to the shopping centre had four lots of people bidding furiously against each other. The agents were beside themselves with delight when the price finally settled at $421,000, some $80,000 over the median price! Another one had three bidders furiously outdoing each other until it sold to one of them for $481,000! Extraordinary I thought.

So another Saturday morning in early May I was looking through the newspaper and noticed a unit in the same block as the one I missed out on for $350,000. I drove to the site just as the first opening was starting to find a stream of people inspecting. It was in the same condition as the other one, needing a refurbishment of the kitchen and bathroom, and the price was $340,000. This was right on the median price of a few months previous. At this stage two other people were letting the agent know they would like a copy of the contract. I quietly said to him after they had left that I would take it for the asking price and settle with cash in 28 days. He agreed to put this to the owner and came back to me the same afternoon with an acceptance. I did not have all the cash but knew I would be able to borrow what I needed, and I arranged it within a week. The property was already tenanted for $265 per week. I decided to keep the tenants on the same rent for a few months' as the market had gone very 'soft', for yield. I felt if I waited six to twelve months and then did a refurbishment I would be able to more certainly gain a better rental return.

NAME WITHHELD

CHAPTER 14

Doing Homework

A few days after my meeting with Jack a large envelope arrived in the mail. Accompanied by a 'With Comps' slip were a set of notes Jack had written about buying property during an early session he had had with our Wealthy Friend.

They were detailed notes and I later discovered that Jack, as any good planner would, had taken a tape recorder with him when he was talking with our Wealthy Friend and later transcribed the notes word for word.

I thought that I knew everything about researching but Jack's notes proved there was obviously much more ...

Prior Sales in the Area

'You need to be 1000% au fait with what's going on in your suburb. You need to get to know the suburb like the back of your hand.

'You can easily get the information you need electronically.[4] Such reports contain such valuable information as sales history, in some cases dating back two decades; type of building; features; size and type of title.

'You will discover from these reports what the property you are looking at buying last sold for and when it sold, and, perhaps more importantly, what properties in the suburb have just sold for.

'You need to know what else is for sale in the suburb so you can do a comparison, and you need to know the rental returns for similar properties. Do not believe the agent, find out yourself.

'Understand vacancy rates. If you can't get access to vacancy rates, attend 'open for inspections' on rentals in the area. See how many people turn up. If you have 20 people turn up to inspect a unit when it's open for inspection for rental, then you know that the vacancy rates are going to be fairly low. If only one person turns up, then you know that the vacancy rates are going to be fairly high. Simple but important.'

Do a Body Corporate Search or a Strata Title Search

'Your solicitor can arrange a body corporate or strata title search.[5]

'The body corporate search or the strata title search will tell you what special levies have been raised only on units; who's on the body corporate; the building's condition; disputes between the owners and the body corporate; and other important information like the state of body corporate accounts and if any of the owners owe significant sums. You can usually only get them on units that are currently for sale.

Arrange a Building Inspection

'It never ceases to amaze me: people who buy investment properties and don't do a building inspection. If you're a builder you're the only potential buyer who doesn't need to get building inspections. Everybody else should get them (and some builders I know should probably get them anyway!).

'Learn what to look out for, though, before you get the building inspection done. Tag along with a builder or building inspector when they do the first inspection for you and find out what you can look for yourself. Find out what rising damp looks like; find out what concrete cancer looks like; find out what the building inspectors look for. This knowledge enables you to dismiss some buildings before spending money on an inspection and will eliminate about 80% of the properties you are considering.

When you get a torch out and look under the building yourself and see any of the dangerous symptoms, what do you do? Just keep rolling. Your inspection doesn't mean that a building necessarily has rising damp or concrete cancer, but you don't have time or money to pay $200 or $300 for a building inspection on each property you consider. Only get building inspections on properties you have first checked yourself and would seriously consider buying.'

Check out the Council Zoning

'Check out what building and development applications have been granted or are being sought in the area. Now, this is crucial research because development applications can dramatically increase or decrease the value of your property.

'Get to know the local town planner, they are critical to your success. Take them out for lunch. Ask them what their vision for the local area is, what they want to see done, how they want to see the property improved.'

The next sheet of paper, I discovered, was written by my Wealthy Friend. It was headed 'How I Met Jack'. Well, here were new revelations!

'I bought a building in a trendy suburb and I went to see the local town planner. I took him out for lunch and I said. "What do you want to do? What are you employed in? What are you interested in doing?" He was talking about streetscapes and this type of thing and how he didn't have much money. I said, "Well that's interesting ..."

'My building was in a tiny little street, only four blocks long, so I went to a contractor and found out how much it would cost to completely rip out all the footpaths, put in paving, put in nice trees, chairs and stuff like that to streetscape it. He quoted me $100,000.

'So I went back to the town planner and said, "Jack, I'll do you a deal. You want to see streetscaping. I would be prepared to streetscape this whole street for you if you allow me to put one extra storey on top of my building." And he said, yes.

'On top of my building I was able to put in two $400,000 apartments which cost me $280,000 each to build. So I was up $240,000 for the cost of $100,000. That's $140,000 clear isn't it? Sounds like good money to me. Now that was just on the first day.

'A year later those two extra apartments were worth $500,000. So 10 years down the track I have effectively got myself $920,000 for the cost of $100,000. That's a good investment to me!'

Lesson

Know your turf. Do your homework and find out all you can about your chosen area, including future plans by local councils or body corporates.

OFF THE PLAN

I bought an off-the-plan two-bedroom unit on the twelfth floor as a first home buyer for $300,000 in the Rockdale area right next to the station. One and a half years later it's already gone up in value to approximately $385,000 and still rising. Developers of a building going up across the road from it are selling one-bedroom units on the ground floor for $305,000 and up. Most of these units won't even see the sun. So my unit should rise in value even more.

LINDA, NSW

CHAPTER 15

Property Prices

I had already had instruction from my Wealthy Friend and his town-planner friend Jack on following the Laws of Money Magnetism and seeking suburbs with high growth. Now that I was getting closer to buying, it seemed my Wealthy Friend thought I was still a little underdone.

'If you're going to select property that's going to go up well, you need to know what impacts property prices,' he intoned. 'There are five main factors:

Sales Demand

'Number one is sales demand. Simple, grade-eight economics ... Sales demand pushes prices up. And this is the most important thing we need when we come to buy property. We need to be buying in an area where there's a big sales demand.

'There is a lot of belief out there that interest rates and inflation push prices and they certainly do. But the most important driver of property prices is sales demand. If we can pick suburbs where there is good sales demand, where there has been a history of sales demand, and we can expect in the future that there is going to be good sales demand, then we have probably bought a potentially successful property. We could buy the worst property in that suburb, but if there's good sales demand in that suburb, then chances are that even the worst property is going to grow. So sales demand is the primary driver.'

'OK,' I said, enjoying my private clinic, 'If more people want to buy in a suburb than there are properties available, the law of supply and demand means that house prices will rise. So if we buy where people are buying, we stand to do well.'

'Spot on.'

'I remember the mid-1990s in the Eastern Suburbs of Sydney. I'd never seen anything like it. I remember one specific unit that I went to purchase. It was a three-bedroom apartment in Darling Point. My valuer had put it at $550,000. I reckoned that the maximum that I'd pay for it was about $520,000. The opening bid was $650,000 and went all the way up to $880,000 before it was sold. Just unbelievable. There was about a 12-month period in Darling Point where it was basically throw-money-at-property time. He with the biggest bank account won. Something like that is repeated in many places from cycle to cycle.'

Rental Demand

'The second driver of property prices is rental demand. If you find suburbs where a lot of people want to rent, that means a lot of landlords will want to buy. And inevitably sales demand will be pushed up.

'It is interesting how much investment property prices are driven by rental property prices. If a property is worth $200,000, what could we, as a rule of thumb, say that that property is going to rent for?

'$200 a week,' I replied having heard this before.

'Exactly. And if that property goes up to $225 a week in rent, what can we say about the value of that property?'

'It's probably gone up to $225,000 as well?'

'Precisely. So if we buy in a suburb where there is good rental demand and rental prices go up, they will pull the prices of property behind them. If there's a strong rental demand in a suburb, that means that the rental prices will continue to go up, and that will attract more buyers which will continue to push prices up and so on.

'We don't want to be buying property in suburbs that have big vacancy rates. The average vacancy rate we're looking for is no more than about three to six weeks a year, which is about average. Make sure you allow for about four weeks per annum that you won't be receiving rent in all your projections and budgets.

'If you're finding you're having difficulty renting your property, drop the price by $5 or $10 a week. That will frequently get a tenant into it. That $5 or $10 a week doesn't mean much to you, but it can mean much to the tenants.'

Trends — the Driver of the Drivers

'The driver of the first two drivers is population and trends. The capital cities are benefiting enormously from the massive drift from the country into the suburbs. And the massive drift from the suburbs into the city. It seems everybody wants to get close to the centre of town.

'This is pushing up the prices of property closer to the city and draining country areas of people wanting to buy. It is also being encouraged by governments and councils, which don't want to be building more infrastructure further and further away from the city, so they rezone property to fit more and more dwellings on a block.

'Trendy suburbs are those particularly affected by this population movement. The real-estate term for these is 'aspirational suburbs'. Of course, we know that as uniqueness. People aspire to live in them for some reason or another. In Sydney people aspire to live in Paddington because it gives that nice inner-city, 'I'm wealthy' type of glow about it. 'I'm wealthy but I'm not ostentatious.' If you're ostentatious you live in suburbs like Darling Point and Point Piper. But Paddington is 'we've got money but we're not going to flaunt it'. Newtown is bohemian, artists and so on.

'People are attracted to certain suburbs because of what they think it will say to the world about them. And Newtown is a classic example. Thirty years ago who would have lived in Newtown in Sydney, or St Kilda in Melbourne, or New Farm in Brisbane? Nobody. Now they are aspirational suburbs, people want to live there. They're moving in there, they're renovating properties, and the properties are growing.

'Look for upgrading features in town-planning. If they're putting in a new expressway, if they're putting in a new railway, if they're putting in a new stadium, if they're putting in a new X, these upgraded features often mean that suburbs are going to go up in price.

'If you look at Melbourne, you will find the suburbs alongside the new eastern freeway have been growing dramatically over the last few years. They've now become attractive to people because they're quick drives into the city.

'It is the same with the corridor between Brisbane and the Gold Coast and areas along the new M2 and M5 in Sydney. Transport is very important to people who work, and they are prepared to pay a premium for it.

'I remember when electric trains went into Brisbane — those lines where they were added saw house prices jump almost instantly as people had access to quality and relatively cheap public transport.'

Economic Drivers

Inflation

'Most people think that inflation is the primary driver of property. Of course inflation does drive property prices. If inflation goes up 5.25% this year, that means that properties go up about 5.25%. It's a self-fulfilling prophecy. But that growth is not what we're chasing. People make a big deal of inflation growth when it comes to property, but it's irrelevant to us because if property prices go up 5.25%, what else has gone up? Everything. If my property goes up at the same rate as inflation, all I've done is kept in pace with inflation. While I'll happily accept any rise, it's far better if my property outperforms inflation, and the only way to do that is by buying well in the first place.'

Interest Rates

'People think that as interest rates go higher, property prices fall. While this is partially true, generally what happens is that when interest rates get too high, demand slackens off so property prices flatten.

'On average, over the last 50 years Australians have paid 9.8% per annum interest rates on their housing loans. Even today, compared with other countries, Australia pays very high interest rates. But against average Australian interest rates, less than 8% is pretty low.

'By the time interest rates get to 9% or 10%, certainly demand for property has slowed. That's when it's better to be lending money out than borrowing, so people start putting their money into cash and buying shares (this is like lending money to a company).

'When demand really starts to slacken off is when interest rates climb to 11% or 12%. Then affordability disappears and people stop buying. Prices stagnate and people who can no longer afford the repayments have to sell their properties. This can push prices down in the short term. Quality growth suburbs are often impacted less by this but prices can go down temporarily there too. Because most people can't afford to sell property at a loss they hold on. After a while things equalise and demand equals supply and prices stagnate.

'This has an interesting stabilising effect on property prices. Even though prices are down because people are inclined to hold on to their property during these down periods, the pricing volatility is very rarely noticed, so it is rare that people lose money by selling. Contrast that to shares, where people rush to sell during pricing downturns. That's why graphs charting property prices generally flatten even though there is downward movement in some property sales, whereas share price graphs are all over the place, revealing volatility. However, if people adopted the same strategy with shares as they do with property — holding during down times — the volatility in shares would largely disappear.'

Lesson

The fundamental laws of supply and demand apply to property. A limited supply of sought-after land or housing will drive prices up.

LOCAL KNOWLEDGE WINS

We were looking at the Central Coast as a good capital growth area with a much lower entry point than Sydney beachside suburbs. The problem with researching the Central Coast is that one postcode covers a lot of different suburbs, so it is hard to pick the best growth area from an available capital growth report. Nonetheless, I drove up every weekend for a month or so to research the area with my wife (six months pregnant) and three-year-old son. We had come to the point after discussions with several local agents, where we'd decided that Umina Beach was suitable, and we then went off to have lunch in a local park.

My wife thought it would be a good idea to ask some of the locals what they thought of the area and entered into a conversation with an old lady who told us that Ettalong Beach was a much better prospect, especially with the fast ferry to Sydney planned to depart from Ettalong wharf. Not one agent had mentioned this little gem, so off we went to Ettalong Beach and within one week had secured a great property. Twelve months later the ferry is approved to go and we have enjoyed roughly 30% capital growth. Sometimes local knowledge is the best knowledge.

CRAIG & ROBYNE, CHERRYBROOK, NSW

CHAPTER 16

Let's Go Shopping with the Second Secret of Money Magnetism

I awoke with a start, my hand fumbling to find the ringing phone. Like most people woken in the middle of the night I was alarmed that something grave might have occurred.

'Wake up,' said a voice which through my sleepy fog seemed only just vaguely familiar. 'We're going shopping!'

'Who is this?' I asked, also alarmed by the perky tone, at this time of the night.

'It's me. Come on the early bird gets the worm,' said my Wealthy Friend. I looked at my clock and it said 6.51 am. For somebody used to getting up at about 10 am it *was* the middle of the night. 'I'll see you in half an hour,' said my Wealthy Friend, before hanging up.

'There are no worms in their right mind up at this time of day!' I thought to myself, as I stumbled into the shower. Exactly 30 minutes later my Wealthy Friend pulled up in a mid-range Mercedes Benz. 'New car?' I asked surprised because I thought it was a big step down from his Rolls.

'Property car,' he replied, 'Just the right combination of "I've got more than enough money to afford this but not enough so you think I won't be negotiating the price!"' I rubbed my sleepy eyes, managing just a small smirk at his joke.

'Don't worry, you'll spark up when you meet Pauline, my real-estate agent.'

Now, my so far limited experience with real-estate agents was of middle-aged balding and sweating men or young sharks wearing cheap suits, ugly ties and even cheaper shoes, so I could hardly imagine a real-estate agent generating enough interest in me to actually wake up. 'What exactly are we going shopping for?' I asked dubiously, worried that I may have to shout my never-spend-a-penny Wealthy Friend yet another small treat when it was the week between pays and all I had left in my wallet was about $2.17.

'Property of course — I am going to demonstrate the Second Law of Money Magnetism — you *do* remember what that is don't you?'

'Value adding — a person is rewarded in direct proportion to the amount of value they add into the system.' I said by rote, having learned all my Wealthy Friend's laws and rules, afraid that I might be 'excommunicated' at this late stage for forgetting or muddling one. While he never actually seemed angry with me, it was obvious that he condemned himself every time one of his 'students' didn't get something he had explained. He took his teaching role very seriously.

We pulled up in front of a block of apartments with a 'For Sale' board out the front. The description read, 'Renovators delight! Turn this 3-bedroom apartment with all the right features — northerly aspect, view and parking — into your own masterpiece.'

I was about to read the rest of the details on the board when a sporty little convertible raced around the corner and came to rest opposite where we were standing. Out of the car emerged (quite a feat if you have ever tried to get out of a tiny convertible in any form even remotely simulating elegance) a woman so perfectly groomed and so stunningly gorgeous she could have been straight out of the pages of *Vogue*. Everything about her was immaculate and, as she lifted her sunglasses up into her hair, I swear it gleamed.

And she was walking straight towards me! By now I was convinced I was dreaming — that I hadn't woken up at all. Her shoes were highly polished, her slacks beautifully cut, everything about her was refined. 'Hello, I'm Pauline,' she lilted, as she held out her hand towards me.

I tried to move but I simply could not. My Wealthy Friend leaned over, closed my jaw, which had dropped to the floor, wiped a small amount of drool from my lips and lifted my hand to meet hers. 'This is Peter,' he said, mildly amused.

I managed to say something barely intelligible and Pauline seemed either not to notice my transfixed state or pleasantly ignored it, making me feel both totally at ease and an utter imbecile all at the same time. 'Come on inside, Peter, and I'll show you this little renovator.'

Once we were inside I certainly agreed that it needed renovation but could not be swayed, even by the amazing Pauline, that anybody would actually be delighted to do it.

It had vermiculite ceilings, mission brown walls, orange shag pile carpet, louvred doors in the kitchen, and came with its own endless supply of cockroaches. I was amazed to learn that Pauline believed the dump would fetch $220,000 to $230,000 at auction.[6]

But Pauline and my Wealthy Friend were not done — they had three more 'renovator's delights' to show me, all in varying degrees of disrepair.

My Wealthy Friend set me the task of noting down the 'saleable' features and attributes of each property and everything that needed to be done on them, which I did. However, what I found far more fascinating was that despite the fact that Pauline was driving a convertible with the roof down on quite a windy day, whenever she arrived her hair was always perfect! Always.

It was just like one of those movies where the actress wakes up with perfect hair and makeup or steps out of the exploding, burning building with not a strand out of place. To this day I have not figured out how Pauline achieves this amazing feat of personal grooming. I have never seen her with even one hair astray!

'And now, we're going to an auction', my Wealthy Friend announced at the end of our tour.

Another new experience for me — they were really adding up since I had met my Wealthy Friend.

When we arrived at the auction, Pauline was already there (hair perfect of course) and talking to an also immaculately presented man, who, I would later discover, was the principal of the agency and the auctioneer.

Little flags saying 'Auction Here Today' fluttered out the front and were obviously doing their job because a small crowd had gathered.

This property was completely different from the ones we had just seen. It was sparkling. Everything appeared brand new and you could still smell the paint drying.

I looked around as my Wealthy Friend got engaged in conversation with Pauline and the good-looking, well-dressed man. I began to think that being good looking was a mandatory qualification to work for this agency!

I noticed that the apartment was about the same size as the ones I had just seen but, as I have already mentioned, this one had been fully renovated. I tallied up the features and attributes of the apartment and I realised that this one could have been any of the apartments I had just seen before, only fixed up. It was almost like I was witnessing live 'before and after' photos.

'There you are,' my Wealthy Friend interrupted my thoughts. 'There's somebody I'd like you to meet. This is Luke, the decorator. He'll teach you the art of refurbishment.'

'Well, hello! Come on, I'll give you a good seeing to,' said Luke as he minced off in the direction of the kitchen.

'So how do you know my Wealthy Friend?' I asked Luke.

'Oh,' he said, while adjusting his bandanna, 'I do all his trick and flicks.'

'Trick and what?' I asked quizzically. I *had* come from the country but I wasn't a redneck and thought I was up on the lingo.

'You know, trick and flick. Fix and flog. Tart up and go.'

'Renovate and sell?'

'If you must,' he smirked, showing his obvious disdain at my lack of savvy. 'He buys, I renovate, he sells. It's simple. So simple I was even thinking of pinching it. You know, pick a daggy old house, kick out the residents, do it up, and sell it for a packet, making a fortune. I can just see the tears and drama of it all now. I just need a catchy name!'

He leaned in close and whispered in a conspiratorial manner, 'You're not in TV by any chance are you?'

'No,' I whispered back.

Luke winced in obvious disappointment, 'It's waaay ahead of its time anyway.[7] And what do you do?' he asked.

'I'm a check-out operator.' I swear I heard Luke gasp but he didn't move his lips so maybe it was something else.

'So what do you see here?' he grunted.

'An apartment?' I answered, ignorant of what was expected of me.

'This, my good man, is a perfectly balanced and harmonious interplay between light, space and colour to stimulate the mind and senses into a magnificent reverie that deceives a soul into believing that a fortune has been spent on the perfect environment for them to exist in. So much so that they are destined to part with significant sums of moolah to make it their own. I can see we have much work to do with you!' he intoned, still with disdain.

'So,' I asked in my customary way to ensure I understood, 'the renovation, while looking fantastic was achieved on minimum budget to create maximum effect in order to get the potential buyers to pay more for it.'

'Yes. I think he's getting it!'

'We do a bit with paint, a bit with finishes and a lot of magic to create a look that people either couldn't or are too busy to create themselves. Of course we are onto blocks now, but we still do the occasional single apartment when the opportunity presents itself. Rent or sell, it doesn't matter. The most important thing is that we dramatically increase what we get for it without spending too much.

'We prefer to call them rejuvenations rather then renovations. You know, just slap on some makeup and lippy and get them back out on the street workin' it!' he said with a laugh.

'What's the difference?' I asked.

'It's all about the cost and the amount of work involved. A renovation implies that there is a complete make-over. Gutting the place and starting again. Renovations are invariably expensive and time-consuming. What we do is much simpler. We avoid anything structural, anything that will take a long time, anything that we don't understand or can't estimate the cost of just by looking, and anything that is going to cost money but you can't see.'

'What do you mean about not seeing it?' I asked.

'Well,' said Luke, trying not to let his obvious disapproval shine through, 'just imagine you looked at a house that needed a new roof which cost $15,000, but the house itself was in very good repair — you know, fresh paint and carpet, needing no interior work — versus one that was structurally sound but looked awful — but nothing $15,000 worth of paint, carpet and so on wouldn't fix ... Which is the better buy?'

'Aren't they the same? In the end you have to spend $15,000 on each to get them to the same condition.'

'Wrong!!' exclaimed Luke with just a little too much relish for my personal taste. 'The house that needs the cosmetics is a much better buy. You see, everybody *expects* a house to have a good roof. If you spend $15,000 on that it won't make one cent worth of difference to the sale price, or if anything it certainly won't increase the value of the house more than the $15,000 you had to spend on the roof.

'Spend the $15,000 on making the place *look* fabulous — better than the one with the shonky roof — and you've probably added $20,000, $30,000, or maybe even $50,000 in value to the house. You see, most people don't have much imagination. They look at a pretty house that needs a new roof and they can call in a builder to estimate how much that will cost — easy. But if they see a place that looks like a mess, most people can't see past the mess to how fantastic the house underneath could be.

'Once we reveal that beautiful "inner" house, people are amazed at how fantastic it looks and imagine themselves in it. And *that*, my dear boy, they are prepared to pay for.'

'And we are about to find out how much,' interrupted my Wealthy Friend. 'The auction is about to start.'

'But *we* were only just getting started,' I protested.

'That's OK,' I'm sure if you shout Luke a frappé or a latte, he'll be happy to give you a lesson in rejuvenations. But for now, let's pay attention to the auction.'

By the time we got there, the auctioneer had already started. He was polite and enthusiastic, encouraging people to bid, helping those who were nervous, and edging the price up.

Pauline was walking briskly between bidders, talking to them quietly, each time generally resulting in a hand raised to make another bid or a head nodding. Pauline said something to each that made them smile and then moved on to the next person.

I was fascinated as the price started at $230,000 (or about the buy price of the previous similar properties we had seen) and went up to $257,000.

There was a slight pause in the bidding when nobody else was putting their hand up and the auctioneer and Pauline's best skills didn't seem to make any difference. Pauline then headed to my Wealthy Friend who was standing there observing but not obviously participating. 'It's a good price for this stage in the auction,' she said quietly so nobody else would overhear.

'Yes. What's happening with your bidders?' he replied.

'I have three yet to come in, the last couple have probably about $5,000 or $6,000 to go and a couple of dark horses.'

'OK, well, we're over reserve so let's put it on.'

By now I was a little lost and would obviously have to ask my Wealthy Friend what all that was about, but for now I thought it prudent to sit back and watch.

Pauline nodded to the auctioneer. He smiled broadly as if he were waiting for this moment and loudly declared that the property was 'on the market'.

This seemed to cause quite a stir and bidding furiously went up another $19,000 in small amounts until finally the property sold at $276,000.

Pauline and Luke both offered congratulations to my Wealthy Friend and, as he walked off to do the paperwork with Pauline, it dawned on me firstly that he owned the property (call me slow) and, secondly, that he probably made a handsome profit if the figures that Luke had been talking about were true.

'So, what did you think?' asked Luke.

'Great. How much do you think he made?' I asked.

'Well, he bought the apartment for $205,000. My budget was originally $15,000 but we went over by $2,000. Stamp duty, legals and holding costs were about $11,000. And selling costs would be about $9,000. All up the costs were $242,000 so the profit was $34,000. Not bad for three months' work.'

'Not bad?' I exclaimed, 'That's more than I earn in a year!'

I was getting more enthusiastic about this property business by the second, and I was certainly seeing how exciting value adding was.

'Come on,' said Luke, 'After all that excitement I could do with a latte. Your shout.'

I was starting to get used to those two words.

Lesson

The Second Secret of Money Magnetism — Add Value.

People need help to see what can be made of a structurally sound but messy dwelling, and that's where value can be added. A limited outlay in smartening up a property and giving it a desirable look can pay much greater dividends.

MESS IS MONEY

Here are the details of what I have been able to achieve. I have massaged some of Peter Spann's rules to suit my individual circumstances.

Property 1: Small beach shack on valuable waterfront land — Phillip Island Victoria.
Used Peter's ideas of creating an expensive look at a reasonable price.

100% equity before rebuilding	$230,000
(redraw facility in place prior to building)	
cost of initial purchase four years ago	$135,000
Rebuild/furnish costs	$210,000
Bank fees/quantity surveyor etc.	$2,000
Value now	$650,000
Profit since building	$208,000
Equity now	$470,000
(Have put in extra money while waiting for next project)	

Property 2: Double story property in same area 20 years old
This property was in a mess and smelt terrible. Mess is money. Had been rewired restumped and replumbed. Divorce after many years;

wanted quick settlement. Could oblige. Used redraw facility for deposit and costs.

Cost of property to buy	$397,000
Refurbish (polish floors etc.)	$4,000
Stamp duty and bank fees	$21,800
Total cost	$422,800
Value now (three months later)	$490,000
Profit	$67,200
Equity	$170,000

(Have put in extra money while waiting for next project)

Total profit on both properties	$275,200
Total equity	$640,000

The profit has been helped enormously by the huge capital growth in the area, in recent months.

ANDREA, VIC

CHAPTER 17

Renovating for Profit

Of course, Luke took me to the trendiest, grooviest, most expensive coffee shop in town. I was beginning to wonder if I could even afford to learn!

After Luke's latte and my iced chocolate arrived, he began to describe to me how to successfully rejuvenate a property for profit. 'Look,' he said, 'people love renovating but most of them don't know how to make a profit out of it. They spend too much, take too much time and renovate to their own taste, not to the taste of the market.

'And then they get all excited because the property has gone up in value, but what they don't understand is that if they had spent far less and just waited the same amount of time as it took them to do the renovation, they probably would have had the same increase in the value of the property. They would have been much better to have 'rejuvenated' as our Wealthy Friend does.

'There are four types of rejuvenation,' he went on ...

The Paint and Patch

'This is where the property has no structural problems but is not well presented. Paint, carpet, fixtures and fittings are all this one needs, and maybe a tidy up of the garden. This means that we can add a bit of flair and get some good capital gain — a rejuvenation.

'As I mentioned, most people don't have much imagination so they pass over these properties, but they are little gems.'

The Fixer-upper

'This is where the property is rundown and needs updating. It has all the features of the paint and patch but also needs a new kitchen, bathroom, and so on.'

The Mother-in-Law

'This is where the property has a problem of some sort, like cracked walls; or it needs a new roof, or extensive electrical or plumbing work; or worse, it needs some structural work.

'Remember, none of these costs will add value to the property. They are often expensive and hidden, which means that nobody will pay us more for a property just because we have done that work, so in fact these things put us back.

'In other words if you buy a house for $300,000 and it needs $50,000 of purely structural work to be done, it will still only be worth about $300,000. So you have lost $50,000 before you start!'

The Bulldozer

'This property requires complete renovation or needs to be demolished. Surprisingly, sometimes these properties are even more valuable than the others, because if they are in a good location, they allow people to start again and build what they want rather than be restricted by the existing property, especially if that property is protected by some form of council provision or heritage requirement.'

'Some people will buy these properties in fantastic positions and deliberately allow the house to deteriorate to the point where it is condemned to allow them to get around heritage provisions. This is one of the few examples I know of where demolishing something adds value, but it certainly is not for us.'

'So,' I asked, 'which is best?'

'Ideally,' replied Luke, 'we are looking for properties requiring paint and patch or fixer-upper renovations only. The level of renovation you take on depends greatly on your level of skills, knowledge and contacts, but most people can easily handle these types of rejuvenations given some planning and flair.

'What we are trying to achieve is a 'designer' look at a budget price. We want *wow* factor. We want potential tenants or buyers to be walking through the property saying "Wow, isn't that great", "Wow, I would like to live here", "Wow, a brand new x", and so on.'

'But I don't have a creative bone in my body,' I exclaimed.

'Then you may need to engage a designer.' If that was a sneer I saw, it softened. 'Stay away from architects and interior designers who do big projects. These rejuvenations are intended to be inexpensive. It takes a unique designer to create a look for you that is fantastic *and* cheap, but once you've found your designer, get them to pick the kitchen and bathroom, colours, fixtures and fittings — things like taps, door handles and so on — then just use the same design for all your properties. Remember to get the designer back every couple of years to update the look.

I must have had a doubtful expression because he continued. 'If you don't want to use a designer, get magazines and cut out the styles that appeal to you. Put them in a scrapbook so you can show tradespeople exactly what you want. Tradespeople can also help explain what will and won't work so use them to sound out ideas. The magazines often have trades and suppliers guides as well.

'Spend a lot of time going around to trade wholesalers. All you need is a company or a business card that says you are a designer and you can buy the goods wholesale — this can save you 10% to 50% on the cost of your fittings.

'Look, here are some basic guides on rejuvenations.'

Floors

'Floors are *very* important because they are so obvious and take up so much space. The timber look is always very popular, from the real thing to a linoleum copy. The new linos are fantastic and you can even instal them in flats and apartments where you are not normally allowed to have timber. However, if you can have a natural timber floor throughout then use it.

'Where you have concrete or an uneven floor you can instal what is called a floating floor, where timber is placed on top of battens to even it out. Unless you are handy leave this to the professionals regardless of how easy it looks on the box in the hardware store. It is complicated. Try to avoid timber in wet areas however unless it is properly sealed.

'Carpets should be plain rather than patterned. It takes a skilled eye to pick a pattern that will work well and not alienate most

Bye carpet if plain + reasonable

people. Nevertheless, try to avoid standard commercial carpets which are bland and have no feel to them. Copies of quality carpets are the best way to go. Again you are looking for a designer feel without the cost.'

Walls

'Choose warm colours for walls but avoid large expanses of yellow, as this colour can be irritating. Select one or two walls in your property as feature walls. Paint the feature walls in the current *en-vogue* colour. This is a very cost-effective way of making your property look up to date, and if the colour goes out of fashion you can repaint that single wall very cheaply.

'All architraves, doors and skirting boards should be painted in high-gloss white enamel. This is one of the few paints that doesn't vary in consistency and touch up can be quite invisible. Every time a tenant leaves a property, you can simply walk around with a tin of high-gloss white enamel paint and touch it up.

'Paint ceilings in flat ceiling white. White lightens a property and makes it look larger.'

Fittings

'Real "designer" fittings are very expensive, but the good news is that as soon as a design becomes popular it is usually copied. These "rip-offs" range in price and quality, so choose good copies of fittings. If you shop around you should find copies of expensive fittings that are almost indistinguishable from the real thing. These can be as little as 25% of the cost of the real fitting giving you a "designer look" at a fraction of the cost.

'Lighting is very important. Buyers and prospective tenants notice both the lighting effect and the fittings. Decent lights only cost about $60 to $80. The right lighting in a property will definitely add to the designer feel and the sale or rental value of your property.

'Door knobs and handles are also critically important. People notice them, and they finish off the entire look of the property and compliment its paintwork. They also contribute to the designer feel.

'A cheap knob might be about $2, an expensive one about $10. While there might be 20 or 30 knobs/handles in a kitchen, plain ordinary kitchens can be made to look very stylish by the additional of expensive door handles and knobs.

'Many people go for the cheapest possible window coverings but this is a mistake. Coverings such as vertical blinds and curtains are difficult to maintain and clean, and get damaged easily. Timber or metal Venetians are generally the best overall window finish available. They fit with most styles of property and they give the property a clean and streamlined look.'

Kitchens and Bathrooms

'Kitchens and bathrooms are critical to the overall design plan but both are very expensive to replace, so you need to be clever in your approach. Look for properties with bathrooms that are rundown and tired, but can be brought back to life through simple and cheap cosmetic changes. Try to avoid extensive plumbing works by keeping the bathroom in its same layout. As soon as you have to do plumbing you may as well rip out the whole bathroom and start again.

'Use bathroom resurfacing rather than replacement. Many people have never heard of this. Instead of replacing the bath, shower, basin and tiles, they can simply be re-enamelled. This is a very simple process by which the enamel is sprayed onto the surface and then baked on.

'Re-enamelling can be done in 24 hours and the reputable companies that do it offer guarantees ranging from 10 to 25 years. They can do any hard surface (although some are reluctant to do floors) and it makes a bathroom look absolutely brand new! And the best news is that it can cost up to 75% less than replacing the tiles.

'Often by resurfacing tiles, bath, and shower, replacing the shower screen and updating the vanity, you can have a new look bathroom for one-third of the cost of a "new" bathroom and it looks just as good.

'Keep tiles white. You can always paint the walls if you wish as it is easy to redo, but sparkling white always looks clean and fresh. If you need to retile, use the "tile over" technique, in which you simply place the new tiles over old ones. This saves the time and

get Addresses of whole folers
to get wholesale — Use STAR HOLDINGS
Ace ? furniture

Renovating for Profit **91**

cost of removing the old tiles (always expensive), waterproofing and retiling. Most people won't notice the difference and it will save at least 30% of the cost of starting from scratch.

'Use stylish and interesting fixtures and fittings, including knobs, taps and shower heads. This will give you a magic designer look at a small price.

'Like bathrooms, a good kitchen can make or break a rejuvenation. And like bathrooms you don't have to replace kitchens if they are in working condition but outdated. You can "transform" them. There are specialists who will come in and relaminate surfaces so that they look new.

'If you *are* replacing, buy kitchens wholesale. The wholesalers supply the retailers and the only difference is a flash showroom. Wholesalers are manufacturers, so don't expect much assistance with design, but you will save between 30% and 50% if you are prepared to do this work yourself. And because kitchens are expensive that can add up to many thousands of dollars.

'If you need to, go into the showrooms and get ideas and then go to a wholesaler to build the kitchen for you. Alternatively take pictures from magazines to show what you want. You can find wholesalers listed in the *Yellow Pages*.

'You only need a kitchen to last around 10 years, so lashing out on the most expensive high-quality equipment is a waste of money. It is more important to make sure it looks good and covers the basic needs of the tenant or buyer. Remember that this may vary dramatically from area to area. For example, a one-bedroom inner-city Sydney apartment hardly needs a kitchen, whereas in areas like Perth and Brisbane people are used to having a full kitchen.

'Remember also that with an investment property you are not building your own dream kitchen and it doesn't need to have everything you would want. Dream kitchens can cost tens of thousands of dollars once you put in all the appliances and labour-saving devices. In a "trick and flick" the objective is to create the *wow* factor without blowing the budget.

'Generally you should include dishwashers as these are now considered a standard modern appliance. Otherwise decide on the appliances and requirements of the kitchen based on your marketplace. And with such small margins on them, there isn't much benefit in buying appliances from a wholesaler because the retailers buy in bulk to get margin. The best place to buy appliances is from factory seconds sales and scratch-and-dent warehouses. These appliances often come with small blemishes and scratches but often in positions that are hidden after they are installed. Sometimes the appliance itself is perfect but the box has been damaged, yet you can often pay up to 30% less than retail.

'Avoid coloured laminate cupboards as they generally look cheap. If you are going to use laminate, choose a timber style or timber veneer.

'Don't go to the effort of installing pantries (or built-in wardrobes) and specialist fixtures and fittings like you might have in your own home. They do not add value. Always remember that people will spend on average no more than five minutes inspecting a property before they rent, and about 15 minutes inspecting a property before they buy. Only the most pedantic people will even remember such things from an inspection and, quite frankly, they will never buy or rent one of these properties. Leave those tenants or buyers to somebody else.

'Most people are prepared to pay more to live in a nice-looking property and these are our market.'

Exterior

'In the case of brick homes, bag rendering is the best way to update the property. In the case of timber homes, simply repaint them when required.

'Some people avoid timber houses because of the painting, but modern paints will last two decades, and timber houses often have more "character" than brick houses and people love "character".

'Choose paint colours to suit your marketplace as in the case of interior colours. Avoid using bright colours on large expanses of the exterior but use them on trims. That way you can update the trims along with what's fashionable, and keep the main part of the house the same, saving you money over the long term but still keeping the property fresh and up to date and appealing to buyers and tenants.

'With landscaping, stick to Australian natives and fill the areas around garden beds with bark. Try to keep the grassed areas to a minimum, as they require maintenance, and tenants (if you are going to rent your property) sometimes don't look after them well.

'Paving courtyards and paths can be a good idea. Modern stencilled concrete can be a cheap way to replicate paving at a fraction of the cost.'

Security

'Security depends greatly on your area. If you are going to rent your property, you have a common law obligation to your tenants to make it secure. In some areas like the inner city, security is extremely important, so it is advisable to provide your tenants with good security so they feel comfortable.

'You also have a common law obligation to your tenants to ensure that you have all the appropriate fire regulations requirements in place.'

Luke had to rush off to some glam fashion parade so he left me with the bill and to contemplate his advice.

While I had never tackled a renovation before I did pick up a number of magazines from the newsagent on my way home and was convinced I could do it myself.

Lesson

Rejuvenation is not demolishing a property or changing its whole character. It is adding sparkle and polish to enhance existing features.

$35,000 PAY DAY

We settled on a unit in St Kilda, Victoria, in August. It's right on the beach, in a block with a sauna and a great pool. We paid $225,000 for a one-bedroom unit with its own laundry, and it was previously rented for $200 per week.

We replaced the bathroom vanity, the kitchen and appliances, retiled the bathroom floor and walls, laid a floating floor in the main room, and had timber venetians installed.

After four weekends, a few days off work, and $12,000, we have had it revalued at $260,000, and we have it rented out at $265 per week. I will be proudly hanging (a copy of) our 'pay' cheque for $35,000 in the office! I haven't calculated it out fully, but I think it's costing us less than $30 per week to own.

By showing the 'before' photos to the quantity surveyor, we are able to write off $4,000 worth of kitchen appliances and old fittings, on top of the usual depreciation schedule.

KIMBERLEY & PAUL, VIC

CHAPTER 18

Knowing Your Price

It wasn't long before my Wealthy Friend noticed my new interest in interior design magazines. 'What most people don't know is that you make most of your money when you buy,' he pronounced one day when he saw me clutching a stack of *Home Beautiful*s.

'How is that?' I asked perplexed.

'Well,' he said, 'Think about it. Before you *buy* a property you need to know exactly how much work is needed; how long that work will take; how much of it you can do yourself; and how much it will cost you to have the work done. This allows you to calculate your purchase price and whether you are likely to be able to profit from the purchase and rejuvenation, and therefore whether you should go ahead and buy.

'Yes, OK,' I agreed.

'Calculating the maximum purchase price of a property is critical to your success if you are going to try to profit from value adding. This is how you do it,' he said, getting quite technical.

Estimate the Renovated Value

'Look around at other properties similar to yours that have been renovated and sold in the area. Ask agents and valuers. Get to know prices yourself as well but don't rely on "gut feel", get the facts.'

Estimate Your Purchasing Costs

'Include costs like stamp duty and council adjustment; interest to be paid during the renovations (when no rent is coming in); and professional fees, such as solicitors', designers', planners', and architects' fees.'

Estimate the Cost of Renovations

'Once you have established what you can do yourself, estimate how much you will have to pay for builders, tradespeople and materials. Make provision for overruns and unexpected work.

'Generally the total renovation should cost around 5% to 15% of the value of the property in most areas. Any more and you are probably overcapitalising.'

Set a Profit Margin

'If you don't add in a profit margin there is no point in renovating.

'Subtracting all these costs from the estimated renovated value gives you the maximum amount you should be paying for the property. Let's look at an example.'

He set out the following sum.

Estimated renovated value	$300,000
Costs	$10,000
Costs of renovation	$25,000
Profit margin	$25,000
Your maximum purchase price	$240,000

'Every dollar you spend over this amount is going to come off your profit, and every dollar less is going to go straight onto your profit.

'Once they get enthusiastic enough to start, many people then go overboard and end up paying far too much for the property thinking they can make up the difference in the renovation. This is simply not true. There is a maximum amount the property will be worth regardless of what you do to it, and this is set by the market.

'Any more spent on the property is a waste of money as it won't give you any more profit. This is called overcapitalisation. You have to spend a certain amount on your renovation, but there is no way your renovation can make up any overspending on the purchase of the property.

'One way you *can* save is by being prepared. Holding time — when you're paying interest and not getting any rent — is very expensive. Interest will be your biggest cost outside the actual renovation itself. The quicker you can get the work done the more profit you will make.'

'So organise any applications required to carry out your renovations before settlement. If appropriate, try to negotiate an extended settlement on the property so you can have all your approvals done prior to settlement. Settle on Monday so your tradespeople can start on the Tuesday and no days are wasted. Have your tradespeople ready to start then.

'My final suggestion —not that you seem to need it —' he said, eyeing my magazines, 'is that you spend a lot of time planning your design before you start.'

Lesson

Emotions have no place when you are buying investment property. This is straightforward, but so many people allow their investment property decisions to be dominated by their emotions. You are not going to live there, so do not overcapitalise. Every dollar you spend over your estimated costs — including property price and renovations — will come off your profit margin.

QUICK CAPITAL GROWTH

Since I started attending Peter Spann's seminars, I've bought two investment properties, so I have three altogether worth about $950,000. The properties have all been excellent. I bought in West Footscray last year at $242,000, spent $25,000 and now have a value of about $350,000; and I bought in East St Kilda at $220,000 now the property is worth about $290,000 to $300,000; and my original property in Middle Park I bought for $165,000 and it's now worth about $340,000.

GREG, VIC

CHAPTER 19

What Tenants and Buyers Don't Like Outside

My Wealthy Friend had already told me that he did not manage his substantial portfolio of property. 'Too much bother,' he had said. 'People ringing up at 2 am in the morning to tell you that their hot-water system doesn't work. Saving 4% or 5% on management costs isn't worth the hassle.'

But I wanted to know what tenants and buyers didn't like in a property and so he introduced me to his property manager, Mary.

Mary was bright and professional. The type of person who did everything with a smile, but you could imagine would be quite tough if she needed to be.

She quickly confirmed my Wealthy Friend's uninterest in managing property as an intelligent strategy. 'People think property management is just collecting rent, so they can't understand why it is good value to employ a managing agent. You'd think it would be easy but it is complicated these days, with the law, tax, and people expecting so much. I have no idea why anybody would want to do it themselves. When a self-manager gets their first big dispute that gets to court, usually they will be ruled against because they were not aware of the law in the first place. This is a costly reminder to leave it to the pros. I get paid for it and some days *I* don't even want to do it!'

While Mary's list of tenant dislikes may seem obvious, my Wealthy Friend encouraged me to use them as a checklist to make sure I didn't get carried away when buying.

'They don't like busy roads, they don't like to be next door to schools, industrial sheds, sporting complexes, shopping centres, commercial buildings or public toilets. They like to be a block away from these things but they don't like to be next to them.

'They don't like noise. Always check your property at different times of the day and different times of the week. A quiet street can turn into a rat race on Friday night; or Monday morning can be hell near a school but quiet on a Saturday.'

I found it hard to believe that people would overlook such basics but Mary went on. 'I actually had a client who bought a property in Brisbane with a new fence at the back. They told me they were painting it the day after settling on the property and suddenly heard an enormous roar. And of course the fence was hiding the train line behind it.'

That must have been a very poor pre-purchase inspection!

'People don't like the railway at the back fence, although they don't mind the bus at the front door.

'I had another client with a property in Cleveland in Brisbane. It's out on Morton Bay. The interesting thing about Cleveland is that it is right on the water, but when the tide goes out there is about 300 metres of mud on view.

'Cleveland was meant to be the capital of Queensland but when the first governor got there, they let him out and he fell into the mud. Took about half an hour to get him out, and he turned around and went up the river and said we're going to do it here.

'So they had this beautiful house in Cleveland. And I was the property manager. What to do with all that mud?

'Well, of course, you only ever showed the property when the tide was in. So people thought, "Oh this is beautiful", but when the tide went out there were all those metres of mud behind the house.'

Other things people don't like are big unit complexes on either side and, as I said, they don't like being in industrial or commercial strips.

'It may sound obvious but it is amazing the number of people who buy property and overlook these things, usually because they are blinded by the price. There eyes are so full of 'bargain' that they fail to see the mud!'

I made a mental note to always look out for mud.

Lesson

Don't be blinded by price. If the price of a property is low, look around you. Is there something out there tenants would not want to live next to?

SLEEPS SOUNDLY

Shortly after attending your seminar we bought our first property using information from the course. We bought an old ex-Housing Commission home, spent $12,000 doing it up, put it on the rental market and got $170 per week. Now it's worth almost double the purchase price, the rent is paying off the mortgage very nicely, and I've not lost a night's sleep in the process. I have done the same three times now and I'm looking forward to the next. Both my wife and I still have our day jobs and our marriage is as good as ever.

COLIN

CHAPTER 20

Say Thanks to the Tax Man

My Wealthy Friend had changed tack. 'One of the easiest ways to lose money with property investing is by not claiming all your deductions. Many people claim significantly less back from the tax man than they should. To make sure you are set up properly, I'll send you across to meet Bruce, the quantity surveyor.'

I met with Bruce, on site at one of my Wealthy Friend's properties where he was apparently preparing a report.

'Hi,' he said when he saw me, 'you must want to know the answer to the magic question?' Not knowing what the magic question was, I nodded in agreement.

'Everybody wants to know how to beat the tax office,' he said. 'I presume you're here because you asked our Wealthy Friend how to pay less tax?' Seeing I wasn't paying much tax, it wasn't top of mind for me, but I hoped that some day I would be earning a packet so I played along.

'Well, let me start by saying, no matter how hard you try, no matter what way you give it a go, you can't beat the tax office. You know what they say, the only two things that are inevitable in life are death and taxes.' He paused long enough to allow me to laugh and I politely obliged.

'There are, however,' he continued, suddenly serious again, 'many ways you can legally minimise your tax through investment property. And that's where I come in, I'm the tax minimisation man!' he said with the kind of flourish that implied he was a form of superhero. I was just happy he appeared to be wearing his underpants inside his shorts!

'The easiest way to understand tax minimisation is to see owning investment property as similar to owning a business. The tax office allows business people to claim a tax deduction for expenditure incurred while earning an income. And the tax office allows property investors to claim the expenses in owning a property as tax deductions as well.

'These things include interest, management and other professional fees, advertising, travel to inspect the property, rates and statutory expenses. All of these can be claimed as immediate tax deductions but, of course, in order to claim these deductions we have to actually expend the money.

'There is a "magic" tax deduction that owners of investment property can claim that doesn't need them to expend cash at all — depreciation. How do you think it works?'

'Um, land goes up in value, buildings decay and so go down in value?' I offered.

'Right. The tax office deems this to be a loss of capital over an extended period, and so allows us to claim a tax deduction for this loss. Let's say you buy an investment property for $250,000, and the land value is $150,000. That means you are paying $100,000 for the building. You are allowed to claim 2.5% of the cost of the building every year as a tax deduction, so every year you get a tax deduction on this property of $2,500 for depreciation and it costs you nothing out of your pocket. Buildings are depreciable over 40 years, so you can claim the tax deduction for 40 years until theoretically the building is worth nothing.'

'So where do you come in?' I wondered aloud, revealing my scant acquaintance with making both income and tax returns.

'You can claim depreciation allowance on renovations as well,'[8] Bruce explained. 'The annual depreciation allowance on some items can be as high as 37.5% over three years.[9] As these items make up the largest part of a depreciation schedule, depreciation allowance is almost as good on renovated property as it is on new.

'If you borrow the cost of the renovation, this adds to the costs of servicing the loan, but it enables you to claim a double tax deduction for the interest and the depreciation. As a quantity surveyor it is my job to put a price on your renovation and work out for you the amount you can claim on your tax for depreciation.

'Some people rely on their accountant for this but it is a specialised area, and for a few hundred dollars the deprecation schedule that a quantity surveyor will provide for you will generally find more legal tax deductions than anything else.

'People give their quantity surveyor copies of invoices or receipts or even their own estimations if receipts are not available.

'Once you get to know your quantity surveyor, they can also give you advice on how to renovate your property to maximise tax deductions through depreciation.

'Many people buy new property just to get the tax benefits of depreciation. While getting tax deductions is never a good reason to invest, obviously having depreciation allowance where you can claim tax deductions with no money out of your pocket makes it much cheaper to own investment property.'

I was listening carefully. I was determined to invest and determined to be rich. It sounded like advice for me. 'So you're saying I should buy and renovate — just like my Wealthy Friend?'

'Yes, but consider this. The benefits of depreciation allowance in new property versus renovated old ones are often overstated. Here is a comparison of the cash flow between two properties at the same price, one new, and one renovated old.

NEW		RENOVATED OLD	
$200,000 apartment		$170,000 + $30,000 renovation	
Interest 8%	$16,000	Interest 8%	$16,000
Buying costs	$2,500	Buying costs	$2,500
Total	**$18,500**	**Total**	**$18,500**
Rental $230 wk	$12,000	Rental $250 wk	$13,000
Shortfall	$6,500	Shortfall	$5,500
Land	$80,000	Land	$80,000
Building	$90,000	Building	$90,000
Fit-out	$30,000	Renovation	$30,000
Depreciation		**Depreciation**	
Land	–	Land & Building	–
Building @ 2.5%	$2,250	Renovations:	
Fit-out @ 10%	$3,000	$10,000 @ 2.5%	$250
Total depreciation	$5,250	$10,000 @ 10%	$1,000
		$10,000 @ 20%	$2,000
		Total depreciation	$3,250

TAX SAVINGS CALCULATION

Salary	$40,000		Salary	$40,000
Weekly tax	$203		Weekly tax	$203

Deductions			**Deductions**	
Shortfall	$6,500		Shortfall	$5,500
Depreciation	$5,250		Depreciation	$3,250
Taxable income	$28,250		Taxable income	$31,250
New weekly tax	$119		New weekly tax	$140
Tax saving	$84		Tax saving	$63

Weekly outgoings			**Weekly outgoings**	
Interest	$308		Interest	$308
Buying costs	$47		Buying costs	$47
Less:			Less:	
Rent	$230		Rent	$250
Tax save	$84		Tax save	$63
Weekly cost	$41		Weekly cost	$42

'So, in this example it is obvious that through the higher comparative rents and the depreciation allowance on the renovations, the cost to service an older renovated property and gain all the benefits of higher capital growth is just $1 more a week!

'However, let's look at the growth potential of the two properties, rounding the figures to the nearest $1,000.

NEW		**RENOVATED OLD**	
Yr 1 @ 5%	$210,000	Yr 1 @ 15%*	$230,000
Yr 2 @ 5%	$221,000	Yr 2 @ 8%	$248,000
Yr 3 @ 5%	$232,000	Yr 3 @ 8%	$268,000
Yr 4 @ 5%	$244,000	Yr 4 @ 8%	$289,000
Yr 5 @ 5%	$256,000	Yr 5 @ 8%	$312,000
Yr 6 @ 8%	$276,000	Yr 6 @ 8%	$337,000
Yr 7 @ 8%	$298,000	Yr 7 @ 8%	$364,000
Yr 8 @ 8%	$322,000	Yr 8 @ 8%	$393,000
Yr 9 @ 8%	$348,000	Yr 9 @ 8%	$424,000

NEW		RENOVATED OLD	
Yr 10 @ 8%	$376,000	Yr 10 @ 8%	$458,000
Equity	$176,000	Equity	$258,000

*The 15% growth in the first year for the renovated old property is due to the renovations. It then grows at the average 8%. Growth of new property is usually slower for the first five or six years before it reaches the average.

'For just $1 a week (or $520 over the period of the projection) you have $82,000 in additional equity with the renovated apartment!'

'That's quite amazing,' I said, genuinely impressed that such a small percentage in growth rate could lead to such a big difference over time.

'Of course, all of this means,' said Bruce, only mildly upset that I had interrupted him in what was obviously a lead-up to his big finish, 'that people can earn income *tax free*!' My blank look indicated to Bruce some further explanation was warranted ...

'OK, so you know that there is this thing called a "tax-free threshold" where the first amount of earnings doesn't have tax levied on it?' So that explained why I paid so little tax!

'It keeps nudging up, but let's just say that it's $5,000. That means the first $5,000 you earn is not taxed. If you had an investment property that had $5,000 in depreciation allowances, that means you could earn $10,000 and not pay any tax. Get it?'

'I think so,' I said, 'The first $5,000 is tax-free anyway and the second $5,000 is tax-free because of the $5,000 in depreciation allowances from the property.'

'Exactly, so for every $1 in depreciation allowances (and any other non-cash deductions) you have in property you can earn $1 tax free.'

'So,' I went on, 'If you own 10 investment properties and claim $5,000 each year in non-cash expenses (depreciation), you could earn $55,000 a year tax-free (about $5,000 per year in the tax-free threshold and $5,000 x 10 in depreciation allowances).

'If you own 100 investment properties and claim $5,000 each year in non-cash expenses, you could earn $505,000 tax-free (about $5,000 per year in the tax-free threshold and $5,000 x 100 in depreciation allowances).'

'You've got it,' he said, putting up his hand for a high five. All of a sudden I understood what my Wealthy Friend meant when he said, 'The tax office is your friend.'

When I mentioned this to him later he said, 'Look, I don't like paying taxes, who does? But it is the government that is responsible for determining how much tax you pay, not the tax office. If you want to change your taxes, we live in a democracy, change the government. I think you'll find the tax office doesn't care how much tax you pay, just that you follow the law. And I also think you'll find, if you want to ask for it, the tax office will readily assist you in following the law, even if that means you pay far less tax. It's just up to you to ask.

'And while dealing with all the paperwork, the occasional audit and understanding the constantly changing tax law has been tedious, over the years I have found the people at the ATO ever willing to assist me in following the law and where possible, legally reducing my tax.'

Lesson

Returns from property come mostly from capital growth. But using tax deductions for depreciation helps your income to go further.

TAX REFUND

I came to a Peter Spann seminar with one property in hand at Bondi Beach and almost paid off after a few years of killing myself. After learning that 'good' debt is good, I bought a second investment unit in Bondi Junction: a one-bedroom, $185,000 real dump. I was going to renovate but the tenants who were paying $200 per week begged me to let them stay and offered me $230 a week and they cleaned it up for me. Nine months later that property is worth $270,000. Not bad for signing a piece of paper!

I then used the equity in the first property to purchase a two-bedroom property in Marrickville for $230,000, which I rent out for $210 per week. It needed no work and the tenants signed a one-year lease for a $10 per week discount. I guesstimate that this property is now worth $280,000 only four months later. I am going to receive a $4,000 tax refund thanks to the strategies used and next month I plan to purchase a unit in Queensland. My friends laughed at me for spending $1,000 on seminars but so far thanks to them my net worth has increased by $135,000 in a year. Who's laughing now?

SIMON, NSW

CHAPTER 21

How to Purchase a Property for $35 a Week

Even after all this research, I wasn't convinced that I could afford a property. It all seemed so daunting. No wonder my Wealthy Friend had said that taking the first step was often the thing that stopped most people.

'Look, I understand why you are not convinced, but most people spend more on lunch a week that they would on an investment property. Let me show you how the average person could buy an investment property for $35 a week.

Property Investment

Property	$200,000
Stamp duty	$4,614
Legal fees	$1,200
Borrowing costs	$5,000
Total	$210,814

Tax position	Without investment	With investment
Cash inflow		
Salary	$40,000	$40,000
Rental income		$10,400
Total income	$40,000	$50,400
Less:		
Cash outlays		
Interest @ 6.5%		$13,000
Rates		$980

Cash outlays (continued)

Body corporate		$589
Management fees		$741
Insurance		$400
Repairs		$700
Total cash expenses	$0	$16,410

Non-cash outlays

Depreciation		$6,000
Amortisation of borrowing expenses		$1,000
Motor vehicle travel to inspect properties		$300
Total non-cash expenses	$0	$7,300

Total expenses	**$0**	**$23,710**
Total taxable income	**$40,000**	**$26,690**
Tax thereon	**$8,980**	**$4,787**

Cash position

Rental income		$10,400
Tax savings		$4,193
Total cash income		$14,593
Less:		
Cash expenses		$16,410
Net outflow		**$1,817 or $35 a week**

'This is the nuts of negative gearing — your income from your investments is negative, which allows you a deduction in taxable income.'

'I understand that,' I said. 'But what if I can't wait until the end of the year to claim my tax back. I can't afford to pay the difference between the income and the costs now.'

'Well, you are going to love this,' smiled my Wealthy Friend. 'You don't have to wait until the end of the year to claim your tax back. You can claim it back immediately, just by filling in a little form.[10]

'You see, if you *know* that you are going to be claiming an amount back at the end of the year, and you know exactly how much it is, and it is reasonably constant, the tax office will allow you to advise them of this and *not* have that amount taken out of your pay as tax each week.

'In the example above, the weekly tax saving is $86. By filling in a particular form the tax office will allow your employer (even if that is you[11]) to deduct $86 per week less out of your pay packet so you will have the amount ready to pay off your interest and other costs. In this way the tax office effectively subsidises the cost of owning property — this means it is significantly more affordable and, if you want, you can buy more property faster.'

Now I was excited. I didn't earn much but I knew I could afford $35 a week. And while this amount obviously changes with all the variables, it is simple to do the calculation for yourself or with the help of a tax professional. You will usually be pleasantly surprised how little owning an investment property will cost.

'But,' I asked my Wealthy Friend, 'what if the government takes negative gearing away?'

'Well, that's a possibility, but it's not really logical. The only time the government tried to, it crippled the economy, forced rents up horrendously, and did not provide the increase in tax expected because so many people sold their investment properties. It was such a disaster the same government brought negative gearing back in and made the changes retrospective to try to fix any damage caused.

'Even if the government does change the law and you had to pay the full amount, in our example you'd be paying $121 a week to own that investment property or $6,292 a year. The property would be growing at about 8% a year on average so you'd still be about $10,000 a year better off in your first year, $11,000 in your second year, and by year 10 your capital growth would be $32,000, so you'd be $28,000 in front that year alone, and that doesn't take into consideration any increase in the rent. If rents went up at about 9% a year it would only take five years for the property to go cash-flow positive and then all the capital gain would be yours as pure profit.'

'Yes, I see. While it would make it harder without the negative gearing benefits, it would still be worth making the sacrifice to own the property.'

'You bet ya!' exclaimed my Wealthy Friend.

'But what if the government raised stamp duty or land taxes?'

'Governments change the laws all the time. Most of the changes have very little impact in the long term — which is where we are looking.'

By now I was aware that there were often traps in every strategy, so I stopped to think if there were any holes that I could spot. It sounded too good to be true.

'What's up?' inquired my Wealthy Friend.

'I am just trying to think of any pitfalls.'

'Good work, expect the best and plan for the worst! To be honest, most people can only use negative gearing benefits to own three or four properties before they are actually paying no tax at all.'

'That comes under my idea of a good problem to have,' I said.

'Yes, but it does mean that you would have to fund 100% of the cost of the property from then on without any tax benefits. And there are some negative gearing no-nos.'

HOW TO BUY YOUR PROPERTY FOR NEARLY NOTHING

One of the most exciting moments for me came when I started looking around for a high-yield form of property investing and found it sitting under my nose: commercial property trusts.

We have already noted in chapter 4 how a property trust can grow well and, based on a 12% per annum yield on a $15,000 investment, fully fund the negative cash flow of a $200,000 property. But, even better, a commercial property trust can also be geared, further reducing your outgoings. If you could achieve 15% yield (higher risk but possible) while paying 7% per annum interest on your loan, you would only have to contribute $10,500 (based on 30% deposit) of the investment to almost cover the cost of your property.

So for every property you buy, you could simply put an appropriate amount into a commercial property trust to offset any negative cash flow.

> The added bonus of this strategy is that as rents grown in your residential property (most property takes between three and five years to go cash-flow positive), any surplus cash flow is yours to pocket or can be used to fund even more residential investment properties. *Plus* you will be getting some capital gain on your commercial property trust and this will be increasing your cash flow and equity. Add it all up and it soon becomes a very exciting strategy!

Negative Gearing No-nos

'Negative gearing should not be seen as a strategy. It is a consequence of your strategy.

'If you want to buy high-growth properties and you don't want to sacrifice low risk, then your return is going to be less than on some properties that may be cash-flow positive but have lower growth.

'So the strategy is high growth, low risk, and the consequence is that you will have to contribute to the costs of owning that property. And this is the consequence of your well-thought-out strategy of sacrificing return for capital growth.

'The "negative gearing" term comes from the fact that you are borrowing to buy an investment (gearing) and your income is less than your costs (the negative part). In order for the strategy to work, however, the capital gain on the property *must* exceed the cash-flow negative amount. And exceed it handsomely, otherwise there is no point. That's why we must do so much research to ensure that we have the best chance of buying property that will out-perform the average by growing well.

'You should never buy a property on the tax benefits alone. This would be the second greatest mistakes of investors. Getting enticed by the tax benefits and forgetting about the growth, return and risk prospects of the property.'

'Are people so concerned about the tax they are paying that they would make such a big mistake?' I asked.

'It would seem so,' replied my Wealthy Friend. 'And there are many schemes, both shonky and fully legal, that will relieve you of your money so that you pay less tax. People forget, however, that the amount they lose is deducted off their income for the calculation of tax, it's not returned to them. So if they lose $1, the maximum tax benefit is about 48 cents. It's only when they have to hand over hard-earned cash to make up for those losses that they realise their mistake. That's why growth of the asset is so important. If the asset grows you can get ahead. If it does not you are simply going backwards faster.'

'Ouch!'

'Oh, yes. There are people out there who own all sorts of weird and wonderful "investments" like frog farms, ostriches, land in the middle of the desert, and so on all in the name of saving tax. I even know of one scheme that tried to sell bottled air! And the first these poor folk know that they have "bought a pup" is when the tax office disallows their claim and not only have they lost their money, they have lost their tax deduction as well.

'And again, that's why investing in good growth property is so attractive and is the best tax-minimisation strategy for most people. You can get good growth, a reasonable return, low risk, *and* tax benefits.'

'Let me see if I've got it,' I said. 'If the strategy is going to be successful we have to find high-growth property. In return for low risk we may have to sacrifice some rental return and therefore we may have to pay some money out of our pocket to own this type of property — if we are going to borrow money to do so. This is called negative gearing. But the good news is, the government allows us to claim this negative gearing off our tax so it makes ownership much more affordable, and so as long as the capital growth on the property is handsomely exceeding our outgoings, we are making profits and we are in front.'

'You're getting good,' said my Wealthy Friend, paying me an extreme compliment, 'but we've missed one thing in our cash-flow discussion, can you pick it?'

I thought for a while but couldn't come up with anything.

'What about the rent itself? In the example I just gave you, we didn't take into consideration that you may be able to increase the rent after you have done your rejuvenation. With the increased rent, many people find that the cost of owning their investment property can be much less. For some, it can even be cash-flow positive!

'That's why the 'rejuvenate and rent' strategy is so good. Good growth, cash flow, and tax benefits are all possible if you do it right.'

Now I could see why so many of my Wealthy Friend's 'students' were so happily getting on with the business of making wealth.

'So I guess you're ready to learn about the leverage component of investing — finance?'

I knew this was coming, and since I had had it drummed into me that borrowing money was bad, I was rather uncomfortable.

Lesson

Taking full advantage of all the tax concessions can mean that your property costs you as little as your weekly lunch money.

FROM JOBS TO FREEDOM IN TWO YEARS

Since doing Peter's seminar, our lives have changed considerably, all from the information we put to work from his seminars. I was working as an interior designer for architects, and my husband had been running his own handyman business for the last eight years. We have, 12 months ago now, sold the business and I gave up work. We now buy property, rejuvenate it and either sell (as few as we can) and keep most. Doing what we love *everyday*, living *a life of choice*, spending every day together — our lives are so easy and fun. We work when we feel like it and rest when it's hot. We go to lunch during weekdays and take as long as we like. We went skiing last year for our holiday, and I have just spent five weeks in Newcastle with my sister, helping her recuperate from open-heart surgery, prepared to pay for large medical bills should her insurance not cover them — something I would not have been able to do had I worked as an employee for someone and been without wealth.

Last year we made $50,000 from one property rejuvenation in three months, and rent went from $150 per week to $270 per week.

We are currently rejuvenating a once-grand large old Californian bungalow on a 1000 square metre block, which we plan to sell for approx $150,000–$200,000 profit in six months. We are doing this without putting a cent of our own money in, and being able to live in a grand old house rent-free.

The profits from this house will go into our trading portfolio to give us financial freedom for the rest of our lives — all in two years (sometimes I think what's taken us so long?).

We have another investment property waiting for us to rejuvenate when we have finished this one, one which we purchased eight months ago and only settled on in November — growth before it's even ours. by the time we have finished, we will have made approximately $120,000 in 12 months from the purchase.

We are now invited to be guest speakers at property investment seminars, and teach others what is possible, as well as consult to others rejuvenating.

My sister has now moved to Perth to live with us and learned about wealth creation. It is amazing that I have inspired her and can affect her life too.

All along the way we have a plan and are totally focused and passionate about what we are doing and where we are going.

ROWENA & CHRIS, PERTH, WA

CHAPTER 22

Leverage — the Third Secret of Money Magnetism

My Wealthy Friend read my face and raised his eyebrow in a way that suggested I should tell him what was troubling me.

'It's just that I need to know more about finance — I still can't quite get my mind around how Glenda and the other people you have introduced me to have borrowed so much money. I thought borrowing money was bad.'

'Some borrowing is bad. There is good debt and bad debt. Bad debt is where you borrow money for depreciating assets that have little or no worth once they are paid off (if ever). People borrow money to buy a couch and pay ridiculously high interest rates on credit cards or on consumer borrowings only to eventually pay off the loan and have the asset worth nothing and probably needing replacement. That way people constantly chase their tails with debt, never getting ahead, always paying things off and going backwards doing it. If you borrow money this way, you'll find it very hard ever to be wealthy. The best advice I was ever given was to never get a credit card or take out consumer finance. The amazing thing is that for the same repayment, or sometimes less those people could have bought an investment property.

'Good debt is where you are borrowing money to buy an asset that is returning an income that is greater and/or growing faster than the interest costs. That way you are getting ahead,' explained my Wealthy Friend.

'Right, so borrowing sensibly for appreciating assets can help you become wealthier faster, but I still don't understand property finance.'

'Well you need to meet Eddie. I'm sure I have his card. Yes, here it is.'

The card read 'Eddie Rice, Finance Broker', and his office was on my bus route home from my Wealthy Friend's place. I was eager to hear what he had to say.

Eddie's suburban office was modest but busy. About 20 people were constantly answering phones and all the interview rooms were full of customers applying for loans.

I was surprised that Eddie could see me straight away and when I commented on that he replied, 'Don't do any of the actual work myself. Supervise, manage, motivate — that's my job. Hasn't our Wealthy Friend taught you the Secrets of Money Magnetism yet?'

'Yes, he has. So you're applying the Secret of Leverage?'

'Absolutely. No need to do anything yourself when other people can do it for you. Especially since they can do it better.'

'You mean your staff are better than you?'

'Oh yes, well certainly at the day-to-day work in financing. Of course, I had to get the knowledge of how to build, run and maintain a successful business, but they know more than me about finance any day.'

'So why did you pick finance then,' I asked, curious to increase my knowledge.

'People hate the banks!' he said with enthusiasm.

He must have noticed the mystified look on my face because he went on, 'It's silly really, because banks lend money to people like you and me to help us buy things we want and need, and also for assets that will make us rich. But to most people it seems that the banks are uninterested in helping them. Most of their customers would prefer to deal with staff like mine who care and are actually interested in helping their customers become more successful in life. We offer exactly the same products as banks, in fact most of our brokering business goes to the banks — after all money is money — but our people seem better at caring. All the banks seem interested in is making a profit.

'So our Wealthy Friend sent you here to get a loan did he?'

'Um, I suppose, but he did give me a big lesson about the Laws of Money Magnetism before I left, so I guess I'm actually here to learn more about finance.'

'Good answer,' laughed Eddie. 'He's really got you hooked hasn't he?'

'I don't understand?'

'Sorry, just a bit of my natural scepticism kicking in — I'm working on it. I just meant that when I first met our Wealthy Friend I was really sceptical. I must admit it took me many years to believe everything he had to say, but now I'm a convert. His knowledge has made me millions of dollars. Even the other day I was offered over a million for a small share of this business — now that's leverage!'

I had to agree. Even though Eddie was acting a bit oddly, always moving in his chair and never sitting still, I was warming to him.

'Using OPM — other people's money — is of course one of the ultimate financial leverages,' continued Eddie, seemingly without taking a breath. 'Once you know how, it's easy to get, it's virtually unlimited, and there's always more of it out there than you will ever be able to use. Can you remember what our Wealthy Friend has to say about leverage?'

'Leverage is the most powerful of the Secrets of Money Magnetism. Use it wisely and it can make you rich. Use it stupidly and it will make you poor — fast!'

'A good summary', said Eddie with a smile on his face.

'I think,' I said, 'if you apply it to a good business, or a good idea, or a quality investment opportunity, then it helps you get to where you want to go faster. But our Wealthy Friend also warned me that the consequences could be dire if I applied it to a bad investment or idea.'

'Exactly, and it's the same with finance. Use it to acquire a quality asset that returns more or goes up in value faster than what you have to repay, and you'll get rich much faster than if you had paid cash. But use finance to buy an investment that doesn't have that potential or to buy things that depreciate to no value or have no tax advantages and you will get yourself into trouble real fast.

'It is leverage that makes property so attractive. Most financiers like financing property. It's tangible, it's easy to value, its price doesn't fluctuate erratically and, because people get very attached to it, they tend to do everything they can to repay the loans, so the default rate is very low. That means they will give very high loan-to-valuation ratios.'

'Loan to whats?' I asked.

'Oh sorry, I'm going too fast. It's all got to do with risk. If you expect a financier to take a big risk they'll charge you more. The smaller the risk, the lower the cost. The three things you have to consider when borrowing money are:

- What security or collateral the lender requires to give you the money. In other words what items of value you are prepared to offer the lender if you don't or can't repay the loan.
- How much deposit you have to put in — how much you have to contribute yourself to the purchase.
- How much it will cost you to borrow the money.

'Quite simply, the better your security, the less deposit you will need and the less it will cost you.

'For small loans the collateral might just be your good name, your credit history or your employment. That might be enough to convince a lender to loan you 100% of the purchase price without any other security. This is called your "covenant", or the trust that they place in you to repay the loan. The better your covenant the more they will lend you with less security and at lower cost. It works on the principle that people do not want to tarnish their good name by not repaying loans and, of course, the "better" your name, the less you'll want to tarnish it, so the more you'll do to make sure the loan is repaid to keep your reputation intact.

'For some loans the only security a lender may need is the actual thing you are purchasing. This is why, when you come to borrow money for an item like a car, all the financier will look at is your covenant and take the car itself as security. Because they know that the car will go down in value they want to make sure that you have a steady job, you haven't moved house much in the past (so they know they can find you) and that you have a good credit history (you've repaid loans before). If you can't prove this they'll charge you more for the loan because it's a higher risk to them.

'When you come to buy something that is more expensive still, like a house, they will want you to have "skin in the deal".'

'Huh?' I said with all the intelligence I could muster.

Eddie smiled, 'I know it sounds complicated and there's all this jargon, but stick with it — you'll get it. Most people allow their confusion to hold them back. People are afraid of looking stupid. I guess it's something drummed into us as kids when we get picked on at school for answering questions wrongly and looking silly. We get afraid to ask questions and so maintain our ignorance. Our Wealthy Friend taught me to persist in asking questions, even at the risk of appearing ignorant.'

'Oh yes,' I said, 'I remember him saying, "Better to appear to be ignorant that to ever remain ignorant!" So what do you mean by "skin in the deal"?'

'It means you have something to lose if you don't repay the loan. The more "skin" you have at risk, the more you are likely to repay. When it comes to borrowing money for property purchases, "skin in the deal" usually means a deposit, or the amount that you have to contribute to the purchase. The higher your deposit, the more "skin" you have to lose and the lower the risk to the financier. The lower the risk, the lower the cost of the loan.'

'OK,' I said, slowing him down so my mind could take in everything he was saying, 'so, the lower the risk to a financier, the less a loan will cost you?'

'Yes, that's it.'

'And you lower the risk by:

- having a good credit assessment by having an income and loans that you have repaid before;
- giving the lender "security", by giving them something of value to sell if you don't repay the loan even if that is the purchase itself; and
- by having "skin in the deal" or contributing part of the purchase price yourself.'

'Spot on,' said Eddie, obviously pleased with himself.

'So what was that "loan to vacuum" thing?'

'You mean the loan-to-valuation ratio. That's simply how much of the purchase price, or more accurately the valuation of the property, the financier is prepared to lend you.

'Let's say the property is valued at $100,000. If the financier is prepared to lend you $80,000, that means the loan-to-valuation ratio is 80%. If the financier is prepared to lend you $90,000, the loan-to-valuation ratio would be 90%, and so on. What's left over is the amount that you have to contribute — or the deposit.

'Most financiers in Australia will lend about 80% to 85% of the value of a property if the property is the only security you are providing. That means that you will need to have a deposit of 15% to 20%. We can talk about how you can get that in a minute.

'If the financier doesn't like your security — for example it doesn't like lending on rural property or some commercial buildings — it will require you to have more skin in the deal. Usually it will only lend about 60% of the valuation of those types of properties.

'If you provide more security or a better covenant the financier will lend you more. One common way to provide more security is mortgage insurance. If a mortgage insurer is happy with your covenant, it will agree to repay the loan to the financier if you don't. Of course, you have to pay for this but it may mean that you can borrow more — 90% or 95% are not unusual and in some circumstances you could even borrow up to 100% with mortgage insurance.

'Another common way to provide more security is to have another property involved. If you are prepared to "risk" two properties to borrow money to buy one, the financier is happy because you have a *lot* of skin in the deal and will often lend 100% or even more of the purchase price of the property. It may be prepared to lend you enough to pay for all the costs of purchase *and* a renovation.

'Of course, if the financier is worried about your covenant it may not lend you more money, it might load your interest by charging you more, or it might require more security. But if you are prepared to look hard enough and know all the options, it is rare that somebody can not find some form of finance at some price to facilitate the purchase of a property.'

'You mean, a financier might even lend money to me?'

'Yes, I'm sure we can get you a loan.'

'Fantastic. Now, I understand that borrowing money is leverage but you also said that leverage is why property is so attractive — can you explain that to me?'

'Of course,' said Eddie, 'Do you know much about the share market?'

'Not really,' I said, hoping it wasn't a prerequisite to learning about leverage in property.

'No problem — generally people say that the share market outperforms property because of its return, which averages about 11% per year over a decade.'

'Oh, I have been told that property averages 8% growth so I can understand their point.'

'Yes it does. So investing in shares would seem like the better option up front wouldn't it?'

'I guess so,' I said, wondering why I was now bothering with property.

Eddie must have sensed my quandary as he went on to explain. 'And that's where most people leave it, but in order to understand the power of investing in property we need to understand leverage. When you borrow to buy property how much of your own money do you have to "put down"?'

'Between 5% and 25%.'

'Good. Most people start out with 10% deposits and then, as they buy more property and the financier gets stricter as the amount of debt increases, they end up with 20% or 25% deposits. So $10,000 would allow you to buy a $100,000 property using a 10% deposit. What would be the actual growth on that property if we assumed 8% annual growth in dollar terms?'

'OK,' I said, nervous that I had to do maths, '$100,000 times 8% equals $8,000 per year?'

'Excellent, but you have only had to put in $10,000 of your own money to get that $8,000, so what is your return on the $10,000 you invested?'

'I think it's 80%,' I answered, still worried about my maths skills.

'Bingo!' exclaimed Eddie, obviously getting excited by this, '80% return. Considering that property is a relatively "safe" form of investment, that's an extraordinary return.'

'Yes, but what about the interest you have to pay on the loan?'

'Good question. Yes, that does have to be factored in, but the rent you receive from your tenants and the tax deductions you'll get go a long way to paying that interest for you, and sometimes you'll even be in front, so anything left over is pure growth. What would happen if you had to put in a 20% deposit?'

'Then I'd be getting $8,000 in growth on the $20,000 I put in, so that would make it 40% growth.'

'Again, a very high return given the level of risk involved in property wouldn't you say?'

I was beginning to see his point. 'But can't you borrow money to buy shares too?' I asked, still a little sceptical.

'Yes, it's called margin lending. I won't bother going into all the details because I just want to use shares as a basic comparison, but let's look at the two.

'Margin loans allow people to buy shares. However, unlike property the price of shares fluctuates on a minute-by-minute basis, so the financier is always recalculating the loan. Just like buying property you need a certain amount of "deposit" to enable you to buy the shares. If the share price goes down, your financier will require you to keep the same deposit proportion in the loan, so you will need to give them cash or sell some of your shares. While this seems simple in theory, it means having to inject cash that many people don't have or sell shares at suddenly reducing prices to top up the loan. This can be very stressful for novice investors like you.

'Because of this many advisers say to limit margin lending to about 50% of the value of shares you want to buy. If you have $10,000 to invest, that means you would only buy $20,000 in shares. If your annual growth was 11%, that would mean $2,200 in growth compared to the $8,000 you were getting if you invested the same amount in property. And most people would far prefer 80% return to 22% return. Wouldn't you?'

'I sure would!' I replied, 'But does property ever go down in value?'

'Property can go down in value, and there are other experts who can tell you more on that — I am sure our Wealthy Friend will get you in touch with them — but that is much rarer than with shares. Also, the amount of the loan is not often recalculated by the bank, so you are not always being called upon to top up the loan. In fact, it is only usually in extreme circumstances in property investment that you will be required by a financier to add more cash into the loan. So, while the returns that can be had by using leverage to buy property are higher than most other forms of investment, the lending environment is also more stable. Provided you don't go silly and borrow more than you can afford to repay, this makes property a very good investment for both long-term growth and easy management of the loan.'

'Ah, but my Wealthy Friend has taught me that leverage can increase return but it can also increase risk — so there must be some risks to borrowing money?'

'Yes, and it's very wise that you ask that question. Many people borrow money with no real idea of the risks involved, and it is just pure luck that saves them from getting into trouble. You already know one of the risks of borrowing. That property can go down in value.'

'So let me see if I understand using leverage to buy property:

- To buy property you generally need a deposit. A financier will lend you the rest.
- The amount of deposit you need depends on the amount of the loan, the quality of the asset backing the loan and your ability to repay.
- The more skin in the deal (deposit) you have the easier it will be to get finance, but a mortgage insurer can also help lower the deposit on a loan, even though it comes at a cost.
- Using leverage can dramatically boost your return and, although there are risks involved in borrowing to buy an investment, property is a relatively stable lending environment.'

'You've got it,' said Eddie, obviously pleased that he was such a good teacher, 'OK, I think you are ready for "deposits".'

Lesson

The Third Secret of Money Magnetism — Leverage.

Leverage — borrowings — applied to acquire a quality investment that returns more or goes up in value faster than the repayments required will bring wealth much faster than paying cash. Leverage applied to depreciating investments will accelerate losses.

PROPERTY BEATS FAST CARS

Only three years ago we bought our first home and borrowed $96,000. We then thought we would add a pergola. We started what was to be a simple renovation and it became a major redevelopment of the property. I worked three jobs at the time and did not sleep very often but, after 12 months of blood, sweat and tears, we finished our project. The nice thing about all of this is Jackie and I got married and enjoyed our renovation experience, which we have been told is not the norm for couples. We then went to the bank and asked if we could buy a present for ourselves as a kind of reward.

The bank manager, whom we owe a great deal of thanks to as well, guided us through our first remortgage program. We thought only of the WRX with which to measure our success and forgot the true value of property.

This was when I found an article of Peter Spann's and read how we may be able to apply the rules we had used to buy the car to gain financial freedom. I spoke to Jackie and, although sceptical at first, I managed to get two of our friends to come along to the introduction night. Wow! Did we get fired up! When returning to Ballarat, we contacted the bank, organising for a valuation to be done asap.

We then spoke to our good friend (bank manager) and asked if we could apply for a line of credit loan. To our total disbelief, our property was valued at $280,000. We only owed $112,000 and we had a redraw of some $150,000 with which to invest. We then attended 'Property Magic' and learned from Peter how to use this line of credit to our advantage.

Applying the rules of position, position, position, I studied our area very hard and bought at auction one of those special bargains which only dreams are made off. The position is three residential doors from some sought-after land. The two blocks three doors up from our block just sold for $405,000 and $435,000 for a 701 square metre block. We purchased our property 14 months earlier and paid $180,000 for 506 square metres. We had our property valued last week and the staggering figure of $300,000 was given. This is land value as the house is somewhat yucky.

We also bought a property last year with equity of $115,000, which is now approximately worth $125,000 and we have not rejuvenated it yet. Jackie and I hope to purchase another property in the next month. This is worth $140,000. We are really impressed with our property portfolio. It has grown from one house valued at $96,000 to four houses worth approximately $900,000 in equity. We are so proud of our achievements to date.

DAVID & JACKIE, VIC

CHAPTER 23

The Endless Deposit

'Right,' said Eddie, obviously sympathising with my glazed look after all these figures, 'I know this can be tedious, but it is critical that you understand it if you are going to be successful at property investment.'

'It's OK,' I replied. 'I just never was really good at figures.'

'Do you want to know a secret?' he asked with a conspiratorial tone that would not allow me to resist.

'Of course,' I said.

'Some of the richest people on the planet can't do maths properly. Many didn't even graduate from high school. Why, even our Wealthy Friend needs a calculator to add up!'

Now there was something I didn't know.

'But,' said Eddie, 'it didn't stop them getting rich, did it? They compensate by surrounding themselves with successful advisers. More importantly, once you get the basics, you don't need much more. Are you ready to learn about deposits now?'

I nodded. Thank goodness I didn't need to be a maths whiz to 'get' this stuff.

'All property investment needs some form of deposit if you are going to borrow for your investment,' he went on. 'Some people have to save it if they don't already own property.'

'That's like me,' I butted in. 'I have been saving for ages and all I have is $9,000.'

'Congratulations,' rebutted Eddie. 'That's more than most people save in a lifetime. And, if you took out some mortgage insurance, that would be almost enough to buy a $100,000 property.'

I hadn't thought about it that way before. The sum of $9,000 didn't really seem enough to start but now I was realising that my dream of becoming a property investor wasn't that far off.

'Most people who come to me already own their own home or an investment property and so they can use available equity,' he went on.

'Equity is simply the valuation of your property minus the outstanding amount of your loan. So if your property is valued at $300,000 and your loan is $100,000 you have $200,000 in equity.'

'Right,' I said. 'So how do you use equity?'

'It's easy,' said Eddie. 'You can refinance to "draw down" up to the agreed loan-to-valuation ratio of the property and use it as a deposit on investment property. So $200,000 in equity could be used as four x $50,000 deposits or ten x $20,000 deposits and so on.'

'I understand, but how do you "draw down"?'

'Let's say your property is valued at $300,000 and the loan on it is $200,000 and the financier will allow you a loan-to-valuation ratio of 80%. You can borrow $240,000, which is $300,000 x 80%. You already have a $200,000 loan and so there is an additional $40,000 available to you which your financier will allow you to draw down through a line of credit or redraw facility. You can use this as a deposit on the loan for another property.'

'So you mean the financier will just give you the money?'

Eddie laughed, 'Sort of. They will lend it to you. But that's OK, because you already own the underlying asset and you are only using the money to buy a quality asset that is appreciating in value. If worst comes to worst you can simply sell the investment property to pay back the loan.'

'What about people like me who are starting with a cash deposit?' I asked.

'Well, if you buy a property today for $250,000 with a 20% deposit on an interest-only loan, and that property grows to be worth $300,000, even though you haven't paid anything off the loan you can still borrow an additional $40,000.'

With that Eddie drew a sheet from his desk that had some typed numbers on them. 'It might be easier if I show you an example,' he said, thrusting the paper under my nose.'

Drawing Down Equity: Example 1

Purchase price (purchased 10 years ago)	$200,000
Current situation	
Valuation of property (when revalued)	$460,000
Mortgage remaining	($60,000)
Equity in property (appreciation deposit)	$400,000
Keep 20% equity in property (20% x $460,000)	$92,000
Calculations	
Value of property	$460,000
Less remaining mortgage	$60,000
Less 20% equity requirement by financier	$92,000
Available to be drawn down	$308,000
Drawing Down Equity: Example 2	
Purchase price	$200,000
20% deposit/equity	$40,000
Mortgage	$160,000
After 1 year	
Value of property (e.g. 10% increase)	$220,000
Equity in property (Deposit)	$60,000
Keep 20% equity in property (20% x $220,000)	$44,000
Calculations	
Value of property	$220,000
Less remaining mortgage	$160,000
Less 20% equity requirement by financier	$44,000
Available to be drawn down	$16,000

'OK, so in that last example, the financier will allow me to draw down $16,000 to use as a deposit to buy a second property?'

'That's right, so effectively you are borrowing 100% of the purchase price of the investment property. This allows you to continuously borrow money to buy investment property as long as the properties you buy keep going up in value.'

'That's great, but won't I run out of money to pay back the loans?'

'Eventually, yes, that's called serviceability. Most financiers will allow you to use a large portion of the rents you receive — generally up to 80% — to help with serviceability. So if you run out you just wait.'

'For what?' I asked.

'For more rent. As the rents go up, your properties become cash-flow neutral. When this is the case, you can borrow more money. Some people who get impatient sell a property for cash, but properties are hard to replace.'

'So how many properties do you think I could buy using this strategy?'

'Potentially unlimited … Just imagine this. If you are starting out with $100,000 equity, that would be enough to buy three $200,000 to $250,000 properties with 10% deposits, allowing borrowing to pay costs too. Do you know how much those properties would cost you to service?'

'Well,' I replied, 'I have seen an example where you can own a property for just $35 per week.'

'That sounds about right,' confirmed Eddie. 'My clients who are using this strategy report back various amounts, but generally the cost is no more than $50 or $60 per week for the average investment property, some much less, and some report they are actually making a few dollars a week after all costs. But let's use your $35 per week example.

'This person has bought three properties so their servicing costs would be $105 per week. If that was the end of their serviceability, some people would think their investing would stop there too. But, as the properties grow in value, so does the equity. As the rents go up, so does serviceability. If you're getting $200 per week rent on each property, you only have to get a 17% increase and you're cash-flow neutral again. That's usually only two to three years of normal rent increases.

'Now that those properties are paying for themselves, you can afford another $105 per week in repayments, or three more properties. Where do you think the deposits are going to come from for them?'

'If the rents are going up then the property is going up in value too. I guess the deposits would come from drawing down on that equity.'

'That's it,' said Eddie, picking up the pace now that he was confident I was getting it. 'With the deposits fully funded from equity, and no more out of your pocket because the rents on the first three properties are now cash-flow neutral, you now own six properties for a weekly cost of just $105. Now you're stuck for serviceability again, so it's the waiting game.'

'Waiting for the rents and equity to go up,' I chipped in.

'Exactly. A few more years pass and rents and equity have both gone up. How many properties can you buy now?'

I thought for a bit and realised the answer was 'Six!'

'That's right,' said Eddie, sharing my obvious excitement. 'The rents on the first three are now cash-flow positive, so that will fund an additional three, and the rents on the second three are cash-flow neutral, so you can afford three more with your $105 a week serviceability. A couple more years and you could buy 12. A couple more years after that it could be 24 more properties.'

'Wow, that's 48 houses in 10 years.' *if all goes V. well*

'Yes, and all with no money out of your pocket for deposits and only $105 per week.'

'If it was 48 properties, that would be over $10 million in property, all with $100,000 down and only about $105 per week. Or cut that number in half and make it 24 properties at say, $225,000 average and they'd be worth $5.4 million. Or cut it to a quarter and it would still be 12 properties worth $2.7 million. *WOW!* That's amazing. But the most amazing thing is you've convinced me that even I could do that!'

'Yes, you could,' said Eddie, quite chuffed that he had explained it well enough for me to understand.

'But hold on a minute,' I said, stopping dead in my tracks, 'I thought you said we effectively borrowed 100% to fund these properties?'

'Yes,' said Eddie with a tone of voice that implied he knew exactly where I was headed with this.

'So that means, while I may have $10 million in property I have no equity? That doesn't sound all that exciting.'

'Ah, you forget that time passing adds value.'

'I don't understand?'

'Patience Grasshopper.'

I was just old enough to remember the TV show that he referred to but the saying did not diminish my frustration. 'I still don't understand.'

'Well, you have $10 million in property which is growing all the time — let's say at 8%. Wait another year and you'll have $800,000 in equity. Another year and your equity will go up by $860,000, making a total equity of $1.6 million. Another year means another $900,000 in equity, which means, just 13 years after you started with only $100,000 in equity and no more than $105 per week in costs ($70,980 in total across the 13 years), you will own $12.6 million in property with $2.6 million in equity. You will be a millionaire *and* you will be growing your asset base at the rate of over $1 million a year! All you need is the right strategy and a bit of patience.

'Even if we take your most conservative example — 12 properties worth $2.7 million — in year 11 they will be worth $2.9 million; in year 12 they will be worth $3.1 million; and in year 13 they will be worth $3.4 million. So you will have gained $700,000 in net worth for $105 per week.

Now, I'm not saying everything will always go as smoothly as that. There's going to be some ups and downs, sometimes the rents won't go up as fast as you would like, and property growth does stagnate every few years, but I am sure you get the idea. Even if things only went half as well and you ended up only with $500,000 in equity, it would still be a 500% return on the original $100,000 equity you started with. Neat hey?'

'Real neat! Now I understand the power of leverage. There must be other ways to start without equity though?'

Eddie thought for a moment and then said, 'Yes there are. All are higher risk than what we have just spoken about ... I wouldn't use them if you were risk-averse — use the savings for a deposit method under those circumstances — or if property was flat, but if you are really keen to get started and property is in a rising market, which happens about four to five years out of 10 usually, then there are other ways.

'If you think laterally and break some limiting "rules" you may be able to borrow the deposits as well. Some financiers will allow high-income earners with stable employment to borrow up to 110% of the value of a property.

'In quiet market places you may be able to access vendor finance, where the seller funds part or all of the purchase price.

'You may be able to purchase the property pre-valuation — where the valuation for the property is well above the purchase price allowing you to borrow more than the purchase price. This can work where you are intending to rejuvenate the property.

'It may be possible to take out a personal loan for the deposit and the legals. Even though this is very high leverage, if you were thinking about borrowing money anyway, it is sometimes better doing this than spending the money on other things that go down in value.

'If you are young and just starting out, you could use the cheap rent you are getting at home to build an investment portfolio.

'If you own your own home but haven't any equity yet, you could take in tenants. You can claim part of the costs of owning the house as a deduction to help you save.

'You could bring forward your inheritance and access the funds in your parents' home; 60% of people who buy their first home are helped by their parents. Parents who have worked all their lives to pay off their home and may be from a different era might be sceptical at first, but you need to approach this as a business proposition — prove you have a plan to implement.

'Nonconforming lenders offer what are called "no-doc" and "low-doc" loans (at somewhat higher interest) to people who are unable to prove serviceability — their ability to repay — by providing tax returns, proof of employment or savings history. The lender is simply taking it on faith that the borrower will repay.

'I am sure there are many, many other ways to get in the game if you are prepared to think laterally. These ways may be unconventional but they can work if you are prepared to take the additional risk and put in the additional effort to make them work.

'Before we're done I just wanted to mention two other uses of equity most people don't think of.

High Equity, Low Income

'Now some folks have got heaps of equity but no income. Capitalising interest is a strategy that enables you to access the funds in your property with no income.

'If you have considerable equity, financiers will allow you to draw down a line of credit to pay the interest on your loans. So in other words you can borrow the money to pay the interest.

'If somebody's going to approve you to capitalise the interest, you're going to have to have a personal relationship with them or you're going to have to convince them. This is very common though. Lots of my clients who've got heaps of equity have done it. Many of them were knocked back eight, nine, 10 times before they found somebody who'd be prepared to do it for them. But, if you've got no income, I for example presume that you're not working, so you've got the benefit of time. You just keep going and knocking on doors until somebody says yes. And eventually they will say yes.

'Wear your suit, pretend you own the empire, imagine you're Darth Vader. Breathe heavily!' Now he was getting carried away.

'Capitalising interest enables you to buy property and fund it during the cash-negative period through additional borrowing. Let's say you have $500,000 worth of equity in your property. A lender will allow you to borrow $400,000 against that equity. You leave $100,000 in your account to pay off the interest, and you take the $300,000 out and invest it. This is a high-risk strategy but it works if you're buying quality growth assets.

'You know, some of us have been dealt a bad hand. You're still playing poker, aren't you? What wins poker games? Good hands? Good playing wins poker games. I used to love playing poker. I was eight years old and I was the best poker player on the face of the planet. I used to play poker with my dad and his friends all the time. And my bedtime was eight o'clock and they thought that was fantastic, because I used to beat them all the time and that got rid of me. People who play poker win by playing the game not by having a good hand. And so if capitalising interest gets you into the game, it might just work for you.

'It will only work as a short-term strategy, though, so the property *and* the rents have to be growing, otherwise you will be losing money at a faster rate due to the compounding effect of the interest on interest.

'The second "fun" thing you can do with equity is to fund lifestyle. Although it is not advisable to do this until your drawings are a very small fraction of your assets, this for many people is a fantastic way to fund your retirement.

'I had a client come to me who was 72. His only asset was his own home, which he had bought in Sydney in 1951 and paid off many years ago. Due to natural growth it was valued at almost $2 million. He was on the pension and struggling and was thinking about selling his home, but he was very active and sharp-minded and told me he was planning on living until he was 100!   *or REVERSE MORTGAGE*

'I asked him if he was prepared to take a bit of a risk. He said, "At my age I can afford to!" And so I suggested, rather than sell his house now, we draw down on equity to fund his lifestyle. He decided he wanted to live it up, so we started with a $1,200,000 line of credit. The plan was to draw down $80,000 a year and capitalise the interest.

'In 10 years he would have drawn down the full amount of the line of credit but the house would then have grown to be worth about $4 million, so he would still have $2,800,000 in equity. If he wanted to he could keep on going. If it all became too much he could sell the house, repay the debt and live off the remaining cash.

'Well, he loved the idea and we set it up straight away. Some months later he sent me a postcard from Hawaii and told me he had a new lease of life. He was travelling around the world, was dating a younger woman (in her fifties), and having a ball. In his P.S. he mentioned that because he was actually borrowing money to live on, he was still eligible for the pension! Now *that* was a happy customer.'

'I'll bet,' I said, excited that in 10 years even I might be able to have millions of dollars worth of property.

CASH-FLOW POSITIVE PROPERTIES

In recent years there has grown a school of thought promoting cash-flow positive property. It stems from the lowering rental returns received during the fast-moving growth phase of the property cycle and it's very simple to understand.

When property grows in price quickly, rents do not keep up. Owners who have had their property for some time are slow to move rents up. New entrants into the market are buying at higher prices but need to be price competitive on the rents and so return suffers. If this is coupled with low interest rates, more people buy homes to live in, reducing demand for rental property and depressing prices.

But like everything, this is cyclical and short lived. Low rental yields (comparative to property prices) are usually only prevalent for two to three years out of a 10-year cycle. Eventually interest rates rise, owners start moving rents up and yields return.

However, inexperienced investors coming into the market late in the cycle (when growth is high and rents slow) are unaware that rents will only be down for a couple of years. So, out of the closet and dusted off is the argument that buying positive cash flow property is better than sacrificing rental return for growth. This standard argument is that making money is better than losing money, and if you take it on face value, we would all agree, but here's the problem ...

To *find* cash-flow positive property at this stage in the cycle you need to head bush. At the beginning of the property cycle it is possible, by using the value-adding strategies in this book, to generate a high enough rent to have the property go cash-flow positive from day one, even with quality property in prime locations. As the cycle moves on, locations close to capital cities (always the best to buy when growth is your aim) become less attractive in terms of rental yield and high rents start moving away from the city.

This is known as the concentric circles principle. Throw a stone into a pond and you see concentric circles of ripples from where the stone hits. It's the same with growth and rental prices. Eventually, to buy property that is going to be cash-flow positive, you need to buy further and further from capital cities (and therefore further and further from the properties most likely to produce exciting, long-term capital growth). So people chase the circles. And because they are rewarded with cash flow and a growth boost (even though it is a fraction of what they would have received by buying prime property at the same time in the cycle), their strategy is validated.

RIPPLE EFFECT

COASTAL + MINING REGIONALS are VG

Better to Balance: ⚠ -ve
Several ⊕ cash flow properties
+ 1 ⊖ " " "   wot good CG
+ Buy + REJUVENATE Policy To ↑ Returns + CG

The Endless Deposit **137**

The problem is that property in these country and marginal locations grows at a lower rate than their city counterparts. And if there is no capital growth there is little argument for substantial rental increases over the years of ownership either. This means that a property in a marginal location that starts out cash-flow positive to the tune of $50 a week may very well only be cash-flow positive to the tune of $100 a week in 10 years. Whereas a property in a prime location that starts out cash flow negative to the tune of $50 per week and achieves the average capital growth of 8% per year may well end up cash-flow positive in three years (therefore negating the advantage of the marginal property) and at the end of 10 years be returning $200 per week and have doubled in value.

To further support their argument, proponents of the cash-flow positive style of property investing say that the wealthy do not use negative gearing. This is only partially true. What occurs is that the wealthy have got that way by buying quality assets and holding onto them. This means that they generally have held the assets that make up their wealth for a long time and that the loan-to-valuation ratios have lowered and rents increased, making their investment cash-flow positive. But their original intention was to buy prime property close to capital cities to hold for capital gain. I do not know a single substantial rich person who owns substantial amounts of property in country towns. Full stop! (They may owns farms but they even run those as tax deductions!) So while the argument that wealthy people have cash-flow positive property is true, they did not buy the property in the first place to only get cash flow; they bought it to get capital growth.

The other argument I frequently hear is that if you have cash-flow positive property you can buy unlimited amounts of property because you are earning money not losing money. If only this were true! You still need deposits, the bank will still discount the rent you receive by up to 20%, and you still need to be able to prove serviceability on the full loan with your income. And what if interest rates go up while you are not watching? There goes your cash flow and now you are stuck owning a property with dubious capital growth potential at a time when the only benefit to owning property is the capital growth.

Proponents still manage to get around this by using a complex strategy called 'wrapping'. This involves buying a property and immediately on-selling to another person (usually somebody who cannot get finance the traditional way) while offering a form of vendor finance. Say you buy a house at $250,000 at 7% interest. You

NB
Ripple
Effect
applies
to good
regional

?
Noosa
Byron
Mandurah
etc

True

then look around for somebody very keen to own their own property but who can not get finance through a bank or traditional lender. You offer to 'sell' the property to them for $300,000 at 9% interest so you make an immediate 'profit' of $50,000 and you get to pocket the difference in the interest rates. People who favour this type of activity love it because the risk is primarily with the 'buyer'. They don't get to own the property until it is fully paid off or they buy you out of the contract. If they default you keep the house and they lose all of the money they have paid you. But now that non-conforming lending has hit Australia, I can't see why this style of borrowing would be attractive to the buyer. If somebody can't get a non-conforming loan (those guys will loan to just about anybody — at a cost) you would really have to wonder why you would be giving them a loan to buy your property.

I must say I am not a fan of this style of investing. To me you lose the most important thing of all, and that's the capital growth. The legal framework is also very complex and fraught with danger for the novice. However, if it does appeal to you there are now a number of books written on the topic so good luck!

To me, cash-flow positive strategies simply do not produce a high enough return on capital invested. Let's say you go to the country and buy a house worth $150,000. At 80% loan-to-valuation ratio and 7% interest, the interest cost is $8,400 per year. Add in rates and maintenance at say, $2,000 per year, and your total costs amount to $10,400. Rental returns seem higher in the country, so say you can get $220 per week in rent you are making $20 a week. So for a capital deployment and risk of $150,000, you are getting a measly $20 per week or about 0.7%. And that's if you get 100% occupancy, there is no change in interest rates or costs and nothing major goes wrong with the property (or the town it is located in).

You could argue that your only contribution is the $30,000 deposit, so your cash return is really 3.5%. If you put that same $30,000 into high dividend-yielding shares (say one of the big banks), you would probably get the equivalent of $40 per week — double the amount from the country property, plus you get the potential of 11% per year average capital growth, and there are no hassles with managing the property, maintenance, tenants, paying rates, dealing with banks and so on.

(But I guess that's the topic of a whole new book! Look out for my next one on creating wealth through the share market.)

I have made this argument very strongly over the years so the cash-flow brigade have countered with, 'Yeah, but what if you don't like shares?' My response of 'What is there not to like?' usually drags out all the arguments made by those ignorant of how to make money in shares, like 'Well, I've never seen a house go broke.' Fair enough, and this *is* a book about property, so look at my comments on high-yield commercial property trusts in chapter 4.

/ PAY OFF OWN HOME QUICKLY

Lesson

Once you have equity in your property, you can draw on the excess for a deposit on your next property investment loan, thereby using other people's money to 100% finance your growth. This means you can continuously buy property without money out of your pocket for deposits.

PROPERTY BETTER THAN PUMPKINS

At long last we have stopped procrastinating and have bought our first investment property (18 months since doing Peter Spann's courses). Not only did we buy one, we brought three.

It was more a getting over the emotional attachment to money and worrying about what others think than not being able to afford it. Now we can see we can't afford not to. No wonder you love property so much as it was fun 'playing the game.'

Our first property was listed for $269,000. We paid $255,000. Our second property was listed for $189,000. We paid $175,000 and managed to get the real-estate agent to pay for the building report and white-ant inspection: a saving of $450.

Our third property was listed for $165,000. We paid $155,000.

So far all it has cost us is the stamp duty, as our farming property is valued at $1.2 million and we have used some of the equity in that.

We have cut our market-garden business in half this year so we could have a life and get some time to become wealthy and, with the price of pumpkins this year, we could still end up making just as much profit for half the work. Now all we need to do is implement the next stage of the plan and stop physically working altogether.

NEVILLE & TANIA, QLD

CHAPTER 24

The Most Important Person in the (Lending) World

I was reflecting on Eddie's advice with my Wealthy Friend when Leon came into the room. 'I guess by that eager look on your face you're here to learn from our Wealthy Friend,' he said. 'And coincidently I am fresh from revaluing one of his properties. Our Friend calls me the most important person in his lending world. I'm not sure I'm that important but I am the valuer.'

'He's very important,' responded my Wealthy Friend. 'Valuers determine how much your property's worth and, as such, how much you can borrow. Go ahead, Leon, and let us know why the valuer is so important.'

'The financier will want the property valued by *their* valuer. This is critical for you to understand if you're going to buy a property. However, if you know a couple of things about valuers, it's easy to manoeuvre this to your advantage.

'Firstly, if the bank commissions a valuation, the valuer works for the bank. So we do not want the bank to commission the valuation, we want to commission the valuation ourselves. If we commission the valuation, the valuer works for us. Most people think, "Well, if I just go out and get a valuer, the bank won't accept that valuation". And that's partly true, so this is the way that we get around that …

'Lenders have a group of valuers they give their work to, which are called their panel valuers. Most have five or six different firms they send their work out to, and many valuers act for many different lenders. The bank will accept a valuation from *any* of their panel valuers.

'All you need to do is find out who is on the panel of the financier you want to deal with. Ask your lender or ask the valuers themselves who they work for. From that list of five or six, you need to find one valuer who works with you really well. It may cost you a little bit of money up front but it is really worthwhile.

'Get all panel valuers to do a valuation on your property then pick the one that gives you a good valuation and you get on well with. The financier will be happy to accept their valuation, and every time you want to buy another property or extend your line of credit, call that valuer to do the valuation on it.

'That valuer may work for a dozen different financiers. Tell them that the valuation is for bank finance but to leave the financier blank. They will then do the valuation for you and you will have a signed sworn valuation to use in negotiations with all those banks that they are the panel valuer for.

'Once you've got the best loan deal, you then go back to your valuer and say, "Now, what I would like you to do is nominate the Irrational Australia Bank as my lender on the valuation." They then tender it to the financier on your behalf.'

Leon excused himself from the room. I was to meet him many more times over the passing years and truly understand why the valuer is so important.

'I can assure you that your relationship with your valuer is 10 times more important than your relationship with your bank,' went on my Wealthy Friend.

'If you have a good relationship with a valuer and they are prepared to give you good valuations on properties, that will open up a dozen different financiers to give you money.

'When I get a property valued or revalued, I take Leon out to lunch and I have all the research done for him so he doesn't have to do any work. I have the prior sales in the area; I have other properties that I can show him; I have got photographs of other properties that have sold in the marketplace. I tell him what I'm going to do to the property, how I'm going to renovate it, exactly how much I'm going to spend, what it's going to look like when it's finished. I give him comparison rentals in the area for properties that have been finished like my property. I give him all this information.

'He then gives me his valuation and I go and negotiate with the banks. Whenever I finish a property, I always invite him to the house-warming party. How often do you reckon a valuer is invited to parties?'

'Not that often I suspect.'

'So I invite Leon to my house-warming parties. I send him birthday presents, Christmas presents, I find out about his family, about his children. Every time I see him I ask him about his kids.

'I've built a good relationship with him. Now when I ring Leon and say, "Leon I've bought another property", what question do you think he asks me?'

'How much is it worth?'

'You got it! So I ring Leon and say, "I've just seen another property in Paddington."'

'How much is it worth?'

'"Oh well, Leon, you know a heck of a lot about property in Paddington. You know I've bought a few; you know you're the guy who knows everything, but I would reckon it'd probably be between, $580,000 and $610,000?"'

'"Yeah, I think $610,000 is fair, I'll give that valuation to you."

'Now, that valuation is critical to me because it establishes to the bank how much that property is going to be worth after I've finished my renovation. If I'm smart and a good negotiator, the bank will lend me the money to buy the property and to do the renovation.

'Think about this: I have bought oodles of properties. Leon has done the valuations on every single one of them. Do you think I'm a good customer of his?'

'Yeah, I bet you're almost as good a customer of his as some of the banks.'

'Absolutely. Do you think he's going to look after me? Yes. Do you think he's going to lie for me? No. He's not going to lie for me because that's his job. His job is on the line. He's not going to lie for me and I don't want him to lie for me. What I want him to do is give me a valuation at the upper end of his professional opinion.'

'That make sense. You wouldn't want to deal with a professional who was open to fraud.'

'When you want to draw down on equity to buy more investment property, the first step is always to get a valuation. The better the valuation, the more money you can borrow.

'Don't get it into your head that if your valuer has given you a valuation for $610,000 on a property, that it's actually worth that. Don't think you'll be able to put it on the market tomorrow and get $610,000 for it — that's not what the purpose of this exercise is. The purpose of this exercise is to maximise our available equity.'

Lesson

The only purpose of valuation is to maximise available equity. The higher the valuation, the more equity there is to draw on.

FROM NEAR BANKRUPT TO PROFIT IN EIGHT MONTHS

My wife and I came to Peter Spann's course in November 2000 — and at the time we were a week or so away from bankruptcy. We were over $100,000 in debt, and most of it very very bad debt. Nonetheless, we began putting your strategy into action — first by beginning to pay off all our interest-accruing debts. We had a goal to pay off all this debt and buy our first investment property within 12 months.

We spent that next 12 months researching property, and by October 2001 we had our first deposit (and had paid off about $60,000 of debt). We bought our first investment property in Camp Hill, Queensland, for $194,000.

We'd done extensive research in the area and arranged to meet the bank valuer there. He was stunned at the research we'd done, saying that he'd never seen anyone do so much in all the six years he'd been doing valuations — it was only a single A4 sheet of paper — we said that we believed that the place was worth $210,000–220,000.

A week later the bank approved it for the valuation of $210,000! So we were $16,000 ahead to start off with! (Most people say that that is impossible, that banks never value above a purchase price — well we found that they do.)

By February 2002, without even renovating, we looked at the market and saw that it had moved. We did our second report and asked for a valuation of $240,000 from the same valuer. He then approved this amount! So we got ready to renovate in April 2002.

Still without any money behind us, we asked the bank for an on-completion renovation loan to finance the renovation. We got another valuation for this and asked for $285,000. The same valuer approved this amount and the bank gave us access to $40,000 to renovate. We only wanted to spend $22,000 but, being our first time, we spent $27,000.

After this we researched the market again in June 2002 and were amazed to see that from a certain point of view our house could be worth $335,000. We got our same valuer out again, the fourth time, by now we had built up a relationship with him as Peter had told us to. He loved our renovation and was very impressed. Within five minutes of being there he asked us the magical question that Peter said they would one day ask: 'What do you think its worth?'!

We were stunned. We gave him our report — and said $335,000. He didn't bat an eyelid. The next week we got our confirmed valuation of $335,000! That was only six weeks after his previous valuation of $285,000 for the on-completion loan. We asked for another $50,000, which the bank gave us.

So all up we made well over $100,000 in just over six months.

Admittedly we'd chosen well and the market had done most of that for us, but we were only able to take advantage of that because of Peter's training in the selection criteria.

What this has really taught us is that money *really* is all just made up, just an idea, and that you can make a case for anything.

Since completing renovations in June we've been hunting every weekend for our second property. It hasn't been easy to find one. But just *this week* we signed a contract on our number two.

Having found that *everything* Peter said would happen did happen, we have no doubt about the rest of his strategy, especially if it is followed to the letter.

BARNABY & ANGELA, NSW

Chapter 25

Should I Wear a Suit?

OK, I'll come out and admit it ... My father was a bank manager. There, I've said it. But to be fair on him, he was a bank manager in the days when they were pillars of society. Admired by (most) of the community and respected by all.

A friend recently sent me newspaper clippings from the local paper of a small town where, in the 1960s, my father took up his first managerial posting. It was like our family were royalty. His arrival in town was actually a front-page event. They reported on his business trips to conferences in such exotic places as Brisbane and Sydney, and when he wasn't travelling on business, they even had reports on our holidays! Amazing.

Can you imagine a country newspaper reporting on any bank favourably these days, with banks closing faster than you can withdraw your money, and foreclosures on farmers and small business people? I think not.

I tell you all of this to remind you of the era when you used to put on your Sunday best to go visit the bank manager and to let you know once and for all ... Those days are *over*! They belong in the same quaint place as reruns of the 'Sullivans' and shows where everybody did what father said and teenagers were helpful, angelic people whose only desire was to grow up just like their parents.

In the real world, the modern world, your financier will come to you. They will view you, their customer, as their most important asset and they will look after you with a range of products that suit your needs, and when you say jump, they should answer with 'how high?'.

And in case you encounter one of those financiers which is a throwback to the 'wear your suit and grovel' days, just remember there are plenty more out there, so, before it declines your loan with glee, you should decline to do business with it. Many people for too long have been allowing financiers to dictate the rules to them. It's time for those people to get what they want, when they want it, at a price that is fair.

After my meeting with Eddie I expressed the fact that I was still daunted borrowing money to my Wealthy Friend.

His reply was simple but extended, 'I love finance because finance is the key, the absolute key, to making money. What you can do when you know what you're doing with the right leverage is astounding. You've got to put it together correctly, you've got to make it work yourself, but it's absolutely awesome what you can do with it.

'But, you must be prepared to test conventional wisdom. There's no other part of wealth creation about which people have more rules and more bad programming stuffed into them, than finance.

Today, there is more money floating around out there than at any other time in the history of Australia. All this money that's in the superannuation funds, all this money that you've been forced to put into the super funds. There's billions and billions of dollars just sitting there in the capital market. Now, the super funds have to make some money for their clients, so the capital markets become wholesalers of money at a margin to financiers to lend us.

You must challenge the system, because there are still banks, bank managers, financiers, and financial managers out there who still think the old system applies. They are singing from a very old song sheet. It's like they rehearse it, like they get up every morning and do their affirmation in the mirror 'No. NO. NO!', they say, smiling all the time.

'Some people in the financial industry think that these old rules still apply. They are not going to be the people that are going to give you money. Many people walk out of a financier's office feeling done over. Why? Because they haven't been told the full story. They haven't been told how finance works. They haven't been told the situation.

'Imagine a mower shop. The mowers come in all different shapes, sizes and prices, but the mower man can't dictate to the factory the features of the mowers; he just buys them already built, puts them on the showroom floor, marks them up and sells them, yes?'

I wasn't sure if he actually wanted an answer to his question but while I was ruminating he went on. 'Well, in exactly the same way that the mower man can't determine how the mowers are manufactured, the banks can't determine what features the capital markets put in their loans. But they pretend that they do.

'The banks look for features that help them achieve their goals. And what is their primary goal? To lend you more money. Why do they want to lend you money? To make money. And the capital markets want the money left in your hands, they don't want it repaid, so they are happy to help.'

'Why don't they want it repaid?' I asked, thinking all banks would want their loans repaid.

My Wealthy Friend went on to explain, 'Because they've got so much of it now, what the heck are they going to do with it? And because they can't figure out what to do with it now, the capital markets don't want you to repay it, so they put all these features in it like redraw facilities, lines of credit, mortgage offsets, interest-only loans, and so on, to encourage you to keep the money out. Lenders then repackage it, rearrange it, decide what features to market and what to leave out.

'But what you must understand is lenders buy the money from the capital market at exactly the same rate as everybody else. There's no bulk discount, there's no special services, special arrangements or anything like that, and we can get a fully featured loan, redraw facilities, all that type of stuff, at the same rate the biggest bank can get them. The banks would like to pretend that it's different. Lenders try to persuade you that they're offering you all these wonderful facilities but, as a friend of mine says, '"You can't put an Armani suit on a home loan." It's just money. No matter how hard they try to dress it up, it's just money.

'And it's our job, as investors, to take advantage of every feature, every advantage and every benefit that our lenders choose to emphasise or offer us.

'There are three main types of lenders: traditional; securitised; and non-conforming. Let me just run through the pros and cons of each with you.'

Traditional Lenders

'Traditional lenders get their funds through deposits and through access to their own capital, and lend these "depositors' funds" to clients. They make profits from the differential between what they pay in interest to the depositors and what they charge borrowers to borrow the money.

'This wide access to funds gives banks a sustainable competitive advantage. It allows them to set the price agenda in Australia. Banks offer loans at discounted interest rates to their best customers — that is, the *big* ones because they are able to access funds at a significantly reduced rate, which other lenders cannot compete with. This is the reason 80% of lending is still with the banks.

'The advantages of traditional lenders are:

* flexibility — they have products for almost any circumstance; and
* they are familiar with things like construction and renovation loans, lines of credit, etc (although other lenders are fast catching up).

'Their disadvantages are:

* higher fees and charges, and interest rates for small customers like us;
* cross-collateralisation (which I will explain in a minute); and
* lack of empathy.

'They are best for:

* people with complicated financial structures;
* people in business with existing finance that would need to be dismantled;
* people with large borrowings who can prove serviceability.'

Securitised Lenders

'After the deregulation of the banking industry new lenders came into the marketplace and secured funds through a process called securitisation. 'Funds are originated through the capital (or cash) markets wholesale at the cash rate (an interest rate set by the Reserve Bank) and retailed to consumers after a margin is added.

'These days the money market is funded largely by superannuation. The financier packages up the money into different sorts of loans with features designed to get you to borrow as much as possible for as long as possible.

'The advantages of using securitised lenders are:

- they usually have the lowest interest rates;
- minimal fees and charges; and
- they can loan up to 95% of an investment.

'The disadvantages are:

- lack of flexibility;
- strict lending criteria;
- the fact that all loans need mortgage insurance (at present there are only two mortgage insurers, so it's not a very competitive market meaning a lot of people who can easily fund a mortgage get knocked back by the mortgage insurer before they even start).

'Securitised lenders are best for:

- people with exemplary credit ratings;
- simple financial structures (PAYE or straightforward businesses producing taxable income); and
- people borrowing for one to five investment properties.'

Non-conforming Lenders

'These lenders are called non-conforming because they specialise in lending money to people who do not conform to traditional and securitised lenders' rather strict credit and lending policies.

'They include specialists who offer what are called 'no-doc' and 'low-doc' loans to people who can not substantiate their earnings; solicitors and accountants who pool their clients' funds to offer them a higher return than normal investments with first mortgage security; and mezzanine funders who secure their money from venture capitalists who want a high return.

'They get their funds from various sources including private funds and capital markets. They offer alternatives to financing for the borrower when other traditional or securitised lenders are not flexible enough.

'The advantages of using non-conforming lenders are:

- highest flexibility;
- they are often able to tailor loans to suit the borrower;
- some do not require substantiation of ability to repay the loan;
- suitability for short-term finance for projects or until businesses can produce adequate documentation and tax returns; and
- they lend large amounts.

'With money this easy to get there are some disadvantages:
- because of higher risk, their interest rates are higher (usually between 2% and 12% above the standard variable rate offered by most lenders, depending on product and requirements);
- they sometimes have high loan-to-valuation rates, but mostly they start at 80% (some 75%, occasionally 90%); and
- they are savage with defaults.

'Non-conforming lenders are best for:

- self-employed people (or low taxable incomes or have no income assessment notices);
- casual or contract workers;
- people with no savings history;
- people with low income and high equity;
- people with a history of credit problems;
- older people; and
- new Australians.'

(Although it is a bit out of step with the story, I want to mention that my first ever property loan was through a specialist non-conforming lender who used money from a church to lend to people like me. Even God wanted me to succeed!)

How to Determine the Interest Rate

'It's easy to determine the theoretical maximum interest rate to pay. The Reserve Bank decides on the cash rate — generally the interest rate that is paid on a 90-day bank bill. Lenders set their rates from that. Australian lenders add about 1.5% to 2% margin to the 90-day bank bill rate to determine their standard variable rate, so by calculating this it's an easy guide to rates.

'The thing is, banks used to make much more margin than this when their primary practice was lending through depositors' funds. Only about 25% of lending today is done through depositors' funds. Seventy-five per cent of lending is done through securitisation.

'Because securitisation came into place, all of a sudden the lending environment became very competitive, and the banks had to find a new way to keep their margins up. And the new way they found is fees and charges. Some people, usually the banks' best customers, can negotiate these out, but as Eddie has already told you, usually, for most people, the cheapest source of money is the securitised lenders, not the banks.

'Bank fees and charges may look tiny, but when you add them up, they can reach considerable sums of money. But like everybody else, the banks have to look competitive, so what they do these days is take the 90-day bank bill rate — let's say it's 5% — they add their 1.5% margin on it and they advertise their standard variable rate as 6.5%.

'And then you look in the paper at any of the non-bank lenders, and you'll see that they are advertising their rate at 6.75%. And so you're saying, 'Well, why the heck would I go to one of the non-bank lenders with all their stringent lending criteria when I can just go to the good old Irrational Australia Bank, the Collecting Wealth Bank, or Wesuck, and get the full service banking?

'But what you're missing is all the fees and charges that many of the banks charge you on most of their products. So you can't just accept the advertised mortgage rates.

'What you need to look for is the real rate of interest, what is known as the average annualised percentage rate or AAPR. The AAPR takes the advertised interest rate, adds all the fees and charges to it, averages it out across the average period of a loan, generally seven years, and compares rates.

'Say the advertised rate is 6.5% at Financier A and 6.75% at Financier B with no fees and charges. On the surface, Financier A

Need this to look @ REFINANCING

looks cheaper but let's calculate the AAPR on a loan of $300,000 over seven years.

	FINANCIER A	FINANCIER B
Interest	19,500 p.a.	$20,750 p.a.
over 7 years	$136,500	$141,750
Application fee	$500	–
Monthly service fee ($8 p.m.)	$672	–
Statement fee ($2.50 p.m.)	$210	–
Discharge documentation	$780	–
Early discharge penalty	$3,250	–
(2 months' repayments)		
Total cost	$141,912	$141,750
Cost p.a.	$20,273	$20,250
AAPR	6.76%	6.75%

'So Financier A is actually *more* expensive than Financier B and will continue to be more expensive the longer the loan operates.

'The financial institutions are required to give you all the information that you need to calculate the real rate of interest for yourself, but they are under no obligation to make it easy for you! You will find that all the information needed to calculate your interest is in your mortgage contract. But when you come to read your contract you may find it's on pages 1, 2, 3, 4, 5, 6, 7 through 10, 10 through 20, 20 through 38, there's nothing on page 39, but pages 41 to 57 have got heaps of information on them, and then there's nothing on page 58, that's just a blank page, left there deliberately, and then on pages 61 to 492, you'll find more information. It's all in there. But if you can calculate it, you're better than me.

'Luckily the AAPR is regularly published in newspapers and is available free on websites.[12] When you do actually bother to get the AAPRs, many times you'll find that the banks are considerably more expensive than the securitised lenders.

So, if the current standard variable is 7.75% and the fees and charges add 2% to the rate, what is the real rate of interest? Lo and behold it's 9.75%, what the banks have always got back on their money, back to the good old days before deregulation. What the banks have done is convince the population that interest rates are considerably cheaper when in fact they're getting the same return they've always got. Clever isn't it (if you are a shareholder; rotten if you are a loans customer).

'And yet, 80% of lending is still done through the big banks, and our real interest rates are still some of the highest in the world because of this "lack of competition".

'Now, I'm not saying the big banks don't have their place. As I've mentioned already, for many people they are ideal. It's just that you have to look with open eyes at the alternatives. Look beyond the traditional lenders and you might find a much better overall package that suits your investing aspirations.'

Lesson

Lenders are not all the same. It pays to shop around to find the lender that best suits your personal circumstances.

MILLIONAIRE BY 32

In March 2000 I attended Peter Spann's seminar in Melbourne. I had by that time already acquired a couple of investment properties but felt unsure about how to progress things from there and was concerned about what may happen to the residential property market given that the scaremongers were already talking doom and gloom at that time.

Naturally, after the seminar I was entirely pumped and on the prowl for further investments. Two days afterwards, my father rang me as he walked past a group of two-bedroom units in Mornington, Victoria. All six units were for sale, strata-titled and fully let. The position was close to the beach, the main shopping centre, and in a street with a number of new houses and new unit developments.

The units were constructed in 1981 and had not really had any meaningful renovation done since construction. Although looking a bit tired, they were structurally strong. They were clustered as three blocks of two units, and each unit had a carport that could later be easily built in as garages.

My initial reaction after a 'drive by' inspection was that the units would be too expensive for me: probably $100,000 each. I rang the agent who advised me that they were for sale as a group for $410,000. I struggled to not sound elated!

I made an offer of $370,000 and settled at $390,000 ($65,000 each). I signed six individual contracts to capitalise on stamp duty savings for properties under $115,000 (a practice that has since been stopped by the Victorian government following the introduction of grouping provisions). The six individual contracts saved me approximately $10,000 in stamp duty.

The key to the cheap price was that the vendor lived in Queensland and appeared to have no idea of the value of properties in Mornington. Secondly, she appointed an agent adept in rural property rather than normal residential property. Oh well, my gain! The day I bought it I knew I had purchased well.

I secured the property by putting $1,000 down on my credit card (the agent protested but accepted eventually and I obtained my 1,000 Fly Buy points!). Secondly, I paid about $600 for a deposit bond in lieu of the $38,000 residual cash deposit. Finally, I used the equity in my home as second mortgage security for the 20% deposit on the loan, and therefore effectively financed 100% of the purchase price.

Actually receiving finance approval and purchasing the property was an incredibly satisfying experience. It would not have happened if I had not invested $48 in a 'Welcome to Wealth' seminar.

After two months and some very minor cosmetic work in two of the units (one was vacant at settlement, so I renovated it — carpets, paint, blinds — and then moved one of the existing tenants into it so I could renovate his in a similar way), I had the property revalued. $535,000! I immediately sought the discharge of the second mortgage on my home.

In March this year, I purchased a new home for myself and sought to refinance my entire portfolio. The Mornington property was valued at $950,000, and the valuer commented that there is considerably more upside in it with further refurbishment.

So, the bottom line is: my personal cash outlay on the property was $1,000 as a deposit (and I got Fly Buy points on it!), $600 for the deposit bond (again on credit card), and $15,000 in renovations, and ongoing property maintenance costs (which are minimal). The property is fully let and is cash-flow positive. In effect, I have received a capital gain of $560,000 in two years from an investment of $16,600!

This is the best of my stories, but I have a number of property investments all of which have seen stunning capital growth following the buy, renovate and hold method. Since attending 'Welcome to Wealth', I *have* become a multi-millionaire. I have paid cash for a new Porsche and live in a million-dollar home with virtually no direct debt on it. I could now retire if I wanted to, at the age of 32. The funny thing is, though, the greater the success the more motivated I am to keep going, work harder at it, and make more! Not because I love the money, but because the feeling of satisfaction and the enjoyment from creating a great property out of an old shack is just immense. I absolutely love it!

BRENDAN, PORT MELBOURNE, VIC

CHAPTER 26

o Wants to Lend Me Some Money?

It was time to apply for my loan. My Wealthy Friend suggested I go back to see Eddie.

Eddie had already worked out that because I was only working part-time and had no real assets my best bet was to apply for a low loan-to-valuation ratio of 80% so, allowing for costs, that meant I could just afford a $30,000 property. I had no idea where I would find a $30,000 property when most properties I was looking at were well over $100,000, but I was determined and ready to go ahead and apply for the loan.

'Right, before we pick a lender you have to decide what features you want and what you are prepared to pay for.' I was confused. I understood the 'features' bit, but what did he mean by 'what I wanted to pay for'?

'Some things you generally have to pay for, like solicitors' fees and valuations, some features are optional, and some lenders charge and some do not. I say 'generally' because some of my clients have been able to negotiate these things out. Let's go through them.'

Things You Generally Have to Pay For

Solicitor's Fees

'You will probably have to pay solicitor's fees. Not your solicitor's fees (you have to pay for them too), the lender's solicitor's fees. The lender will normally charge you somewhere between $350 and $500 for its solicitor to prepare the documents for the loan. This is a highly complex process which is well and truly worth $500 because you know that the 18-year-old junior in the solicitor's office fires up the computer, opens up the Microsoft Word document, types in your name and then prints it out. Which of course is well and truly worth $500.

Valuation Fees

'You will normally have to also pay for the valuation on your property. Valuation fees and solicitors' fees are usually covered in the application fee, which sounds like a fee you pay when you apply, but actually you pay it after the loan is approved and you have decided to go ahead with it. But some financiers are even waiving the application fee in an attempt to get business. Often the banks will waive the application fee if you are a good customer or are bringing a substantial amount of business to them.

Always negotiate. They may say no but often they will say yes.

Mortgage Insurance

'If you are taking out a loan with a securitised lender or with a high loan-to-valuation ratio, you'll probably have to pay for mortgage insurance. Mortgage insurance is required when you're putting down a smaller deposit than a lender normally accepts. Most financiers will give you money without charging mortgage insurance if you put down a 20% or 25% deposit.

'Many financiers will negotiate down to 15% deposit without mortgage insurance, and some of my clients have even been able to get down to 10% without mortgage insurance. However, generally, if you only want to put down 5% or 10% as a deposit, you're required to pay mortgage insurance.

'Most people think that mortgage insurance covers them. It does not. Mortgage insurance covers the financier. It's a one-off cost that you have to pay that covers the financier if you default. The important thing to note is that this mortgage insurance isn't really insurance because, if you default on the loan, the lender will come after you. Don't think that you've got any protection if you've got mortgage insurance, it is the bank that has the protection with the mortgage insurance, not you.'

'So, should I pay mortgage insurance or not?' I asked.

'To me it is a commercial transaction which I simply factor in', said Eddie.

'Let's take a look at, say, a $200,000 loan. The financier says we'll give you 10% deposit if you pay mortgage insurance. So how much is my deposit? $20,000.

'What's the mortgage insurance? Let's say $3,000. So it's $23,000 that has to go into getting the loan.

'Alternatively, if you go to 15% deposit, then you don't have to pay mortgage insurance. So how much money do I have to put down if it's 15% deposit?'

'$30,000,' I answered.

'Right, so in this case I'd go $23,000 versus $30,000 because, once you've put down your deposit, you won't get that back until you sell, and because you are an investor, it is unlikely that you will sell in the foreseeable future. Effectively, the deposit is lost money.'

'So, if I put in $30,000, I don't have to pay mortgage insurance, which is what most people think, but if I pay mortgage insurance of $3,000, I've effectively freed up $7,000?'

'Yes. Under that circumstance, I would say $23,000 versus $30,000 — I'll take the mortgage insurance. Now let's take another scenario. Let's say the financier says you can put down a 10% deposit plus mortgage insurance and the mortgage insurance is $7,000, or you can put down a 15% deposit ($30,000) and no mortgage insurance. Well at $27,000 versus $30,000, I'll probably go $30,000. It's just a commercial transaction.

'While I am sure there is a way mortgage insurance is calculated, there often seems to be no rhyme nor reason, no obvious way that mortgage insurers calculate the cost of mortgage insurance. I have been offered somewhere between $2,500 to $7,000 for mortgage insurance on about the same loan and I can't seem to see any reason between why one was more expensive and one was less expensive. Always ask for the quote and always attempt to negotiate.

'Now the bad news with mortgage insurance is there are only two mortgage insurers in Australia. And what they do is cross-reference your loans between them. So chances are that you're not going to get more loans than about $500,000 or $600,000 worth with mortgage insurance.

'Some of my clients are really clever. They move around really quickly and get five or six loans approved all at once, and they get one loan in their wife's name and one loan in theirs, and I've had some of my clients get up to $1.2 million, $1.3 million, $1.4 million at 10% deposit. But you have to move quickly to do that because the mortgage insurers communicate between each other, and while it's not illegal, the mortgage insurers frown upon it and may make it difficult for you to get mortgage insurance from them again if you do it.

'In my experience it's very hard to get more than about $600,000 with mortgage insurance. After that the mortgage insurers will no longer insure you and that's when you've got to find the 15% 20% or 25% deposits.

'The good news is that mortgage insurance is tax deductible for investors.'

Critical Options You Should Not Pay For

Lump Sum Payments

'Firstly, you shouldn't pay for the ability to make lump sum payments on your loan. If you've got a $200,000 loan and you get, say, a $20,000 tax return — and you haven't made up your mind what you're going to do with it, it's worthwhile putting it into your property loan, so you're effectively getting the property loan interest rate on it, which is better than putting it in a savings account, isn't it?'

Redraw Facility

'When you make up your mind what to do with it, you then draw it out. So a redraw facility is very useful. A redraw facility gives us the ability to move our money in and out of loans, and it allows us to access any surplus money we may have put into the loan.'

A Line of Credit

'A line of credit is a pre-approved facility, generally secured against property, that works like an overdraft. You only pay interest on the amount that you draw out, but you have access to those funds at any time.

'As your equity grows, or you acquire more assets, the line of credit grows as well. So if the property has grown in value and you can prove that to the bank, a line of credit allows you to draw down your increased equity without having to refinance. And you should be able to draw down as many times as you wish with no charges.

'There are a number of ways that you can access your funds — cheque, ATM, electronic banking; however, the most common way these days is through credit card.'

Change the Rate

'You should also be able to change your interest rate from variable to fixed and vice versa without incurring fees and charges. Now, obviously, when you change from fixed back to variable it has to be at the end of the fixed-rate period. So if you fix your loan for three years, you can't change back to the variable rate after 18 months without expecting a fee. That's fair.

'But if you get to the end of your fixed period, you should be able to change that loan back to the variable rate straight away with no fees and you should be able to change from variable rate to the fixed without any fees.'

Terminating the Loan Early

'There should be no penalty for paying out the loan early (unless it is a fixed rate), and no fee to terminate the loan.'

Weekly or Fortnightly Repayments

'If you're making capital repayments, you should be making them fortnightly or weekly. There are only 12 months in the year, but 26 fortnights, so you actually make two extra repayments in the year, and over a period this can dramatically reduce your interest bill. And because most people get paid fortnightly, they don't miss the extra they are paying off their loan.

'Now watch out for the new rort where you go to the financier and say "I'd like to start paying my loan fortnightly" but instead of having you make those magical two extra repayments a year, they add up the 12 monthly repayments and divide the total by 26. So in other words you're not paying any more off your loan, plus you are giving the financier the benefit of your extra funds more regularly.'

Mortgage Minimisation

'Mortgage minimisation is where you have your pay and other income paid into your redraw facility or a special interest-offset account. Paying into your redraw facility can save you a couple of hundred dollars a year. You may as well have this money in your pocket than anybody else's. An interest offset account works in a similar way except the money goes into your bank account and the bank puts the interest that you would normally be paid on that account into your home loan. Again, it'll save you probably a couple of hundred dollars a year, so you may as well do it.

Honeymoon Rates

'The honeymoon rate is a reduced fixed rate of interest for a set period of time, usually one year. At the end of the period it reverts to the standard variable.   *any* CBA WA

'A friend in the business says, "The honeymoon rate is like any marriage: the first 12 months it's fabulous, the rest of it sucks!" While I might not share his view on marriage, he certainly makes his point about honeymoon rates, which rarely have any place in an investor's scheme.

'If you calculate the savings made in the first year and then add them to the cost of paying the standard variable rate to which you are committed for three years after that you will invariably be able to negotiate a better rate overall, or will most often do better just by taking the standard variable rate over the same period.

'And remember you've got no control over what the interest rate's going to be in 12 months' time.'

How to Decide When to Fix an Interest Rate

'Basically, what we want to do is to fix an interest rate in a rising interest-rate environment and stay on a variable rate in a falling or flat interest-rate environment.

'The interest rate cycle is usually about five years. From the time interest rates start rising they take two to three years to reach their zenith and then about two years to fall back to their lowest point. Then they will stay flat for one to two years before they start rising again.

'Amateur investors watch the variable rates for their cue, but interest rates are merely a function of monetary policy. If the Reserve Bank lowers the cash rate, financiers will follow by lowering their variable rates. If the Reserve Bank increases the cash rate, financiers will follow by increasing their variable rates. Not much science in that.

'Professional investors watch the fixed rates. That's where banks employ highly qualified and expensive actuaries to predict what is going to happen in the future and hedge them against losses. If you watch the fixed rates, there is always a good clue as to what the professionals think is going to happen.

'When fixed rates start to rise from their lows at the bottom of the interest-rate cycle, it is time to take notice and consider fixing your loans. Because the interest rate cycle is about five years, a five-year fixed rate is often the best to smooth out the high-interest rate periods.

'In order to continue accessing features of loans that investors need, like a line of credit, it is important to realise that you can not fix the entire amount of the loan. Make, say, 90%, of the loan fixed and make the other part of it variable. That gives you the security of knowing what your payments are going to be and gives you access to all the facilities that you want. With the 10% of your loan on the variable rate, you've still got the line of credit facility that you can draw down. Remember, because you are only charged if you actually draw down loans, if interest rates are too high, simply leave the funds in the loan.

'There is a compensation for high interest rates. When interest rates go up, fewer people can afford their own home, so that creates more demand for rental accommodation. Couple that with the natural desire of investors needing a higher return to compensate them for higher costs and invariably rents go up. If you have most of your loans fixed at that point, the increase in rents can be a welcome bonus!'

'Now, that's good,' I thought. I had already been in his office the better part of a day and my mind was full. I never knew that there was so much to financing. It was even getting dark, but it was apparent he wasn't finished just yet ...

Cross-collateralisation

'Now another thing I need to cover on financing is cross-collateralisation.'

'Fancy word,' I said. 'Is it good or bad?'

'Bad, quite bad. You want to avoid cross-collateralisation wherever possible. Cross-collateralisation is where a financier wraps all of your lending into one and takes security over all your property. It's good for the financier because it has you exactly where it wants you. It's bad for you because if anything goes wrong, you're finished.

'Let's say your house is mortgaged for $500,000, and you want to buy an investment property that's worth $200,000; they now give you a $700,000 loan. They wrap it all together. Then you go and buy another house and they wrap it all together again. Then you go and buy another one and they wrap it all together for the third time. Then you go and buy another one and again they wrap it all together. And then you run out of money.

'So now you have one loan that has all five of those properties on it. That's cross-collateralisation. The financier takes collateral on your house and applies it to the other properties. Now if anything goes wrong, and you've cross-collateralised, what will they sell first?'

'I guess the house,' I said.

'You guess right,' said Eddie. 'That's the first thing that they'll sell. So, to avoid this, if your financier is prepared to (and they want all your business) you can simply ask them to remove the "all monies clause" (which allows them to access any and all assets or funds you have to ensure their debt is paid back if you default), and to not cross-collateralise your loans, so you have independent facilities and independent loans.

'Most financiers are not prepared to do this so you also need a different strategy. One is to go to the financier and say, "See this

$1 million house here, I've got $500,000 worth of equity. I want a line of credit facility to draw down on and access those funds leaving open what you want to do with it."'

'Respectfully decline any offer to cross-collateralise your mortgages and lend you the money for your investment purchases.

'We then take the funds out of that house and use them as a deposit on the investment property, which we fund through a loan from a different financier. Then we use more funds as a deposit on the next loan, and again and again. So we now have five separate loans, none of them cross-collateralised.

'Now if anything goes wrong, what can you do?'

'Sell one of the properties.'

'Exactly. Then if it still goes wrong, you can sell another one. And if it still goes wrong, you can sell another one. And so on, you've now got five lines of defence to your home.'

'But what if you already are cross-collateralised?'

'That's not unusual. In fact, the vast majority of people have cross-collateralised loans because that's the way financiers like to do it. And, in the end, it makes it very easy to get finance. There's no need to rush out on Monday morning and refinance everything. If you got a really bad deal, and you now know that you got a bad deal with your existing financier, yes, refinance it. But if you've got a good deal with your existing financier, just accept that as a mistake and the next property you buy, avoid it. And then the next property you buy, avoid it again. Easy.'

Credit Reference

'Every time you apply for finance, you will be given one of those little privacy agreement forms to fill in. What that does is give your financier permission to report the fact that you have applied for a loan with it to the credit register.[13]

'It is critical that you get approval for your loan before you sign this form and before your prospective financiers lodge any entries on your credit record. If you sign the agreement prior to getting your loan approved, all the financiers you have applied to will report your application and record it on your credit register — "Loan $150,000 with Collecting Wealth Bank", "Loan $150,000 with Irrational Australia Bank". You'll have all these loans that you've applied for and none of them will have "approved" next to them. Eventually you could have any number of applications and banks will simply start knocking you back on finance because they think everybody else has knocked you back.

'Once you actually get your loan approved, you then sign the agreement form giving your financier permission to check your records and they will then report your application to the credit register to be recorded on your file. 'If you do it this way, you'll only ever have "Loan $150,000 Collecting Wealth Bank: Approved". And that's all we want on our credit register.

'The interesting thing is, if you do not sign the agreement and your financier reports that you've applied for a loan with them to the credit register, they are, in fact, breaking the law. If you want to access your file, simply contact the credit register and tell them so. You should do this anyway. They frequently make mistakes. If there are mistakes in your records, you can demand the records be amended. The credit register is required to remove details that are erroneous or non-factual as long as you can substantiate that they're wrong.'

Negotiate Everything and Bend the Rules If Necessary

'Negotiate everything?' I asked. 'Even with a bank?' This was indeed a strange concept to me.

'Absolutely — worst thing that can happen is it says no, and, you never know, there might just be somebody out there who is happy to say yes.

'If you are not getting the response that you want, upscale it. Talk to someone more senior. Just remember that probably nobody in a cardigan is going to approve what you want. Probably nobody wearing a logo on their suit will approve what you want. And certainly nobody wearing a logo on their *cardigan* will be able to approve what you want. You've got to at least get to somebody who's wearing a real suit!

'And you've got to go in confidently. Not like you own the place, but at least like you could afford to if you wanted it! When I applied for the loan on my house, it was three days before the house was due to settle and they knocked it back. They knocked it back! I couldn't believe it. So I stormed into the bank manager's office, sat down and said, "You knocked back my home loan. Why the heck have you knocked it back?"

'He said, "You don't have enough serviceability".

'"What do you mean I don't have enough serviceability?"

'"I'm sorry," he replied, "but you simply don't have enough serviceability. There's nothing I can do." He then ceremoniously lifted up a pile of papers and straightened them by banging them on the desk as if to intone, "the file is closed."

'Well, I got mad. "Look," I growled, "I've read in the papers that this bank is closing branches and cutting costs, is that right?"

'"That's correct."

'"And that it is actively raising profits by getting more business?"

'"Ah, yes," he answered, still not getting my point.

'"May I point out that *you* are a *cost*, I am the *profit*. Your company seems to want less of you and more of me!"

'Well, that amazing piece of rapport building didn't seem to get me anywhere! So I rang the state manager. I opened the conversation by saying, "You must be insane!"

'He, not surprisingly replied, "What?"

'"I am a customer of yours and you people have just knocked back a home loan for me."

'"I'm sure we've got very good reasons," he said.

'"Well, apparently I don't have enough serviceability, but you're insane. I have applied for a $1 million home loan and I've got $1.5 million in my bank account. You're insane!"

'"What's your account number?" he inquired. And with that he put me on hold. In two minutes he was back with, "I'm terribly sorry, you're story's correct, give me an hour."

'An hour later the bank manager rang me back, "Ohhhh, helloooo, just ringing you to tell you that we've reviewed our lending criteria ... your loan's approved. Thank you very much for doing business with us!"

'Every now and again you've got to bend the rules. Now the interesting thing is I didn't need to leave $1.5 million in my bank account for very long to make my point. *About two minutes!*'

'Another time I applied for a loan with a bank and the bank manager told me I didn't fit their lending criteria. When I asked for an explanation I realised everything was just a misunderstanding and I could fix it if I resubmitted my loan application in a different format. He had a different view. "You can't expect me to approve the loan just because you submit it another way."

'Arguing didn't seem to work but on my way home I drove past another branch of the same bank and thought why not? I walked in, asked to see the manager and resubmitted my loan the different way. Lo and behold, it was approved. Easy.

'Don't accept the first thing offered. Tell them precisely what you want and do your own research. Banks *will* negotiate and even if they won't, most likely there will be a product somewhere that precisely suits your needs.

'Know your financier's lending criteria. This knowledge is more accessible as you start to get to know your lender. If you don't meet the lender's criteria, you may have to consider another approach. Read your application form, come back with something new, do something different.

'Remember that you are the customer, you own the transaction, they've got heaps of money and they want to give it to you. You've just got to find somebody who will talk your language. There are about 2,700 lenders in Australia — until you've tried all of them, how can you say that you can't get what you want?

'Now, if you think you're going to go out on Monday to borrow some money and you won't come up against a couple of brick walls, you're absolutely bonkers. Fifty per cent or more of the financial industry still thinks that you have to get down on your hands and knees and grovel to them. This is changing but still 50% or 60% of people want you to play by their rules. Forty per cent of the people out there will play by *your* rules. You've got to find them. So you will come up against some brick walls.

'You've got to remember a few people when a bank manager says no: Colonel Sanders, Abraham Lincoln or Thomas Edison. Thomas Edison invented the light bulb. He made hundreds of attempts before he was successful. By his 300th attempt, he was accused of being insane, with 300 failures to his name and no successes. '"No, no, no," he said. "I am 300 steps closer to getting this thing right."

'Colonel Sanders took 680 knockbacks, before somebody took his chicken recipe. I mean, let's face it, it was chook. And Abraham Lincoln had stood for election 37 times before people elected him to any public office.

'They're amazing stories to read. They tell you to keep on going. And it's the same with finance — keep on going, keep on going.

Lesson

Negotiate everything. The worst that can happen is that someone says no.

DON'T SETTLE FOR 'NO'

I was looking in the Eastern Suburbs of Sydney for an investment unit to purchase in early 2001. After an exhaustive day of looking at seven units, I was driving home when I noticed a one-bedroom unit for sale in Coogee, NSW, which was currently open for inspection.
Immediately upon walking into the unit I realised that this was a great purchase. The building was a 1920s block with high and ornate ceilings and an absolutely fantastic sunroom, which received plenty of afternoon sun and which led on to the living room — very Art Deco.

The sale price was $285,000, which was surprisingly low for the market in that area, and I could not for the life of me work out why the vendor was selling at such a low price (recent sales in the area for the same style property were all going for around $350,000). As a result, I went to the agent and made an offer which he would not accept. He informed me that the vendor was taking the property off the market because there was such a huge interest in it, and he would be putting it back on the market at auction. On hearing this I asked for a copy of the contract, and again the agent acted suspiciously and told me that this was not possible.

Frustrated with the lack of service I drove straight away to the real-estate agency and told the receptionist that the agent had provided permission for me to obtain a copy of the contract, which she gladly photocopied. After passing this obstacle, I noticed on the contract that there was a special clause included which gave the real estate agent permission to purchase the property for himself. Realising this, I knew that the agent was obviously aware that the property was a golden opportunity and he was going to milk it for everything the vendor had.

After deciding that I was going to do whatever it took to purchase the property I looked up the vendor's address in the White Pages but to no avail. I then travelled back to the unit (the inspection was now over and everybody had left) and knocked on the door, but again to no avail. I then proceeded to knock on every door in the block until someone could provide me with some feedback. As it was, the one person who was home happened to be the strata manager, and he informed me that the resident of the unit was a tenant and not the vendor. He was unaware of the vendor's address but knew where the tenant worked. I then proceeded to the pub where the tenant worked and, only knowing her first name, I went to the bar and asked for the lady. Luckily she was there. It took some considerable persuasion on my part to convince her to tell me where the vendor resided. In the end she was unaware of this but knew he owned a restaurant nearby. So back again, I hopped into the car and travelled to this restaurant where I asked for the vendor.

By now it was Saturday evening and, sitting down with the vendor, I made an offer of $300,000 and told him that I had another property which was being auctioned on Tuesday night. Therefore, the vendor had to commit to the purchase and we would exchange contracts on Monday. The vendor was very good about the situation and was surprised to hear that the agent had told people he was going to take the property off the market (which the vendor had no intention of doing).

As it turned out, we exchanged on the Monday and when it came time for the real-estate agent to ring me up and ask me my details to put on the contract he was not impressed, as he knew he'd been done by someone who'd been burned by agents before. It was an exhausting day, but one that I will never regret — the property has appreciated by 50% in only 18 months.

THEO, NSW

CHAPTER 27

To Pay Off or Not to Pay Off?

I still wanted to know if I should pay off my loans. I had heard it might be better not to. So I asked Eddie.

'Generally an investor will want to take out interest-only loans because it minimises the cost of meeting the repayments. Only the interest component of loan repayments is tax deductible — the capital part is not. By taking interest-only loans you can borrow more through increased serviceability, so the less it costs you each month, the more you can borrow.

'If you wanted to borrow $200,000 to buy an investment property, the interest bill on that at 7% would be $270 per week. If you took out a principal and interest loan (where you are actually paying off the principal), the repayments would rise to $526 per week for a 15-year loan term. You could therefore afford to buy twice the number of properties if you took interest-only.

'And worse still, remember the capital component of the repayment ($256 per week) is not tax-deductible, so you have to pay this amount out of money you have already paid tax on. Most people would have to earn about $480 extra a week just to afford the capital repayments.

'Let's compare the results. We already know that quality property doubles in value on average every 10 years. And for ease of calculation, let's say that over the 10-year period the rents earned take care of the interest paid.

'If you bought one $200,000 property and paid off the capital component, you would have paid off about $130,000 of the loan and had to earn about $250,000 to do so. The property would be worth about $400,000 though, so you would have had a capital gain of $200,000. Here's the calculation:

Property's new valuation:	$400,000
Less tax paid on capital repayments:	$120,000
Less remaining loan value:	$70,000
Actual capital gain:	$210,000

'Compare this to buying two properties on which you paid interest only. Your repayments on the interest component would have been $540 per week, or only $14 more per week than if you had bought one property and paid off capital. At the end of 10 years you would still have a loan of $400,000, but the properties would be worth $800,000, making your capital gain $400,000.

'After all that effort you put into paying off capital in the first example, and all the extra tax you had to pay, you would be almost twice as wealthy if you had chosen the path of *not* paying capital off the loan and maximising your purchasing potential by buying another property.

'You might be wondering, then, when you should pay off the loans?'

'Well, theoretically, never.'

'That's right, never. Why would you? The property can sit there growing in value every year while you get tax deductions for the interest repayments.

'Interest-only loans are generally for a fixed period — usually five, seven, or 10 years. At the end of that time, provided you have a good repayment record, they can generally be renegotiated. Eventually you will have enough equity in your portfolio to sell down a few of your properties and use the equity from "pure" capital growth to pay off the outstanding capital component of the other loans.

'There may be other reasons why you might want to scale back borrowings, for example if you want to start earning an income[14] (retirement maybe), you simply stop borrowing to buy property some years before. That way, as the properties grow in value and the income increases, they will go cash-flow neutral and then cash-flow positive, providing you with an income that is indexed for life. Alternatively you could sell some of your properties to pay off the debt and allow your remaining properties to generate you an income through rent.

'Think of it this way: if you are 40 and own your own home, you could afford to buy two or three investment properties right now. Apply the leapfrogging strategy and you could double that amount every few years. Start with three. At 45 you could buy another three. At 50 you could buy six. At 55 you could buy 12. By the time you are 60 you could own 24 properties.

'Say each was bought for $200,000 and they grew evenly across the 20 years, you would have owned three for 20 years, so they would be worth about $800,000 each. You would have owned three for 15 years, so they would be worth about $600,000 each. You would have owned six for 10 years, so they would be worth about $400,000 each. You would have owned 12 for five years, so they would be worth about $300,000 each.

'That would mean you would have $10.2 million in property, and your borrowings on that would be just $4.8 million.

'If you sold the last 18 properties you bought, you could pay off the debt and the capital gains tax and you would still own six properties valued at a total of $4.2 million, clear of debt.

'If you were getting a 5% rental return you would be getting $210,000 a year income. And the rents and the capital value of the properties would be increasing year by year.

'The alternative would be to keep some more of the properties so you could benefit from increased capital growth, and write off the negative gearing component against your rental income to reduce your tax. Let's face it, you could probably afford it! And that's taking a conservative view. With a bit more effort you could probably afford many more properties over that 20-year period.'

By now it was very dark, well after dinner time and, while I was grateful to Eddie for giving up a full day to teach me, if he was anything like my Wealthy Friend I knew I'd have to get out before dinner, but I had one more question. 'I understand now why it's not necessary to pay off capital, but what if I wanted to leave something to my children? Or if I get sick and can't make my repayments?'

'Sounds to me like we're done and you need to meet Igor. He's the man everybody needs but nobody wants.'

Eddie opened a draw and pulled out a business card. Intrigued I read the card as soon as I left the office, but it only had a name and contact details.

I didn't have to wait long to find out more, as Igor called me the next day. 'I heard you're interested in insurance,' he said enthusiastically. Now I knew why nobody wanted him — I guess it was time to find out why I needed him.

Lesson

There is more wealth to be made by not paying off the principal of a loan with income out of which tax has been paid and re-investing that money in more property.

TAKING THE PATH TO SUCCESS

I recently bought a house at Camp Hill, Queensland, for $175,000. I had a rental appraisal which was $220 per week, but I could not find tenants, so I moved in for six months and rejuvenated the property.

The house had two average-sized bedrooms and two closet-sized bedrooms. After days of deliberation, I decided to reduce the property to a three-bedroom ensuite house. When finished, the property was totally rejuvenated for just under $15,000.

The tenants could not move in quick enough, paying $260 per week, which has worked out to be a great return on my $15,000 invested. The property was then valued at $240,000.

Overall my story is not just about a great result in property. For me, it is about changing the path of my life, which is what I am eternally grateful for.

DAVID, QLD

CHAPTER 28

Protection Money

'Everybody needs insurance!' Igor exclaimed, after I asked him why I needed him, 'but nobody wants to talk about it. For some strange reason they think that if they don't ever get insurance they won't ever die!

'Ordinary people see insurance as a cost. Rich folk see it as essential. A cost of doing business — just like protection money. My motto is, "Cover yourself well".

'Why, our Wealthy Friend is one of my best customers. He has a multi-million dollar policy underwritten by Lloyds of London.

I wasn't sure exactly who Lloyds was but it sure sounded impressive.

'Some people still want to think that by the time they die they will be debt-free so they can pass on a legacy to their children. I personally want to spend my last dollar the minute before I die (preferably well after I have received the telegram from the Queen)! The legacy I want to leave to my children is this knowledge rather than a big inheritance. If they know they are going to get nothing they are less likely to want me dead!

'But, all joking aside, I am sure you have seen the results of leaving a lot of money to kids who have to do nothing to get it. Tragedy, disappointment, restlessness and worse seem to dog their lives and remove any happiness they may get from their riches. I believe that the pursuit of money is far more interesting than the money itself. That the journey is far more interesting than the destination. Why deprive your children of the journey?

'Having said that, if you are still intent on leaving a legacy of money to your children, the good news is you *still* don't have to pay off your loans. Let the insurance company do it for you!

'Term life insurance is relatively cheap and you can get cover well into your eighties. If you carried enough cover to pay off your debts, your loans would be fully repaid and all your lovely property would go to your children (or the Happy Valley Dogs' Home) unencumbered.

'I think it's quite beautiful. You borrow a fortune from the bank. You die. The insurance company pays it all back! Perfect — even better if the insurance company is owned by the bank!'

Even I saw the deliciousness in that! 'But,' I objected, 'I don't have a lot of money. What is the minimum insurance I should have?'

'My suggestion is that you should hold as a minimum the following insurances, if you are borrowing money and care what happens to your assets after you die:

- Term life insurance — it works like car insurance with one premium for one year — and pays on the outcome. Make sure you get a policy that is uncancellable and indexed so in case you get sick, the policy still has to be renewed. Get enough to cover all your debts or, if that seems too much, get enough to cover three years of your normal income. That way, any dependants have more than enough time to grieve, get settled and sort out your affairs before they have to worry about repayments.

- Income protection insurance — it pays out if you cannot work, either temporarily or permanently. Many policies are cheaper if there is a waiting period (like an excess on your car insurance). The longer the waiting period, the cheaper the policy. My suggestion is that you make the waiting period about half the savings buffer you have allowed for yourself. Everybody should keep a 'buffer' of cash or redraw for a 'rainy day'. If the waiting period is set by calculating your costs and using up half your buffer until the policy kicks in, you'll still have half your buffer left. Some policies only pay out for a limited period (say two or three years) and while they are considerably cheaper I still prefer the ones that pay out for life.

'You might also like to consider trauma insurance, which pays out a lump sum in the event that you are diagnosed with a major illness (like cancer or diabetes). If you are relatively young and in good health these policies are inexpensive, and while I don't wish illness upon you, they might just be worth it. You can seek the best medical attention the world has to offer and if you recover, you may still have a packet left over to enjoy your "getting well" party!'

I left Igor's office with a referral to a doctor and after being prodded and poked a few times, had my very own insurance policy. And funnily, he seems to know exactly when it is due for renewal for I get a call from him every year. Plus a very nice Christmas card!

Investment Property Insurance

It wasn't all I learned about insurance. 'There's another sort of insurance I wouldn't be without,' my Wealthy Friend observed. 'It's called investment property insurance, or landlord's insurance.

'Investment property insurance covers you for a whole barrage of things that can go wrong with investment property. These include:

- default on rent;
- denial of access by the tenant — when the tenant won't allow you into the property;
- breaking of the lease — when the tenant does a runner;
- departure without notice — when the tenant does a runner without having a lease;
- malicious damage — when the tenant damages the property and then does a runner;
- theft; and
- accidental damage to building — when the tenant steals the oven out of your kitchen.

'Generally the premium is very cheap because the risk of these events happening is actually very low. Your agent or your property manager will be the person who organises investment property cover or landlord's insurance for you. If your agent doesn't get it for you, a number of general insurers provide it.

'Because this insurance is so cheap all investment property owners should have it — again, it provides the "sleep at night" factor. And if your tenants trash your property and you have landlord's insurance, you get a free reno! So, whenever I want my properties renovated, all I do is instruct my agent to rent only to bikers and prostitutes. Pretty well a guaranteed reno. Just kidding!'

Lesson

Life and income insurance let you focus on the here and now in the knowledge the future is taken care of.

A LESSON IN INSURANCE

In early September 2002, one of my tenants vacated one of my properties without notice and left a considerable amount of mess and damage. Fortunately I knew where to find him. I took him before the Consumer, Trader and Tenancy Tribunal ($27) and won. The tenant didn't show up to the hearing. The tenant was ordered to pay compensation of $1044 within three weeks.

Well, three weeks passed and he did not pay. After several attempts to contact this person fell on deaf ears, I was forced to apply at the Sheriff's Department for a Notice of Non-Levy. Cost to me $110. The sheriff went to the tenant's new place of residence and was greeted by a person claiming to be someone else. The sheriff was powerless to do anything, and left without asking for identification. According to the real estate agent who manages the property, the tenant had lied.

I complained to the Sheriff's Department for not doing the job so it sent someones out there again. This time they asked for ID and this time they issued him with a Notice to Pay. By this time a further two weeks had lapsed. It is well worth noting that the sheriff is not allowed to repossess any of the person's items at this stage.

The tenant once again refused to pay, claiming that he was on welfare and could not afford the payment. Mind you he could afford the 18-foot cruiser parked in his driveway. He offered to pay me $500 up front if I just left him alone. A kind of bribe. I declined his offer. Some time later he made another offer, this time to pay in instalments, $40 per month for two years (Wow! Such generosity I had never seen before). Again I refused.

The tenant then had the option to go back to court to try and convince the magistrate to allow him to pay in instalments. Unfortunately I had to be there also to state my case. The roles were all of a sudden reversed.

Another two weeks passed when I received a call from the tenant. I asked him how he got my phone number and his reply was that the sheriff gave it to him. By then I was fuming. I had three little children living with me and he knew where I lived. I will be seeking legal action against the sheriff's department for revealing my whereabouts.

After some haggling back and forth, he offered to pay me $900. Given the circumstances, I accepted his offer. I am so annoyed and frustrated with our legal system. Here is a situation where the law favours the tenant and not the landlord. Unfortunately I did not have landlord's protection insurance. Otherwise this could all have been avoided. I recommend everyone take out landlord's insurance. You never know when this might happen to you.

Even if the person was granted the right to pay in instalments, somehow I doubt that he would make all his payments. If he deliberately stopped making payments I would then have to take him to court again. A neverending cycle.

EVAN

CHAPTER 29

Ways to Buy Property

I was champing at the bit. Primed, ready to go, but ready to go at what? My Wealthy Friend and his friend Jack had shown me how to locate the best suburbs — so that was where to buy covered. I knew I wanted to buy residential property and I knew my price range, including allowing for renovations. And I knew how to get money. But what was I actually going to buy? All these different kinds of dwellings: apartments, houses, old, new ... It was time to talk to my Wealthy Friend again.

'What's up now?' queried my Wealthy Friend, when he spotted me morosely studying the real-estate guide.

'I can't see the trees for the forest,' I said, turning the metaphor around. 'Now that I'm so keen, all I can see is a forest of 'For Sale' signs and I don't know what to buy.'

'The key to buying anything of value that you want to rise in value is irreplaceability. And in property terms that means the three Ps — position, position, position.

'There are two aspects to irreplaceability — desirability and restriction. Land where everybody wants to be — close to water, forest, high spots, manmade facilities and infrastructure, close to work, schools and so on — will go up in value. Restriction comes from the old saying, "They're not making any more of it". In other words, where these features are confined to a small area due to geographical and manmade restrictions — mountains, rivers, oceans, highways, railway lines, bridges, infrastructure, zoning and land-use restrictions. Restriction also comes from development. If there is no free land or no land that allows more housing to be built, then existing properties will have greater value.

'Irreplaceability comes about when desirability and restriction coincide. Let's look at Sydney Harbour — and that's the point —

everybody wants to look at Sydney Harbour! While there is theoretically heaps of harbour-front land it has, over 200 years, been fully developed so it's very hard to find land to build on. This desirability — near the water in the major capital city of Australia — and restriction from full development mean that land on the harbour is almost always going up in value.

'Brisbane has its riverside areas and spots where you can get a breeze, which are always in high demand. Perth has its beaches and the riverside suburbs. Melbourne has its bayside suburbs and so on. Add in access to public transport, schools, hospitals and so on, and it's clear why the inner ring of suburbs 2 to 15 kilometres from the city are so desirable. Some people may desire space and so head further towards the country, but the further you get from the CBD the less restrictions there are on available land and so price growth drops off.

'That's why older property so often outperforms new property — because older property usually is in these highly desirable locations. It is rare that new property is built in these areas because of the extraordinary cost of the land. When the property cycle is in full swing we know that older property can be demolished to make way for newer buildings but it is the land that always holds the value.'

Older Property

'The advantage of older property, then, is high capital growth potential. Generally, older property grows much faster than new property, particularly in the first five years. You're generally buying in established areas and people want to live in established areas; they like trees, they like schools, they like infrastructure, they like transport, they like hospitals and so on. You can add value to such property, which, of course, I love. It also attracts some depreciation allowances and it's not subject to GST.

'The disadvantages of old property are that it requires more work (research, dealing with agents, traipsing around to "opens", managing the renovations, etc) and possibly higher maintenance.'

Redeveloped Property

'Redeveloped property is old property that has been redeveloped by someone else. It is property refurbished, something renovated already. There are a few advantages to that. Firstly, these properties are hard to get, therefore desirable, especially in suburbs of Sydney and Melbourne with high demand and low supply. Secondly, you are buying in established areas. Thirdly, all the work's been done for you.

'There are also often very large depreciation allowances on this kind of property and if it's in a sought-after area, it can have excellent growth. So, if I wasn't going to buy old property and redevelop it myself, this would be my next choice.

'The primary disadvantages of this property are lack of choice, high prices, and not as good a capital growth as a project completed by yourself because the builder takes the profit. The exception to the rule is when there is a quality developer and an excellent designer/architect, so the building has above average design principles, built on land that is genuinely irreplaceable.'

New Property

'The primary advantage of new property is that it allows higher depreciation rates which means higher tax deductibility and in many circumstances better cash flow for people with taxable incomes and with no other ways to reduce their tax.

'If you're going for maximum affordability or maximum cash flow, then you're probably better off buying new than you are buying old. They're cheaper to own generally because they require less maintenance; however, because I generally renovate my (old) properties anyway, I do all the maintenance necessary in the renovation. Some states offer stamp duty concessions on new dwellings, and in theory new property is less work to buy because it is easier to find.'

I recalled the advice I'd received from Bruce the quantity surveyor on growth of old properties, and as if to echo my thoughts, my Wealthy Friend went on. 'The primary disadvantage of new property is that initially it (generally) offers lower capital growth potential than older property in the same area. This is because of supply and demand and price comparison. Because there is usually a lot of new property to choose from, supply outstrips demand, which keeps prices down. There is a lot to choose from so there is also a lot to compare and the properties become very price competitive.

'Generally new property only grows in response to inflation, and we have already noted that while inflation will increase prices it is not the "best" way to get growth because everything else goes up in price at the same time as your property. Because I am generally looking for strong growth from my properties and I am not prepared to sacrifice low risk, I would prefer to go for older property that offers better growth.'

Which Property Performs Best?

'The three types of property that perform particularly well in a rising marketplace are:

- Older property in fast-growth suburbs. Older property has the best capital growth potential of any type of property and if we can get it in a fast-growth suburb, then it should perform exceptionally well.
- Refurbished property in exclusive non-replaceable locations.
- New property in exclusive non-replaceable locations. If you want to buy new, you should be looking at exclusive non-replaceable locations. Such as the Eastern Suburbs of Sydney. In this area it is very hard to get new property. Virtually every property is heritage listed. If you could find a new apartment in a quality development in Paddington, because that's non-replaceable and it's exclusive, then that could be a good buy. But how many exclusive and non-replaceable locations are there? Very very few.'

Which Property Performs Worst?

'The property that performs worst in a falling market is new property in new developments or suburbs.

'Oversupply depresses prices. The need for builders to force demand by discounting depresses prices further and interest rates make it hard for people to buy and profit. Unfortunately, many people who buy their first property, buy when interest rates are low. They can only just afford the property when the interest rates are low and when rates reach 11% or 12%, they're at breaking point and have to sell.

'And they are very likely to be in the same circumstances as five or six other people in the same street, all having to sell their property. Two blocks away there may be new houses that are selling for less than their "old" house. That is a very bad situation to get into, and virtually impossible to get out of.

'The other type of property that falls rapidly in a falling market is luxury expensive property. Now when I say expensive property, I mean expensive compared to the median price. Luxury property in a falling market almost always goes down.

'The reason people buy luxury property has nothing to do with value. They buy it as a statement about themselves and are often prepared to pay millions above the market.

'Such property is also often driven by the share market. People make money in the share market or in business and put it into a lavish house. When the share market goes down and they need to recover their position, they often have to sell their property and then they see prices come plummeting down.'

Property Off the Plan

'Buying off the plan allows you to take advantage of time value and having somebody else add value to the property you are buying by building it. Letting time pass is a 'lazy' way of adding value — passing time does the work, adding 'natural' capital growth.

'The concept of buying off the plan is that you assist the developer by providing cash or (more often) confirmation of a sale so that the developer can go to a financier to get funds to continue the development. In return for this you get a discount off the real value of the property.

'Furthermore, you are buying the property at today's prices in the expectation that by the time the property is finished it will have grown in value and you can profit from that. For experienced investors who know what they are doing and buy from reputable developers, this can be a good way to profit from property in a rising market.

'One of the most successful strategies used by experienced investors is to buy a property off the plan with a deposit bond. Deposit bonds are a product originally provided by insurance companies but are now usually provided by specific deposit bond companies.

'For a fee, usually ranging between 1% and 4% of the purchase price of the property, they guarantee (insure) the developer that you will be able to pay the deposit when the building is completed and ready for settlement. This secures the contract and is sufficient to count as a full sale enabling the builder to count one more pre-sale to secure the funds to go ahead with the construction. It allows the buyer to secure the property with limited funds and gives them time to raise the extra capital/finance. Particularly with a property off the plan which could be many months, even years from completion, this saves a lot of capital being tied up for an extended period. Used like this, and not for speculation, they are worthwhile tools.

'Let's say the property is priced at $500,000 and the deposit bond is at 2%, it would cost you just $10,000 to secure the property. If the bond is at 0.5% it would cost just $2,500. Say then that the property takes 24 months to build and, by the time it is finished, prices of that sort of property have gone up 15%, or $75,000.

'That means at 0.5%, you've put out $2,500 to gain $75,000, or if you have put down 2% you've put out $10,000 to gain $75,000 or a 750% return. Furthermore, if your deposit (not bond) is 10%, it can be fully funded by the growth and you would also have a surplus of $25,000. You put in $10,000, so your return is still 250% *and* you own a property valued at $575,000. This is why people find it attractive.

'It sounds simple on the face of it and it is, but of course what you are giving up when you buy off the plan is control. Once you have bought the thin air of the property, a lot can go wrong before you take possession of the apartment. If you are buying off the plan you are taking a considerable risk, so you are looking for at least a 20% discount off the market.

'Anyone considering buying off the plan should buy only from reputable developers. During property booms many developers start up with little experience of building quality property. People get sucked in with slick sales tactics, apparent benefits and the idea of getting a bargain. For a while they do very well because the boom covers up any mistakes and allows them to make a profit, even if things go wrong.

'As more and more developers come into the market and more investors want to buy, the inexperienced developers gear up their businesses to keep churning out the properties. This leads to oversupply and over-competitiveness.

'The price of your apartment at completion is set by the value of other properties available for sale at that time. Remember supply and demand? If there is oversupply and the developers have started discounting to get business and keep "feeding the machine", then there is a good chance that your apartment may not have grown in price at all and, worse, could be worth less than what you paid for it, meaning the banks may not finance it.

'Developers get into a position where most of their profits go into expansion; they are always chasing new buyers and the temptation is to cut corners. Some developers certainly do this, and frequently go bust. That leaves you with a half-completed property and a lost deposit.

'Another thorn in this strategy is that at the end of property booms the economy has often started to "overheat", and governments respond by interfering in the market dynamic and "slowing" the economy by increasing interest rates. If this occurs when your property is being built, by the time you come to settle on the property, interest rates could be as high as 9% to 12%. Not only will you have to finance the property at those rates (as you will not be able to fix them prior to settlement), people will not be in the market buying. Demand will have slowed and prices will have flattened.

'Now, this isn't a problem with older property because with this type of property supply also decreases. And because 70% of that property is owner occupied, people simply stop selling, happy to wait until prices improve.

'This is not the case with new property. Most developers can't just pack up and wait it out. They have spent all their profits on expanding during the boom and, in order to drive demand, they start discounting and cutting prices on their stock, coincidently this is usually what sends them broke.

'So, if you bought your property for $500,000 two years ago and now they are discounting and selling similar apartments for $450,000, that will lower the value of your property by $50,000. Then the opposite of what you want happens. When you have to settle, not only do you have to come up with the $50,000 deposit, you also have to come up with the difference between what you paid for the property and what the property is now worth — an *extra* $50,000. Plus you suffer the indignity of paying two or three times your rent on interest.

'By clever marketing, people are persuaded that rising property prices are inevitable, and then encouraged to overstretch themselves by committing to many more properties then they can afford on the premise that they will be able to sell them at a profit before they even have to settle. While, of course, this is true during the height of the boom, if you get caught at the end of the boom it can be very costly. For example, someone with $50,000 to invest might be encouraged to put down five deposits to acquire five $500,000 properties instead of one deposit for one property. Well timed this can be an incredibly profitable strategy. *If* the price of the property does go up then the profits can be huge.

'And by now you know that anything that has potentially high returns also has high risk. Increases in property price are not inevitable. With new property, prices can go down.

'If our person bought the five properties the marketers had encouraged them to buy and property prices had dropped by 10%, they are in a mess. They would have to settle (pay for) five properties at $500,000 each. That's $2.5 million. They would need a minimum of $250,000 in deposit for the financier, but when someone is borrowing millions they probably need a 20% deposit and that's $500,000.

'Not only that, the buyer now also needs to fund the difference between their buy price and current market price, as the bank will only lend to the current selling price, so they need to come up with another $250,000.

'They can't sell the properties at their expected $575,000 because prices have dropped from $500,000 by 10%. So instead of a $375,000 profit ($75,000 x 5), they have now effectively lost $625,000 ($75,000 expected profit + $50,000 actual loss on each property).

'And there's the risk. People think they are risking $50,000 to gain $375,000, which is a pretty good return based on the capital committed; however, they are actually risking $625,000 — or even more if prices dropped further — to gain $375,000. And most people simply don't have the $625,000 so they sell their $500,000 house to fund the debt and walk away thrashed in the market.

'Buying off the plan can be an effective way of making money in property *if* you know what you are doing. But like most higher risk strategies it can also send you broke if you don't know what you are doing or if you understate the risks posed in the strategy.

'You also need to remember that even if you get deposit bonds, effectively you're locking up the money that you could have spent elsewhere for three months, six months, one year, two years. Often people say "I bought an apartment off the plan for $300,000 and, by the time it was finished 18 months later, that property was worth $350,000." Well, congratulations, but if they had bought something else for $300,000 at the time, it probably would have been worth $350,000 two years later too, and they wouldn't have effectively tied their money up. While a deposit bond which costs 1%, or a bank guarantee which costs 2.5%, is not tying your money up, effectively you can't use it. You can't go out and buy another apartment because the money has to be available when the property is completed.

'Now, a lot of people will say, that if things go well and the property grows in value, they don't ever have to put the money in. But there are a lot of ifs and risks in that. Even profit on $3,000 for the deposit bond on a property that is going to take 12 months to complete still depends on building it on schedule, on interest rates being the same, on finishes being as good as promised, on the property growing in value.

'Think of the number of ifs in that sequence. Every time you add an if, you're adding an extra risk. If the builder takes an extra six months to develop and build it, or if the builder runs into cash-flow problems holding completion up another six months, it could be another 12 months before the property is completed. And that could mean another 1%, 2% or even 7% in interest rates. If there are any dramas with council or any disputes, that could be another 1% interest. We could get up to paying 10% or even 15% interest on a property that we thought we were going to pay 6.5% on or 7.5% on.

'Does that mean to say that you couldn't make money out of it? No, but I reckon there's safer and easier ways to make money. I could go out and buy the same $300,000 apartment now, add value to it, instantaneously get equity that I can draw down, and, within six months buy another $300,000 apartment. Within that 12 months completion period, the $30,000 that I would have put aside to pay my deposit would probably have grown into three apartments for me if I'm doing it the right way.

'I'd much rather do that than buy off the plan and take the risk — when you're buying off the plan, you're taking 50% of the risk of being a developer! And that's a pretty risky game.

'The only exception to the rule is where an experienced, quality developer sells property off their land bank — in other words, land they bought years previously — in order to benefit from the capital growth in a genuinely irreplaceable and highly sought-after position.

'If you can combine this with buying in an early part of the property cycle you can lock in genuine and exciting profits from the capital growth that occurs during the building period and the value added through the actual building.

'If you *are* going to buy off the plan there are a number of important rules that you need to follow.

- Stick with experienced quality developers. They don't need to be the biggest but they do need to have a long-standing track record demonstrating that they complete their jobs on time within budget, with the finishes that they promised and people like living in, buying and renting their properties.

- A lot of developers put up show boards with really fantastic finishes pictured but when you get into the "finished" block, they're not anything like they were advertised. If you read your contracts, you will see that the developers are frequently allowed to vary the finishes by between 10% and 20%. That 20% can make a hell of a lot of difference in the quality of a kitchen. Be very careful that the builder has a good track record. There's a lot of research to be done when buying off the plan.

- Make sure the developer provides completion guarantees. A completion guarantee is usually provided by the financier to the development. It guarantees that if the builder does go down the tubes there will be sufficient financing to ensure that the block is completed. If you can't get a completion guarantee on the property or if the completion guarantee is provided by the builder, you are taking a considerable risk because builders frequently go bust.

- Make sure the deposit is placed in trust. There are so many developers out there who are taking deposits and keeping them. You should not allow this to happen. Your deposit should be placed in trust.

- Buy in smaller developments. Blocks of four or six are ideal. Where the land the property is being built on is a one-off and where the development is medium density or low rise (three to four storeys) I will make an exception to this rule, but the land has to be genuinely irreplaceable. I hate buying off the plan in big blocks because your sale price is limited by what else is going on in the building. If the block has 500 apartments in it, when you come to sell your apartment in two years time, how many apartments do you think are going to be on the market? One, two, three? Your price on that property will always be determined by the other prices in the building. The same goes for rental? When you come to rent your apartment in a block of 100, how many other properties do you think will also be on the market? One, two, three, four? If your apartment is exactly the same as the one nearby, how can you possibly command $10 or $15 more per week for it? So again, beware of big blocks.

- Get advice from a quantity surveyor. The biggest problems with apartments are noise, room size, finishes, ceiling heights and cross viewing (being able to see into other apartments), and if you are buying off the plan it is very hard to judge these things unless you have a lot of experience, so get quality advice — generally from a quantity surveyor or independent architect.
- Buy in the upper median price range in the building. Don't buy the very best and most expensive apartments in the building. The developers know there will be high demand for them regardless of what happens in the rest of the block, so they price them up. Mostly the apartments that are in the lower median price range in the building will have problems that you won't want to be dealing with when you come to rent or sell the apartment. It's hard to build a large block and make the majority of units ideal. The design skill involved in that is simply beyond most commercial architects. To achieve an overall design they often create odd lay-out quirks which are not obvious on a plan: less than optimal views, too close to the elevator and so on. Developers know this and generally price that 50% of the building a bit cheaper so the units there will sell quickly. The top 25% will sell because they are premium, so they are priced up. It's the 25% in the middle that are usually the best trade-off between value and price.
- Most importantly of all, buy only the number of apartments that you know you can afford to settle on when the due date arrives.

Lesson

Older property has the best capital growth potential and provides opportunity to add value with rejuvenation remembering that rejuvenation costs and depreciation can be tax deductible.

TAKEN IN BY 'PROFIT'

I had placed $500 deposit with a real-estate agent in Parramatta on an off-the-plan unit purchase in Miranda, New South Wales, in September 2001. This was my first investment on an off-the-plan basis! The purchase price was $340,000. There were only ground-floor units available, as I came in at the last sales of the complex of 40. A friend of mine by the name of George had previously purchased a unit overlooking Miranda City on the top floor for $395,000. He was happy with his purchase; however, I was very indecisive. I was always very apprehensive about the dark, unexplored concept of buying off-the-plan. My friend thought I was being way too negative. I was more so, because I had recently lost my job due to health problems. I was relying on making money on a prospective higher valuation after settlement or resale at a higher price. Negative gearing was certainly not going to work for me, especially without a job!

The time came when the builder wanted to settle. I had originally paid a finance company at Parramatta approximately $2,700 for a two-year deposit bond in September 2001. The builder had said that it was a two-year building project. However, the ongoing drastic drought in Australia allowed the builder to complete the job 12 months ahead of time! I therefore unwittingly paid a higher deposit bond premium. At this stage I became very worried. I already had an approval with a loan shark, again at Parramatta. However, I decided to go with a recognised lender, with a lower interest rate and no application/valuation fees or '1% establishment fee'. It was lucky for me, because I found out later that the loan shark was featured on *A Current Affair* for shady dealings. He even borrowed approximately $38,000 from my friend George. Fancy that, a general manager of a lending organisation borrowing from his own clients! When the time came to repay, this guy of course defaulted. The last thing I heard is that George had put the debt collectors onto him! In my due diligence investigations, I checked the credentials of the builder with the Department of Fair Trading. There were no complaints; however, it was his very first project. I was about to pull out but I was reassured by my friend George that I should stick it out, nevertheless. He was sure I was going to make money out of this deal!

Before settlement, I went to the Miranda site, with George and another good friend named Hooi. Hooi was quick to point out many faults for the builder to rectify! One major problem was the existence of a flooded concrete floor area (which was still there two weeks later!) in the main bedroom. The water had already damaged the gyprock and inbuilt cabinets contacting the floors. I later contracted an inspector for $440 to professionally itemise all faults. I presented this list through my solicitor. The solicitor later contacted me to say that the builder would be happy to cancel my contract with no penalty.

The real-estate agent also called me to say that the builder would happily take over, and sell the unit at a profit. The word 'profit' got me! I thought, 'well, maybe I should take the risk and sell at a lower price for a quick sale after settlement. Why let the builder make a profit? It should be me! After all, I'll lose my deposit bond fee, solicitor's fees and 'opportunities'. And I've done it before. I've placed a 0.25% deposit (being .25% on the total purchase price) on an old unit in Penrith, for which I'd instructed my solicitor to carry out the strata report and building inspection and then pulled out at the last minute because of too many repairs. I found out later that the person who finally purchased it, made a cool $35,000 extra equity within two months of his purchase. He also threw out the old tenants and successfully increased his rental by an extra $35 per week. The unit was positively geared from day one! All he did was cheaply tidy up the old unit. I was angry and didn't want to be stupid for the second time!

Well, I finally settled in October 2002, against the advice of my building inspector (who advised me to pull out because he felt that the builder concerned was not aware of BCA standards!). I dragged on the settlement one month over. Why? Because I went yet again, to another lender for a better deal. There was an application fee and valuation fee but no break cost fees and a lower interest rate! I had to pay an additional $2,000 in penalty fees for delaying settlement and had been issued with a notice to settle.

Now I've got a 'nice new unit in Miranda'. Purchase price was $340,000 plus $2,000 penalty fees, $2,000 in solicitor's fees, $10,000 in stamp duty, $2,700 deposit bond fee, $440 in building inspection fee (not to mention the bank and other government fees) and a multitude of rectifications still outstanding. On the day of writing, I inspected the unit and found a large motorised dryer working unmanned in the main bedroom fanning out the damp areas! Some old shelving had been planed in the courtyard accompanied by carpet underlay. So, two weeks on after settlement, I have no tenants and no prospect of selling in the immediate future. I've been told by the real-estate agent that there are only two other units on the ground floor yet to rent. The 'sun over the horizon' does not seem too promising at the moment!

By the way, I found out that my ex-friend George has rented out his unit for $340 per week. Not positively geared, but at least he's got a tenant!

MICHAEL, ST MARYS

CHAPTER 30

The Risks

My Wealthy Friend had given me a lot to digest with his talk of risk. In fact I was starting to feel a little nervous. He must have seen the look of fear on my face, for he went on, 'There are inherent risks in property investing. They're not as bad as everybody thinks but they are there. The best thing you can do is recognise them. Understating the risks — being greedy — is one of the most foolish things you can do.

'We saw some pretty extreme risks taken and understated with our buyer off the plan. They thought they were risking $50,000 for a $375,000 gain — that seems reasonable — a 750% return, in fact pretty exciting. But what we saw was they they were actually risking $625,000 *or more* for a potential $375,000 return — about 60% return.

'The promoters of these schemes rely on the fact that people will allow their greed to overcome their common sense. Promoters say give us $50,000 and you will *make* $375,000 — not that you could also lose $625,000, which you don't have. The problem for our buyer is, firstly, they don't have $625,000 to risk, they only have $50,000; and, secondly, there is no guarantee that the risk is capped at $625,000, and the $375,000 potential return is subject to all those factors we mentioned, such as downturns in the market and construction hiccups, outside the control of the investors.

'When it all goes pear shaped, people put it down to back luck or that they were ripped off and should have been protected. This is not bad luck. Market forces have nothing to do with luck. This is greed, and you can't legislate against greed, and you can't project people against their own stupidity. The fact is that all booms come to an end. It is not bad luck that such people are caught out; it is through lack of research, planning and foresight.

'Buying off the plan has some high risks associated with it that should be recognised. We also saw risks involved in buying commercial and industrial property. The strategy I'm teaching you is based on low risk, which is why we have focused on the property we have.'

'Yes. But there must still be risks in this strategy?' I wondered aloud. 'What else could go wrong?'

'Well, the following things are what people most often worry about. But, as I said, they are not as bad as many people think.'

Your Lender Collapses

'You know, it never ceases to amaze me how many people say 'I'm really worried if I move away from the banks to another financier and they go broke.' Well just remember that you owe them money! Not the other way around. This is a good thing! What will actually happen is your mortgage portfolio will simply be sold to another financier who will operate it similarly to your old financier.'

Interest Rates Rise

'It's very, very simple with interest rates. We lock into interest rates when interest rates are low and when they are starting to rise. You keep them variable when the rates are reducing or are flat. Pretty straightforward but people are often misled. Once you have fixed your interest rate, no matter how high the variable rates go you still pay the same rate. This gives me the "sleep at night factor".

'On the whole, I prefer to pay an extra $10 or $15 a week in interest on a fixed rate in the knowledge that for the next five years those repayments are all I have to find every week to fund my properties.'

Structural Scares

'In other words the building falls down! This can be averted by getting building inspections prior to purchase.'

Can't Find a Tenant

'Good properties in good locations are rarely vacant. Tenants have to give 14 to 28 days' notice in which time you should be looking for new tenants. If you are having problems tenanting the property, as

I've mentioned before, reduce the rent a little. Don't reduce it a lot because you want to keep in the same price bracket as you were. If you still have an extended vacancy period then you have to question the value of that property in your portfolio. Maybe you made a mistake in its purchase? If that is the case, you are probably far better off acknowledging this, selling the property and freeing up those funds to acquire a new better performing property.'

The Tenant Won't Pay

'Your property manager should do a thorough reference check before letting your property which will eliminate 90% of non-payment renters. Professional management will save you time and money in most instances. You should, of course, ensure that you always have approval over your tenants.

'You can recover non-payment of rent from your insurance and from the bond your renters pay before they move into the property.'

Property Doesn't Grow in Value

'Normally this comes back to bad selection. Consider cutting your losses, accepting your lesson and selling. Analyse where you went wrong and start again. Not identifying where you went wrong means you might do exactly the same thing again. That will only lose you money a second time round. You can't make money from property that doesn't grow unless the rents are really high.'

Lesson

Wise investors cover themselves against risk through insurance and through judicious decisions based on market realities.

WATCH OUT! MISTAKES TO LEARN FROM

The first property we purchased was in Brisbane. We were offered this 'wonderful potential' at a 'presentation' in South Yarra in Melbourne by people we didn't know but seeked OK.

After a free flight we were chauffeur-driven in a Jaguar from the airport through some of the best looking streets of Brisbane. The agents then showed us property which was specifically designed for rental and investors. They had all the figures on how it would benefit us by negatively gearing it. The area looked great, the plans looked great and we signed on the spot: $148,000.

The place was rented for $170 per week and we had no problems renting it. There were the usual fees for 'de-roaching' the place every six months and some small repairs.

Our shock came when we wanted to by a second investment property in Melbourne two years later after attending one of the Peter Spanns seminars. We called the valuer and got a valuation of $105,000. The bank had used the equity in our home to finance this Brisbane property. We decided to sell it. After being on the market for over 12 months we finally managed to sell it for $122,000 less agent commission and advertising. A total capital loss of $36,000 plus all the 'benefits' of negative gearing for the time we had it.

Our second property we purchased over dinner. Our friend's husband was a real-estate agent and he mentioned that a property was coming on the market and was to be auctioned in six weeks' time. The sign was being placed on it the next day. We had a quick look from the outside and liked the position, just 100 metres from Altona Beach. We made an unconditional offer to the owner (we knew our financial position beforehand) of $150,000. It was take it or leave it — he took it.

What we did not know was that the tenants did not pay rent and being 'friends' he could not bring himself to evict them. When we took over the property we paid landlords insurance. The first few weeks they paid rent OK, then the excuses stared to come in and the rent fell behind. When they were two months behind we got an eviction notice. We made a claim on the insurance company. Three weeks later the tenants sent the cheque for the outstanding rent.

We spend four weeks in cleaning up, repainting, repairing and changing the carpets for a total of $4,800 not including our time.

The property is currently rented at $230 per week, a return on investment of 7.9% plus capital growth. This property has been valued six years later at $450,000.

We have since invested in other property but now we take care where we buy. We also buy when the property is slightly positively geared.

DUSAN, VIC

CHAPTER 31

When to Buy?

'So surely now I am ready to buy?' I asked my Wealthy Friend, in the same tone as a child in a car forever asking 'Are we there yet?'

'You haven't considered timing yet,' answered my Wealthy Friend.

'I thought you said any time is a good time to buy quality property.'

'Yes, I did and that's true, but some times are better than others. There are a few unique circumstances in which you can actually secure quality property at less than market value. Once the opportunity is gone, so will be the discount price, so when you come across any of these, you have to be ready to act.'

Interest Rates Falling off a High

'Have a look around at property when interest rates have fallen below 9% on a downward trend and property prices are flattening. This can be a very good time to buy property.

'Ordinary buyers take a long time to come back into the market, even when rates are falling, so it can be a year or more before property prices start rising again, especially if rates have gone sky high. People will still be smarting from the high interest rates and with less demand, if you go in with offers, you can often secure good property relatively cheaply.

Property Passed In

'Sometimes a good time to buy is when a property has been passed in at auction. Either the vendor is unrealistic or there are no buyers at that time. Either way, the vendor has just been given a lesson in marketplace reality. Sometimes properties have actually been passed in at auction for higher prices than they ended up selling for.

'Once the auction is over, interest evaporates, buyers move onto other properties, and the vendor realises they can't have it all their own way. If the agent starts to put pressure on them to sell and if they need to sell, they can often be persuaded to sell for less than they could have got if they had used good tactics at the auction. If you wait about 48 to 72 hours after a property has been passed in, the vendor may be starting to get a little bit nervous, and that's a good time to jump in.

'And remember if a property has gone to auction, it has cost the vendor a lot of money. The more time that passes after an unsuccessful auction, generally the more eager people will be to sell.

'Of course, in a fast-rising market this situation doesn't often occur, but you never know your luck with a bad agent, or a vendor who gets caught up by greed and who has had a reality check.'

Quiet Times of the Year

'I went to an auction a couple of years ago on Easter Sunday. I got there about 15 minutes early and, as I was the first person there, I mentioned to the agent that it was a very strange day to be holding an auction.

'He said, "We reckoned that there would be no competition." He was right. There was no competition, there were also no other buyers. I was the only person who turned up. It was very interesting bidding against myself!

'Quiet times of the year are January, for example, school holidays, June to July, Easter, and Christmas time. Why would anybody sell a property during these quiet times of the year? They're desperate. Or they've got a really bad agent, one or the other.'

Desperation Sales

'Sometimes people *have* to sell. They've bought another house and need the sale to settle; they are behind in their repayments and the bank is chasing them; family is squabbling over an estate and the only way they can resolve it is to sell the property and divvy up the cash; legal proceedings, family court matters and so on are all forced sales.

'A lot of people don't like "taking advantage" but we did not create the situation for them and they are going to sell to somebody; so why not us and why not at a discount? It's a great opportunity.'

During Times of Construction Work

'It's amazing how often people sell while major infrastructure improvement is going on around them. Usually just as it is about to be finished!

'People will hold on and on while the world is collapsing around them; a new shopping complex being constructed, a freeway being built; they hold on, then six weeks before the whole project's ready to be finished, they put the property on the market. This is a perfect time to be buying.

'I've frequently picked up property, six, eight, 12 weeks even before construction's due to finish. You buy the property, you do the rejuvenation, by the time the construction around you is finished, you've got a whole new property. Of course, the new infrastructure around you has just added $50,000 to the value of your property.

'In my suburb at the moment, exactly this is happening. I think it's amazing. You drive down the road and there are three developments going on. Plus a restaurant is upgrading and new public park facilities are going in and the construction is this close to being finished. Yet there are about six properties in the road up for sale. It's insane. And they've all gone to auction and been passed in, when exactly the same properties were sold 12 months ago for far more than they have been passed in at.'

Prior to the Agent Even Listing the Property

'If you get to know some agents, they'll frequently ring you up. Remember that little thing known as a business card? I frequently have agents ring me up and say, "I'm having a lot of trouble getting this listing. It's exactly the type of property that you'd like to buy, would you like to have a look at it?"

'I go have a look at it and say I'll buy it for $280,000. They take the offer to the client they're trying to get, they get the sale and the listing all in one. That's happened to me now about six times.

Contessa

'Another version of this is when the vendor wants a "quiet sale". For some reason they don't want to advertise that the property is for sale. Nobody knows about it and only people who know the agents are let in. This is one time to be on the good side of the agents.

'These types of deals don't happen often but every now and again is enough.'

After a Special Levy is Raised in a Unit Block

'Body corporates, the groups that manage apartment blocks, are supposed to have sufficient reserves to meet all anticipated costs, but when something unexpected comes up, like major structural work, or a change in council rules, or new people come into the building and want to do renovations, and the body corporate doesn't have enough money, it raises a special levy.

'This levy forces all apartment owners to contribute to the cost of the proposed works. Sometimes these levies are so high that the owner can't afford them and has to sell.

'You'll often see people selling $200,000, $300,000, $400,000 properties because they can't afford a $6,000 special levy. That's insane. Especially if the work is going to improve the building. Yet people do it all the time, often at a discount because they need to sell fast.

'This can be an ideal time to buy, especially if you can time the rejuvenation of the interior of your property with any building work, and by the time it's all over you have a "brand new" apartment with added value courtesy of the body corporate!

'Because you bought a property when special levies were raised, it is worthwhile getting yourself onto the body corporate or at least attending the meetings. Sometimes you will discover that other people in the building, through no fault of their own, are struggling to meet the levy too.

'When I've been in such situation I've said, "Hey, I just bought apartment No. 7. Would you like to sell to me and I'll pay you the same amount for it?" And people will frequently sell to me. It works well for both parties. They save the hassle and expense of selling through an agent and they get paid market price, because that's what the other unit sold for anyway.'

Lesson

With an average 8% growth, the best time to buy residential property is always yesterday!

Some unusual — often unpredictable — circumstances offer occasional bargains if the buyer is quick to act.

ASK WHY THE VENDOR IS SELLING

One thing we have learned buying investment property, which may seem obvious, is to get us much information as possible from the agent as to why the vendor is selling the property. Usually their responses are fairly standard, but now and then you get more information than you bargained for, as was the case on our latest purchase.

We were looking at a property in Chelsea, Victoria, 200 metres from the beach and close to the train station and shops. It was advertised at $279,000 which, considering that a townhouse could be built behind the existing house, wasn't bad value. New townhouses there were fetching between $320,000 and $350,000. When we asked the agent why the vendor was selling, especially since the house had just been renovated inside, the agent replied that the vendor was going through a divorce, had already purchased another property, and naturally was in financial difficulty. Suffice to say we did not end up paying the advertised price and our first offer of $250,000 was accepted.

JOHN & FIONA, WARRANDYTE, VIC

Chapter 32

Inspecting Property and Assessing an Agent

It was time to get my hands dirty. My Wealthy Friend was giving me a lift to a suburb where there were a few properties open for inspection.

'So, what should you do when you inspect a property?' he quizzed me.

'Do your research. Be prepared.' I piped up.

'Yes. And very practically — take some notes. I take a short checklist with me that prompts me to check things such as how many bedrooms are in the property, what condition it's in, what type of renovations I would need to do. I put down estimates next to each. Here, take this with you,' he added passing over a small box with buttons and a digital read-out screen.

I looked at the little gadget he'd handed me. 'What's this?'

'It's a laser reader like tradesmen use. You put it up against the wall and you press those buttons and it tells you the dimensions of the room you're in — lounge room 45 square metres, for example — and I add that to my checklist.'

'Why is that important?'

'Because once you know how much carpet you need, how much you're going to use, and so on, you can do a rough estimate of how much it's going to cost you to have the place rejuvenated.

'You should also take an assessment sheet and take Polaroid or digital photographs of recognisable features. You did bring a camera didn't you?'

Bring one? I didn't even own one. 'Why?' I asked, avoiding the question.

'When you're doing this in earnest, you might see 30 properties a day, and by the end of that day you will probably be totally confused. It can very difficult to remember which place had which features. Now, what have I said about the agents?' he moved on.

'Agents can be very useful to you. If you get to know the agents in your area and they get to know you as a buyer, they will give you all sorts of information that they won't give anybody else.'

'Yes. I've had agents tell me the real reserve price on properties. I've had agents tell me all sorts of things, why people are buying, what other people are prepared to pay for properties. It doesn't matter whether they like you or not but if they get to know that you're a player, they understand that you are their meal tickets and so they'll start to give you all sorts of information.

'Get to know the real-estate agent and their style. Always ask them what price is expected for a property. Even though, through your research, you should have a good idea of what the property is worth, it's still worth asking the question. You want to know whether they talk the property up or they talk the property down.

'Some agents seem to make a career of underselling property. They are either really bad sales people or just natural pessimists. Pity the poor vendor who lists their property with them, because they are going to sell a good property at way below its fair price. I am sure they serve a place in the market though, probably listing the properties of pessimists who don't think they are worth much or that prices have already started to tumble and if they don't get out now, things will only ever get worse.

'There's an agent I buy property from quite regularly, he's hopeless. Absolutely hopeless. He's so bad it's unbelievable. And I've bought heaps of properties from him. I bought one property in Elizabeth Bay from him, which he said he'd had on the market for ages and couldn't sell. "It was terrible," he said, "and he couldn't get anybody interested." Well it was a little tatty but I had seen far worse. Two bedrooms with nice views and plenty of space. I bought this property from him for $320,000. I spent $20,000 on it and it was valued three months later for $480,000.

'And then he rings me up and says, "We've got this really bad property, I'm sure you won't be interested, the vendor's totally unrealistic, it's like never going to sell, I'm not going to put it to auction, it's really terrible, but you might like to look at it."

'You beauty. Bought another one. I practically don't need to see it, I just need to buy it straight off his recommendation!

'On the other hand, some real-estate agents talk the property up so, when you actually buy it for significantly less than they indicated, you will think that you got a bargain. "Mate, mate, mate, I reckoned this thing was going to go for big buckaroos, but you, the legend, bought it real well, mate!" I can't tell you how many times I've heard a line like that before (and how many agents suddenly become my "mate" when I buy something from them!).

'Some agents talk it down so that they get more people at the auction or putting in offers. Now why you'd do that is beyond me. You only need two people at the auction for it to work. Two people who actually want to buy the thing. Most people are only lookers anyway, but some agents like having lots of people at their auctions for some obscure reason — maybe it's to make the vendors happy!

'I'm going over some old stuff here, but remember to introduce yourself to the agent. Have a business card printed with the name of your company on it, your name and title — Managing Director, Chief Property Buyer, whatever you want — and all your contact details. On the back print something like this:

I buy two to three bedroom terraces under $550,000 in Paddington that are in reasonable condition but need renovation.

'When you go to the open-for-inspection and they ask for your details just hand over your card and say "Here's my business card, you might like to notice on the back what I purchase. If you hold onto it and find any properties that fit this, please give me a call."

'Many, many agents have rung me off my business card. I hand them out everywhere. If I go out to open-for-inspections, I hand them out. If I'm in a suburb and a property is up for sale and I miss out on it, I go to all the houses around it, like the real-estate agents do, and put cards in letterboxes because people will ring you. A lot of people don't like dealing with real-estate agents and they ring directly, so I've often purchased property direct from them on that basis.

'They cost you just a few dollars to have printed up and they save you an enormous amount of time and make you look professional.'

Lesson

If you get to know the agents in your area and they get to know you as a buyer, they will give you information that they won't generally divulge.

IN THE PRESENCE OF GREATNESS

At 31 years of age, I feel I am well on my way to financial independence.

I went to inspect a property in Lower Templestowe, Victoria, having made a suitable time with the agent. The appointment was for 11.30 but we turned up 10 minutes early. The tenant refused to open the door until the allocated time during which period the agent informed me that the tenant makes it extremely difficult to show people through.

Once the clock turned 11.30, the door miraculously opened as if on some kind of timer. Having been told to remove our shoes, we then walked into what would have to be the cleanest and tidiest tenanted property you are likely to find, and this was a single mum with three young kids! Realising that I was in the presence of greatness, I immediately asked her that if I purchased the house would she be prepared to stay on? With that her fierce guard came tumbling down as she feared being told to vacate. With her number now in hand, I left her to negotiate a price and told her I would be in touch.

While final negotiations on price would take nearly a week, I now had the tenant keeping me informed of any further interest in the property — of which there was none. Knowing that I was the only interested party, I had time to not only negotiate price but a four-year lease (she wanted a five-year lease) with a $60 per week rental increase on the already top rental she was paying. She was happy, I was ecstatic!

206 How You Could Build a $10 Million Property Portfolio in Just 10 Years

The property was on the market for more than $400,000.
I negotiated a $380,000 price on six-month settlement. The tenant
was paying $390 per week rent. I negotiated that to $450 per week
on a four-year lease. I negotiated a six-month settlement as that is
when the current lease expired, and it also gave me a potential
upside for capital growth — as Peter Spann taught me!

An identical property went under the hammer last weekend.
I anticipate at least a $50,000 capital gain and I only settled on
my property last month.

While having had an investment property prior to attending
Peter's seminars, the confidence he gave me has seen me enter the
market in a much bigger way than I probably otherwise would have.
In fact, I now have six investment properties in Melbourne (plus my
own home) plus 10 investment properties in the UK that I purchased
with my twin brother and two others.

ANTHONY, DONCASTER, VIC

CHAPTER 33

Buying Through Private Treaty

The term for most real-estate sales is 'private treaty'. This is where the seller (the vendor) lists the property with an agent at a selling price and you, the buyer, negotiate with them for a final price. In a private treaty sale, negotiation is the key, so my Wealthy Friend introduced me to his friend Wayne. Wayne was a top negotiator. His motto is 'Negotiating can be the most profitable activity you ever did'.

'Just imagine you are going to buy a car. The retail price is $33,000. You offer $25,000. The salesperson laughs and it goes around and around in circles for a while, but you end up agreeing on a price of $27,000 with a host of extras that weren't on the table 30 minutes ago. You have just made $6,000 in half an hour. There's not too many activities where you can make that much money. And yet people seem afraid to negotiate for fear of rejection or ridicule. "Negotiate everything" — that's my rule.'

My Wealthy Friend had said to me, 'In property, negotiating is everything,' so when Wayne spoke I paid attention.

'Everybody develops their own negotiating style, but its important for you to start with some tools of the trade. The first, and most critical is acting dumb.'

'That should be easy for me,' I said.

'You'd think so but most people just can't do it. It sounds easy but their ego gets in the way. Most people want to be known as smart. At least they don't want to come across as stupid, and so acting dumb is actually very hard.

'When you act dumb you can ask questions that seem obvious, slow down the negotiations, make statements that leave people aghast and generally put a spanner in the works. Most of the strategies in negotiation need some part of you giving up your ego

Dumb

and shaming yourself to make them work. That's all. If you can do that you'll make and save hundreds of thousands, possibly millions, of dollars over your lifetime.'

'OK, so it's really an act. If I appear a little dumb, people give me more leeway, maybe even divulge information that they wouldn't normally to a "smart" person?'

'Exactly. So let's start with our "Negotiating Tool Kit" and remember that these strategies work regardless of whether you are buying or selling.

WIN-WIN

'To get under way it's important to understand that negotiation works on the theory of "reciprocity". Give and take is the layman's term. When you give somebody something they feel obliged to give you something in return. Give them lots of things and they feel obliged to give you lots of things, or one big thing in return. Your mother used this on you for years to get you to clean your room or to be home by a certain time. In *Silence of the Lambs* Hannibal constantly said 'Quid pro quo Clarice' which is the same thing — you give me something and I give you something. That's why it's so important to always include many different things in your negotiations. The more you can include, the more things you have to "give away" or dig your heals in on. The more you have to give away the more you can expect in return. If you give away a lot, you are building up a "bank" with the other person that you are hoping to cash in on when you have something important that you need from them.

'In property you could include things like settlement time and terms, amount of deposit and the opportunity for the buyer to release that to you instead of it sitting in the agent's trust account, access to the property, fittings and inclusions, repairs, vendor finance (which will sometimes get people up on the price), long settlement but the ability to move in early and rent the property at a low rate from the vendor, options contracts (particularly useful if you intend to on-sell the property), the vendor paying stamp duty, the vendor signing council applications on your behalf, sale subject to finance, building inspection, pest inspection — whatever you can think of really.

'The more you include the more you can give away later if

necessary — just remember the items that are *really* important to you. Use the others to build up your bank, then bring your important items in and don't budge on them. If you are not game to include all the other items, even if you know they are just red herrings, you will not have built up any reciprocity.

'There are five critical questions to ask your agent:

- Why are they asking this price? This gives you an indication of what they may be likely to give on.
- What price did they first list the property at? What price was it passed in on (if it went to auction previously)? What offers have they already refused? This tells you what they were originally wanting and how far they have come down, or what they refused before. Remember just because they wouldn't sell at a low price before doesn't mean to say they won't come down now. I have frequently seen properties pass in at auction only to sell at a much lower price months later after the vendors realised how ridiculous their first asking price was.
- Why are they selling? This reveals their motivation and if you know somebody's motivation it gives you "angles" to work on in your negotiation.
- How long has this property been on the market? The longer it's been on the market the more keen the vendor is to sell. Either that or they are totally unrealistic about their price. There may also be something wrong with the property which you might not have noticed.
- What price will they actually take? Amazingly agents will actually tell you this and sometimes it's even accurate!

'Start by offering an obscure, amount, for example $273,421. This makes it look like you have calculated it down to the dollar. And always use unusual amounts as you go along. If nothing else it will keep the vendor confused as to how you are arriving at your figure.

'Never be afraid to start low. Do your homework and see if you can come up with a price that you think the property is worth. Even if you think it is a bargain at full price always start lower. Some sort of negotiation is expected, and vendors always include a negotiation margin no matter what the agent may say to you.

'Remember "players" always negotiate down to the wire. Get a reputation for being a tough negotiator. Every time you deal with that agent it will get easier. They will remember you and know they have to put in the hard yards to make it work.

'No matter how ridiculous your offer may seem, the agent is required by law to submit your offer, even if they protest and tell you how stupid it is. Once you have made your offer don't budge for at least 48 hours — even if they come back with a counter offer straight away — this gives them time to sweat. Patience really is a virtue in negotiations. Generally, the longer you can wait the better deal you can get. The agent will be keen to progress things rapidly so that nobody goes cold. To a certain degree you want the other party to be cold — not dead, just warm enough to be alive — but the best negotiations are usually protracted.

'The golden rule of negotiation is "Once you have made an offer — he who speaks next — loses." This can lead to some pretty amusing silences but it is important. And this is where your patience can really be tested. Eventually and inevitably somebody must speak and you want that to be the other party. What they say is critical to the progress of the negotiations. If you speak too soon it tells an experienced negotiator you are keen and they will exploit that.

'Avoid all of the agent's excuses — and they will make many. Don't take their comments personally — some will even be rude. If you think you are being played ask for a counter offer — it's a very game agent that will make a counter offer without consulting the vendor.

'Donald Trump, when asked why he was so successful, once replied, "It's because I write the cheque." In other words the best way to get a deal done is to put your money where your mouth is. Putting your offer in writing, especially on a legal contract and adding a deposit cheque to it carries a *lot* of weight. In my experience most people are of the "bird in the hand" variety, and they will often accept your offer, as brazen as it may be, for fear of losing that beautiful cheque if they say no.

'One of my favourite lines when agents are squeezing me on price is: "The property is worth whatever somebody will pay for it.

I've done the numbers and this is all that it's worth to me." That way you are firm without being rude.

'Always go up in decreasing amounts even if you are a long way away from where you are prepared to end up. This "whittling down" of your offers indicates that you are running out of puff and that is always good.

'Be ready to throw in a curve ball. This is always good to get stalled negotiations started again, get things moving in your direction or changing your mind. "Look I'm sorry but I just saw a very similar house with a few extra features that I really like which is a bit more expensive but it might be worth it for me to pay more to get what I want." Or "My wife/husband/children/dog doesn't really like the house. I am trying to talk them around but I think it might be a losing battle unless we can do something about the price."

'If all else fails make a *suicide offer* of 20% to 30% below the listing price. One friend even used a very unique way of negotiating — he would go down in his price instead of up. That always threw people!

'No matter what side of the deal you are on, it's the agents job to "crunch" you or "condition" you as they say. They will use every tactic they can to get you to move in their direction. Remember, if you are selling, they don't really care what price you get as long as you sell. Agents work on a tiny percentage and 2% of $250,000 is almost as good as 2% of $270,000 (only $400 difference) and certainly better than 2% of nothing if you don't sell. They will try to get you to come down, tell you all sorts of things they didn't mention when they were trying to get the exclusive listing from you, suddenly go all sour and pessimistic about the market. I have seen some dooseys — whatever you do don't listen. Remember reciprocity and stick to your guns. When an agent is trying to get me to reduce my price I have two favourite lines: "Time for you to take your negotiator's hat off and put your seller's hat back on. Go in there and re-sell the benefits of this person buying my beautiful home." And the ultimate motivator, "Look, I'm happy to come down on my price if you go halves with me by reducing your commission!" You'll be amazed how quickly they will be motivated to get that buyer to come up in price.

'And if you are buying, they can crunch even harder if you let them — they think they are in a position of power because they have something you want. Just keep blasé about it and play dumb.

'You should practice negotiating *all the time* to build your skill. And never be afraid to throw the curve ball.'

Lesson

Negotiating can be the most profitable activity you ever did. Build up a 'bank' of terms you can negotiate on down to the smallest detail, and don't be afraid to look foolish.'

BEAT 'EM TO THE PUNCH

I decided to invest in a house. I picked St Andrews, which is along the M5 near Campbelltown. I purchased a three-bedroom brick-veneer with fireplace, on a 700 square metre block with a double garage for $176,000. It is near shops, schools and public transport and had existing tenants with children who have been there for five years and want to stay forever. There are also few rentals in the area. The tenants were relieved that an investor bought the house and not a first home buyer.

I raced out to the agents and was the first person through and quickly put a $500 deposit down. I was lucky because the owner of the real-estate agency took me through and I realised later that if he made the sale then he would not have to pay another salesperson any commission. He said that he was only taking one deposit and that it was mine. I knew that about five couples would be going through the house after me and that there were similar houses on the market in the area for $20,000 more. While I was signing for the deposit, the owner phoned the other agents who were taking the other couples through and told them the house was sold. They were furious as they knew that all the couples were eager to buy. The property has risen in value to $260,000+ since I purchased at the end of November 2001 and besides the usual costs of the loan and a few other things, it hasn't cost me much to maintain.

ZDENKA, NSW

CHAPTER 34

Buying Through Auction

'I swear,' said my Wealthy Friend, as we struggled to find a park near an auction we wanted to attend, 'that attending auctions on a Saturday has replaced footy and cricket as our national pastime!' We weren't here intending to bid. Rather, there was another property my Wealthy Friend wanted to buy that was being sold by the same auctioneer. My Wealthy Friend was also coaching me on auction tactics and had said, 'The very best advice I can give you is to know your auctioneer. Good, bad, it doesn't matter. You are not outbidding the other buyers, you are outfoxing the auctioneer. After a while, they all develop their techniques, their patter, into a methodology that they use every time. Get to know their methodology and you can control the bidding. Control the bidding and you control the auction.'

And it was true. At this stage, even though I had not ever bought a property at auction, I had got to know the methodology of half a dozen auctioneers. I had taken notes on their lines, their banter, their timing, how they interacted with agents, buyers and vendors, and I had written it all down in my 'playbook'. The amazing thing is that, after a while, you can almost set your watch by the way auctioneers work a room.

I had seen my Wealthy Friend's agent, John, conduct an auction and was convinced he was the best in the game. When he was auctioning a property it was like a magical dance between buyers, agents and auctioneer. Tens of thousands in bids come and go like it's natural to want to pay a record price for everything he is selling. You almost can't help putting your hand in your wallet and giving him money, he's that good.

And I've seen the worst, berating the buyers, harassing the agents and losing the vendor a fortune because people were unable, unwilling or too frightened to bid. Either way, if you know how they work you are one step ahead of the game.

As my Wealthy Friend would have said, keep that playbook close, study it, add to it and refer to it often and you will outsmart the best of them.

Of course, every now and again, somebody simply has more money than you are willing to spend on a property and you will miss out. That's the time to sit back, relax and just enjoy Australia's new national pastime.

Here's my Wealthy Friend's Top Ten Auction Tactics.

1. Be Organised

If the auctioneer says 'sold' and they're pointing at you, you've just bought a property. That is not the time to be finding out if you can get finance, whether the property is properly zoned or the body corporate has just raised a special levy three times the value of the property! Get all that done beforehand.

Make sure that you have all the finance in place, valuations, building and strata inspections done and auctioneer's playbook well researched.

2. Set Your Bidding Limit

Professionals set a price before going in and never bid above it. The price is based on quality research and backed up by recent sales. This is your upper price limit.

Agents and auctioneers rely on people getting emotional at auctions. The more emotional people get, the less they are in control and the easier it is to sell the property. Good auctioneers work people's emotions to get them to bid higher and faster than they intended, pushing the price of the property to stratospheric heights. I have seen genuine frenzies created at auctions.

The easiest way not to get caught up in this is to know the maximum price you are prepared to pay on the day. To be realistic I will often allow myself a small margin of error — say 10% or 15% in a fast-rising market where I really want to acquire the property, but that's it.

Never tell the agent if you are bidding, how much you will be bidding, how interested in it you are, what colour your underpants are. Tell the agent nothing. The agent has a pretty good idea that you're interested in the property. You've been back to inspect it three times, you've had a building inspector through it and so on, but you don't have to necessarily give away anything that you're going to do on the day of the auction.

3. Arrive Early and Recognise Other Bidders

You've got to be there early to settle down, calm yourself, get the best position and observe other people arriving.

Everybody has their favourite position, but mine is at the front, standing to the right of the auctioneer. This is very distressing to agents, as they view this as their possie. You will see them all line up in their beautifully logo-ed blue suits, white shirts, red ties. Why are they standing there? Because that is the best spot.

So frequently you're going to have to walk up and say, 'Hi, excuse me', as you shuffle them out of the way. And they'll say things like, 'Sir, there's heaps of seats down there.'

'Oh no, I'm fine, thanks'. I've had some agents attempt to physically move me back into the seats. You can stand there if you want to. From this position you can see everybody in the room. You can look them in the face and they can see you bidding. The auction process is nervewracking for most people. Therefore, if you can outstare them and out-nerve them by bidding confidently, then you're probably going to win.

I've never understood why people don't want to be seen bidding. I like to be seen bidding. If you put in good strong confident bids, people will stop bidding against you.

I inspect other people when they're arriving and I make up stories in my head about them — things like, 'OK they're a young professional couple, they're probably buying this house as their first home. That guy looks like a builder. I've seen that person before — I'll have to watch how they bid and get them into my playbook. Have I seen them at the open-for-inspections, are they my competition or not?' The more I get to know my fellow bidders, the less I am surprised. The less surprised I am, the more confident I am in my bidding. Confident bidders win auctions.

Over the years I have loosely grouped people at auctions, based on what I anticipate their bidding tactics will be. It helps me prepare and deal with the various strategies they adopt. If nothing else it is seriously amusing when people act 'true to type' at an auction. Here are some of my 'classifications' (with apologies to *Top Gun*):

The Rookie: is extremely nervous. They usually start out at the beginning of the auction quite calm. They're trying to pretend that they're cool, calm and collected. They're trying to pretend that they're Ice Man but they're really Gone-to-Water Man or Woman. They are actually very nervous, and have often come straight from work. Unfortunately for them, they rarely win auctions and if they do, they will have paid over the money for the property. But it's always nice to see them react with genuine happiness and excitement when they do win.

Ice Man: You don't see them at open-for-inspections, they hide at the back of the auction room, they rarely bid out loud and they come with unexpected bids at really high prices. They sit and say nothing and just when everybody thought it was all over and done with, they come in with the big bids. They're cool, they're calm, they never show their hand but they are easily rattled by those of us who are prepared to bend the unwritten rules.

The Maverick: That's us. We're the Top Gun and we know it. Confident enough to be good, but have had the wind knocked out of our sails enough not to be over-cocky. We've the poise of Ice Man, the skills of the professional investor, but we're prepared to do things differently if necessary to make things go our way. Nobody ever knows what to expect from the Maverick and nor should they. We've always got something up our sleeve (and often it's a Polaroid camera!).

The Meg Ryan: You see these people everywhere — at every open-for-inspection on everything, at all the auctions, at the same cafes you go to get lunch — just like an overexposed celebrity. Are they actually stalking you? But they never seem to buy anything.

In fact, they hardly ever seem to bid and, when they do, they always miss out by a few thousand dollars. They cry when they miss out, but there they are again next Saturday, smiling and waving when they recognise you!

The Admiral: The professional investors, who bid in set jumps, they're looking bored, they're looking uninterested, they're probably not going to buy it but they might if it's looking like going for a bargain. They turn up at all the auctions; they never buy anything because they already own every block in the area that sold for less than market price and they did it before you even knew it existed. They're at the auction to find out how much profit they are going to make when they sell, if they sell.

The Goose: The Goose is my favourite type to have at an auction because they make things entertaining. They are the folk who are saying, 'Is it on the market yet? Is it on the market?' in loud and obnoxious voices.

I remember an auction that I went to recently. I had the chance of buying two properties on the night. For the first property that I was looking at buying, my limit was $500,000 and it went for $520,000. So I missed out on that one.

But there was another one that which was virtually identical and I reckoned that I could probably pick it up because, of the people who had been at the inspections, the only person to outbid me on the last property was the one who had won the auction at $520,000. So I was ready for business. I had my super cool Maverick disposition at the ready, my knockout bid all organised. The auctioneer said, 'Good evening ladies and gentlemen, I'm here to auction XXX, now any opening bid or ——'

What usually happens when the auctioneer says, 'Any opening bid or offer' is silence for the next 5.5 hours. 'Anyone, anyone, anyone?' says the auctioneer doing his best *Ferris Bueller's Day Off* impression. And finally somebody comes in with a ridiculously low bid — '$22,000?!'.

'Well, I was expecting a better bid than that but we'll get it under way at $22,000,' says the auctioneer, grateful that the silence has ended, 'Anybody else?' And then people gradually come in and the auction gets under way.

So, at this particular auction, when the auctioneer greeted everyone, he didn't even get to say 'offer'. From the back of the room, loud and strong, we all heard, '$600,000!'

'What *the*?' And the agent was going, '*yes*' and making fist-punching-the-air movements. And the auctioneer was going, 'Was that $60,000 sir?'

'No, $600,000.'

'Well, fantastic. I'll take just about anything. Anyone? $1,000? $250? $10? First, second, third, all done, I reckon you'd be pretty well done. Sold.' All over in two seconds flat, one bid only, leaving me, and just about everybody else there totally dumbfounded!

And do you want to know the look on the vendor's face? Stunned excitement — I found out later their reserve on the property was just $450,000. I went to the agent, whom I know really well, and said, 'Gary, what on earth just happened?'

He said, 'I don't know but it was bloody beautiful.'

And thought what a great guy this Goose is — he's just increased the value of all my properties in Paddington by $100,000. This guy's fabulous. Went up and shook his hand, and I said, 'Very strong bidding, congratulations.' He was very proud of himself.

Turns out the buyer thought this property was significantly better that the other similar property — worth about $100,000 more. So when he opened at $600,000 he thought he was just doing a normal bid. Got to love them. They *think* they know what they're doing but they only end up embarrassing themselves. Just make sure you don't end up the same! Do your research, act calm and follow your strategy.

The Russian: is prepared to put everything on the line because he doesn't have anything to lose and he's not in the game for himself; he's in the game for the Motherland. We love the Russian because, prepared to buy at any cost, he makes the auction very entertaining.

The Russian is usually a middle-aged man (they're usually men because women aren't this stupid). He is buying the property for one of two reasons: he's either buying the last house for his wife — this is their final house, this is their dream home; or he's buying the first house for his new 21-year-old girlfriend. One or the other.

Basically the motivation that 'the Russian' operates under if it's for the wife is 'Honey, if you don't buy this house, you're not getting any for 15 years!' If it's for the girlfriend, it's 'Honey if you buy me this house you are going to die — from overexertion for the whole of the next 15 hours!' Pretty much the same motivation really if you think about it.

This guy has money and he's got the worst thing on the face of the planet for other buyers: he has the Motherland behind him. You can't win, you can't beat him. The best thing to do is sit back and enjoy the entertainment. He is going to buy that house come hell or high water. If he has to pay $50,000 more for it, that doesn't matter, he's got to have it.

The best fun to be had is when there are two Russian's in the same auction. It's like tennis. I once saw an auction in John Street, Woollahra, in Sydney — a fabulous property which I was going to buy and live in myself. I had it valued at $1.8 to $2 million. So here we are and the auctioneer's saying, 'Ladies and gentlemen, we're at $1.6 million, $1.6 million any further bid or offer, 1.6? Strong bidding up until now, we have reached the reserve ladies and gentlemen, we are going to sell the property today, $1.6 million? I'll take $25,000. Going once, second time, third and final call, are we all done, are we all exhausted?'

And I'm just about to put in my bid when from across the room comes, '$1.7 million'. The auctioneer is impressed by the strong bidding, '$1.7 million. Fantastic, good strong bidding sir, $1.7 million.'

Then another guy on the other side of the room pitches in, '$1.8 million,' and all of a sudden it's property tennis ... $1.9, $2 million, $2.1, $2.2, $2.3 million, all the way up to $2.97 million and a new record for the area.

It was beautiful! The whole auction had taken half an hour to pull up at $1.6 million and in three minutes it ran up more than another $1 million. B-e-a-u-t-i-f-u-l. Always a pleasure to watch.

4. Watch Out for Dummy Bidders

Dummy bidders are usually used by the agent to get the property up to the reserve price. Some people complain that dummy bidders are not ethical, and the practice has such a bad name that some states have outlawed it, but from my point of view if the reserve is realistic and using a dummy bidder gets it on the market, why the heck not?

But be very careful. There are some cowboy agents and, even worse, some silly vendors who use dummy bidders after the property *is* on the market. That is a very stupid and dangerous strategy. Your playbook is your best defence against the dummy bidder. They will be largely ignored by the agent when they bid or the agent will pay them a friendly hello and they will drop out once the bidding gets serious.

Watch how the auctioneer reacts too. If the auctioneer is in on it, they hardly acknowledge the bidder's dropping out. But often these days agents don't even tell the auctioneers who the dummy bidders are.

It is hard to identify a dummy bidder by their demeanour. They can be cocky, unconfident, arrogant, unself-assured, there's no real way of telling how they'll behave.

If I think I have a dummy bidder on my hands, this is what I do. I call the agent over and ask them outright — 'I have seen this person bidding before and I am concerned they may be a dummy bidder — do you have any insight on that?' If you think you are being suckered and you're close to your top money, say to them, 'I'm not sure what's going on here but I'm prepared to put in one more bid, that's it. Do you understand what I'm saying?' You're not accusing them of anything, you're just being confident.

Now if they're smart, they will go over and tell the dummy bidder to shut up. You put in one more bid. If the dummy bidder is stupid enough to bid against you, simply walk out. Walk out. I've had agents run after me, I've had them ring me in my car, and I've had them ring me the next day, but I'm not going to play that game. I am playing for the long term. I've got to get a reputation for knowing what I'm doing and being played by a dummy bidder won't win me that reputation. Walking out will.

5. If the Property is Not Going to Reach Reserve be the Underbidder

The reserve is the amount set by the vendor under which they will not sell. This is usually set prior to the auction but it often changes as the auction progresses and things hot up or slow down. If the property does not reach reserve, despite the best efforts of both the agent and the auctioneer then it is 'passed in'.

The last person who bid before the property is passed in is referred to as the 'underbidder' and in the unwritten rules of the auction is given the first right to negotiate with the vendor to buy the property. This is a very useful right to have, because often you can still secure the property on the day, before other people have had the chance to think about chasing it and they become more of a threat.

If the bidding pulls up below the reserve, the agent will generally negotiate with the vendor in an attempt to get them to lower the reserve. If this fails, they will inform the auctioneer and the bubbly is put back on ice. The auctioneer will clearly announce to the assembled masses that, 'unless there is further bidding the property will be passed in', and then, of course, give the potential buyers the chance to continue bidding.

If it is obvious that the property is indeed going to be passed in, call the agent over and let them know that you want to be the underbidder. Ask them to inform the auctioneer of your intent and ask for a small increment in the bidding, say $500. When that is offered put in your $500 bid.

One of two things will happen then. Either you will be the underbidder when the negotiation begins, or the auction will restart. Either way you are another step closer to buying.

6. Never Put the Property on the Market Deliberately or Accidentally

This is a tactic that a lot of agents use. If the property has not reached the reserve, and you bid in order to be the underbidder, and it's obvious that nobody else is going to come in, the agent will sometimes come up to you and whisper the reserve, perhaps telling you that you are not going to buy it at the price you bid, but if you up your bid to the reserve you stand a really good chance.

Let's say the reserve is $300,000 and your last bid was at $280,000. The agent will come over to you and say, 'Mate, mate, mate, mate, mate, matey, mate. Mate I'm going to let you in on a secret. You wouldn't tell anybody this matey. Nobody will I tell this mate. Nobody on the face of the planet apart from you (and the other 20 people I'm just going to tell). Mate, the reserve price is $300,000. Mate all you've got to do is increase your bid from $280,000 to $300,000, you reach the reserve price, you'll buy it.'

Resist! Never deliberately put the property on the market. Don't do it, because frequently once the property is on the market, the bidding will start up again and you've lost it. You never know what will happen with the property actually on the market.

I've seen people come up and it seems like they're the last bidder, they've increased their bid to $300,000 and all of a sudden — it starts running, people are bidding and they're up to $360,000. If they had just kept the $280,000 bid, the property would have been passed in, they would have gone into negotiation and they probably would have paid $290,000 for it.

Always remember that if the property does not sell, if it doesn't reach its reserve, it is passed in and the last bidder gets the opportunity to negotiate. So be the final bidder if the property is going to be passed in.

But, presuming the property is going to make reserve then ...

7. Don't Bid Until the Property is On the Market

When a property is on the market it means it has reached the reserve price. And if it has reached the reserve price, it will be sold.

Some auctioneers make a big deal of this — 'Ladies and gentlemen the property is now on the market, which means that it is for outright sale. We *will* be selling the property.' This is good for you and other serious bidders because this is the action end of the auction when bids are serious.

Other auctioneers use a technique of through sale where they never refer it to the vendor or announce that the property is on the market. The auctioneer knows the reserve price; they don't refer it to the vendor, and they just keep going until such time as it is either sold or not. When you hear the 'Goose' or inexperienced buyer yell out, 'Is it on the market?' in the through auctions this will only result in snickering and glib comments from the auctioneer like, 'It's been on the market for six weeks — now we're selling.'

We, the Mavericks, prefer to wait until the auctioneer announces it or we have a good enough rapport with the agent to quietly call them over and ask them to let us know when it has reached reserve.

This is always the best tactic and good agents will let their buyers know when the property has reached reserve because they know that that's when the real buyers come out.

8. Go for a Knockout Bid

The person with the most money does not necessarily win an auction, but the person who bids with the most confidence frequently does. Strong, confident bidding wins auctions. So, my favourite tactic is to go for a knockout bid. It works best right at the end of a drawn-out auction when the final bidders are obviously down to their last and I have yet to enter a bid.

When the bidding has pulled up, completely pulled up, there's nobody else bidding, and the auctioneer has got down to, 'second call, our third and final call, all done, all finished?' you look directly at the person who made the last bid. They won't be looking at you. As far as they're concerned you don't exist. They're looking at the auctioneer and what's going on in their head? 'I think I've got it, I think I've won it, I think I did it.'

You haven't said anything. You're standing over there in your possie. Poised, in control, you are the Maverick. You look them directly in the face and you go for a knockout bid.

A knockout bid is usually about two or three times the current increment. By this stage the auction should have got down to relatively small increments.

So if they're going up by $1,000, you could take it up by $3,000, $4,000 or $5,000. Whatever it is, it needs to be a large jump in the bidding.

When the auctioneer says third and final call, and it's obvious it's going to sell, you make your bid, you make it loud, you make it clear and you make it in the full price. You don't offer an increment like most people; you say the full amount of your bid — 'two hundred and eighty-seven thousand dollars', loud and strong, and you never look away from the person who made the last bid.

If you pull that off properly, you will hear the whole room go, 'Oooh'. That's how you know that you've done it well. It's your first bid and if you do it properly, you will only ever make one bid. If it has the desired effect it will literally 'knock out' your opponent.

It is, however, a one-time-only bid. If we use it more than once, we're just going to end up costing ourselves a lot of money.

If this doesn't work we ...

9. Use the Fast Increment Strategy

Let's say you put in $280,000 as a knockout bid, and your competitor comes back with $285,000. Ask the auctioneer for a very small increment, the smallest they're prepared to give you: $100, $250, $500, $1,000, $10,000 — whatever is the smallest increment they'll accept and start calculating inside your head.

If you're at $285,000 and the auctioneer is prepared to take $1,000 increments, you've got your next bid calculated in your head and before they've even finished their $285,000, you say, 'Two hundred and eighty-six thousand dollars.'

Always say out the whole amount, it psychs people out because it makes any amount *sound* like a lot of money. And the better you do it the more likely they are going to turn to their partner, shivering in their boots saying, 'What do you think I should do honey? Oh goodness.'

The auctioneer will be saying to them, 'I'll give you the same courtesy, we'll give you $1,000, will you take $287,000?'

'Oh I don't know, oh, oh,' so they just accept the $287,000. Before they've even got their hand down from making a bid, you're ready with, 'Two hundred and eighty-eight thousand dollars!' The louder you say it, the longer you say it, the more thouuuuuusand dollars you say, the more nervous they will be.

Bid it up really quickly, get them worried that you'll never stop. Bail out if it just keeps going. Stop, shake your head, and pull out, until you get to 'third and final call' and put the other bidder through the whole process again, until you reach your limit.

10. Crazy Tactics Sometimes Work

If all else fails the Maverick does have some tricks up their sleeve.

They break the (unwritten) rules of auctions. They tick everybody off. They may make the Maverick look like the Goose, but they just may win the property. I pull them out of the hat every now and again if I really want the property and nothing I am doing is working. Mostly they work on intimidation and getting everybody off guard. Here's some I've used:

If somebody is pushing me up, I walk over to them. The auctioneer doesn't know what on earth I'm doing. The agents get really panicky. I shake their hand, introduce myself and say, 'I see you're bidding against me?'

'Yes'.

'How much are you going to pay for this thing? Because it would be really stupid for us to bid each other up and I don't want to cost you money if you are just going to end up beating me; and I don't want you costing me money if I am just going to end up beating you.'

If they tell you their price, just go over it and say, 'Look, it's obvious I am going to outbid you, please save me the cost of that by just pushing me up and withdraw now?' You'll be amazed how many times people will stop. Others will get really determined but it will only end up costing them money.

Sometimes I'll simply walk up next to them and watch them bid. Other times I'll ask the auctioneer or the agent to wait and hold up the auction while I make an imaginary phone call to slow things right down and get everybody else in the room jittery (just make sure your mobile doesn't ring while you're making the call!). I've even seen somebody walk up to another bidder and offer them cash in the hand to stop bidding (although I'm not sure if this one is legal)!

Just remember that most of the 'rules' at auctions are just 'folk-law'. Most of the laws only apply to the agents and the auctioneers. Mavericks are prepared to break the rules (not the laws) to push things their way. If nothing else, as long as you buy every now and again, you'll get a reputation for being a bit crazy and that will have the auctioneers and agents nervous every time you walk into their auction room and that can only work in your favour.

Finally, if all fails, it pays to remember ...

The Deal of a Lifetime Comes Around About Twice a Week

Many people get quite upset when they fail to buy at an auction — this is pointless; it happens to professional investors all the time. I would buy one in every five properties I bid for at auction, and this is a good ratio.

Be a gracious loser. Congratulate the winner and the agent. Let them know they did a good job but that you are still looking and give them your business card. Smile, and remember to add what you've learned to your playbook.

Lesson

An auction can be like a magical dance between buyers, agents and auctioneers. If you want to succeed, keep a playbook, study the score, know the characters and choreograph your own steps.

LITTLE FISH ARE SWEET

I had invested $68,000 in a house in Frankston, Victoria, in 1992. This was to help my tax situation, upon advice from my accountant. In 1997 I was retrenched from my Victorian government position. With my payout I looked at further investing in property, as I felt I knew a little about it. I looked around for some time and went to investment seminars, read books, and decided that there were more people that can afford $150 rent a week than $300 rent a week. So with this in mind I went looking for cheaper units that were in a location that had growth potential.

Lots of real-estate agents were on the lookout for suitable property for me. Then one of them rang up: 'I have your units for you. They are in Carrum'. Upon inspection they were four, rundown 40-year-old two-bedroom units fully tenanted with long-term tenants.

The agent said they would sell at auction for about $160,000. I started checking with other agents and decided that they would go for about $200,000. I got a bank cheque for $20,000 dollars but two days before the auction I was called away to go to Dubai in the Middle East.

So my wife, Jackie, had to go on her own. She was terrified, having never been to an auction before. By the time of the auction I had built a rapport with the agent and he was very supportive of Jackie. Saturday 4th. The day of the auction Jackie, shaking in her boots but showing outward confidence, outbid seven other keen bidders, and got the property for $190,500. No one said anything about the fact we did not pay the maximum we had arranged.

We had just settled and the agent, now a confirmed friend, rings up and tells me that the block of five units next door is for private sale. The battle to get the five units was on two fronts: finance and bidding. From the six bidders it came down to two of us. I won in the end for $278,750. In six months, the value of units in this area had gone from $47,625 per unit to $55,750 per unit.

The other bidder, I found out some time later, was my very good friend Jim the plumber. We still joke about it. If we had only known at the time who the other bidder was, I wonder what the outcome would have been.

I got a phone call a few weeks ago from the agent: 'do you want to sell?' A prospective buyer had contacted him and made an offer of $1.1 million for both blocks. From $469,250 dollars to $1.1 million in four years. Excellent!

CARL, CRANBOURNE SOUTH, VIC

CHAPTER 35

Doing the Paperwork

So I was finally going to become a property baron. David, my solicitor, sat next to me, turning pages, pointing to where I had to sign and explaining important passages in the contract.

'There certainly is a lot of paperwork with all of this, isn't there?' I stated.

'Enough to keep me in a good living,' he joked.

There are three very important pieces of paper when you are buying property: the contract; the title; and the mortgage.

The contract is simply the agreement between you and the seller (the vendor) stating the terms and conditions of the sale. Most agents use standard forms provided by their respective real-estate governing bodies. Just because they are standard doesn't mean they don't need checking, however; so make sure you get your solicitor to check them *before* you sign them.

No matter what the agent says the contract must contain *all* the parts of the deal. If you have agreed that the deal is subject to finance make sure the contract says 'subject to finance'. If it does not, you are still obliged to go through with the deal once you've signed. Anything else the agent says, such as what is included in the sale, and all the terms and conditions that you have negotiated, must appear in the contract.

It is amazing how many people sign a property contract and ignore the basic rule that once signed, they are virtually impossible to terminate. There are some 'out clauses' in property deals, but they can rarely be used and it's always best to avoid the need for them by checking carefully before signing the contract.

The title is the legal document that sets out the boundaries of the property, what it consists of and who owns it. At the time of sale, a copy of it is generally attached to the contract. For most people the only time they see the title document (or at least a copy of it) is when they sign the contract because the real title is held by the financier until the loan is paid off. That simple piece of paper — the one that confers ownership — is the entire basis of the capitalist system. Without it the whole system would collapse, so it's rather important in the general state of affairs.

Then there is the mortgage document. Like the contract with the vendor, everything you have agreed with the financier has to be in this document. Check it carefully. The financier will often send you a form document prepared by its solicitors which will frequently leave out important changes to what you have agreed. This can be very frustrating but do not sign the mortgage document until it is complete and accurate. The mortgage is signed by the borrower(s) and, if there is one, the guarantor(s). All parties who sign the loan documents are liable for its repayment and in a very nasty sentence called 'the all monies clause' give entitlement to the financier to go after them in any way it can to ensure the loan is repaid.

I could go on in great detail about mortgages but you need to know one thing: if you sign the thing you have to pay. If you don't pay the financier will find you and then you will pay more. Never sign a mortgage document under any circumstances if you don't understand this. Many spouses, parents, grandparents, friends, business partners and others have lost the shirts off their backs by guaranteeing loans, not fully understanding that if the original borrower does not pay, they automatically become liable. Due to that 'all monies clause' the house they worked for 25 years to pay off, or anything else of value for that matter, is at risk.

Well managed, borrowing money to invest works, and many people need guarantors to help them get their first loan. But it's just important to know what you are getting yourself into. Always remember to allow for the cost of:

- solicitor's fees (conveyancing);
- state government stamp duty;
- loan costs;
- building inspection; and
- strata fees.

They can be a nasty surprise in the hip pocket if you don't budget for them.

Ten minutes and about 300 signatures later I had my first official mortgage and owned my first ever property. I didn't know whether to be excited or terrified!

Lesson

The contracts with the vendor and the mortgagor are legally binding documents on all parties who sign them. They should be checked carefully before they are signed.

FINANCIAL FREEDOM IS WAITING FOR EVERYONE

I am about to share with you how I have amassed over $1 million in cash and equity in the last five years. I left school at 15 after Year 10, and landed a job as a baker-pastrycook. Including the apprenticeship I have done this for 15 long years.

In September of 1996, while sharing a house in Paddington and working in a bakery in the city, I commuted to work via motorbike. As I was riding to work one day through Paddington, a 4WD parked on the side did a 'U'-turn in front of me knocking me across the road into oncoming traffic. I ended up in hospital with three broken ribs, a fractured collarbone, sprained wrists and groin injuries, and had five weeks off work.

Eventually I got back to work but, fearing my financial future, I was immediately drawn to an advert in a Saturday paper for Peter's one-night seminar around February of 1997. It was at the Brisbane Convention Centre. The crowd was enormous, at least 5,000 people.

The funny thing was I sat up in the balcony, and just as Peter was about to speak a man about 50 years old leaned over to me and said, 'I will give this bloke 10 minutes and I am out of here!' Well three hours passed and the man was still there with his mouth literally hanging open, intently listening to Peter's strategies on wealth creation. That first-night seminar to me made complete sense in every part, especially about property, rejuvenation, drawing down equity and leapfrogging into the next one.

Within a week after the first seminar I started house hunting. It took about six weeks of casually looking in my spare time to find the one nobody wanted, a deceased estate, low-set brick bunker a few doors from the waterfront in Redcliffe. It had rusted gutters, wallpaper, lino floors, rats and was so overgrown you could not see the house from the street. My parent came to look with me after I signed the contract on the home and, within minutes, my mother was starting to cry. I was totally embarrassed in front of the agent as my mother started telling me off sternly and then started on the agent with some verbal abuse. Luckily the agent was a good friend I have know for years.

I ended up buying the home for $83,000, spent $5,000 on renovations and lived in it for six months. It was revalued at $105,000.

I bought house number two for $100,000, lived in it for two years, spent $2,000 on rejuvenations, and revalued. I bought house number three for $125,000, and am currently living in it. I spent $10,000 on it and had it revalued at $310,000.

I sold house number one in June 2001 for $135,000, a profit of almost $50,000. I bought house number four in June of 2001 for $78,000, spent $2,000 on rejuvenations and had it revalued within three months at $120,000. House number five I bought for $150,000, spent $5,000 and had it revalued, buying house number six for $205,000.

House number six will be our lifestyle property and in the next eight months we will be spending about $90,000 on it. When finished it will be revalued at around $420,000–$460,000, an estimated capital growth of $130,000 on one residential property within 12 months.

I revalued again this year and am, at present, starting to develop five townhouses on 1,000 square metres. The cost will be $170,000 each x 5 = $850,000. Revalued at $275,000 each x 5 = $1.375 million. So for a 12-month project = $525,000. Rental will be $220 a week and total cost per week with body corporate fees, etc is then $0.

I would like to note that we started this journey only five and a half years ago with only $10,000 in total. I am now 33 years old and have a young family. My wife, Lynda, is 29 years old; Brandon is six years; Mitchell is two years; and Claire is only three weeks old.

Even a baker with a minimal education can go from broke to millionaire in under six years. I challenge every person to do what is right for them to improve their quality of life and strive for dreams as we have. To take charge of their financial future. For me, finishing work this year was a great goal; being able to give our children opportunities; spending quality time with them and world schooling them so they can learn firsthand about history. Our life as we now live it has only been possible from that first night seminar. A night never to be forgotten.

JOHN, REDCLIFFE

CHAPTER 36

To Sell or Not to Sell?

There are few reasons ever to sell quality investment property. I have lost more money over the years in forfeited capital growth by selling than I made on the irresistible offer. It is hard to find good property — if you sell, what are you going to replace it with? If you sell, you have lost the asset and the capital growth from that asset *forever*.

If you need money, you can always draw down the equity in the property. Agents' commissions, advertising and selling costs, and capital gains tax will often come to a greater percentage of the equity than the loan-to-valuation ratio, so then it doesn't make sense to sell.

There are, however, some reasons why I would sell:

1. If I made a purchasing mistake. *problem property*
2. If I received a ridiculously high offer for the property.
3. If I needed the cash and borrowing against the equity wouldn't work *Rationalization of property portfolio*

If you find you do need to sell, there are 10 top tips you should take note of.

1. Get the Right Agent

The agent is responsible for at least 50% of the success of a sale, so it stands to reason that you should choose them carefully. So many people select their agent by foolish criteria, such as that they charge the cheapest commission; they have the biggest ads in the paper; or their office is close by. Rather than have these qualities, your agent should:

- genuinely like your property;
- think the price that you want is reasonable and attainable;

- have sold your sort of property before (preferably recently) and have maintained a list of buyers they can contact;
- follow up on all leads diligently;
- build a rapport with you that is strong enough to prevent you from making big mistakes, but open enough to allow you latitude to bring your ideas into the marketing campaign.

Just in case you are tempted to sell your own property to save that tiny 2.5% — don't. While I am sure it can happen, it is rare that a 'Fisbo' (for sale by owner) will outperform a good agent selling the same property. A good agent can earn you their commission and more in a good selling campaign. Selling yourself to save money is false economy as far as I am concerned.

If you genuinely think nobody can do as good a job as you of selling your property, do your research first and make sure you know what you are doing. There are many specialty books written on the topic.

2. To Market to Market

In a fast-moving or rising market, auction is invariably the way to go. Certainly auction any property that is hard to value, unique, highly appealing to the marketplace, or expensive.

A lot of people don't like auctions because they are stressful. They are only stressful if you make them that way. Set a reasonable reserve, do everything you can to assist the agent in getting the hype going during the marketing campaign. Buy yourself a bottle of Champers and crack it before the auction starts (not too much now — you need to have some of your wits about you!).

Be reasonable but don't allow the agent or auctioneer to bully you or put too much pressure on you. Don't be afraid to put the house on the market if it is just shy of its reserve — most times that stimulates the bidding again. I have seen properties passed in at auction only to sell months later for *less* than the figure it was passed in at. And, finally, don't be upset if the property doesn't sell on the day. That's when the agent starts earning their pay.

Any property that is common for the area, easy to value or you want to sell without the hassle of a full-blown marketing campaign is probably best sold through private treaty where you set your price and negotiate from there. All the other forms of sale — sealed auction, by tender, and so on are too far outside most buyers' comfort zones to participate in, so you are only cutting off a large percentage of your market.

3. Open that House

Open-for-inspections always work better than inspection by appointment for all but the most exclusive and expensive properties. If you are genuinely worried about security, pack up anything expensive or fragile and store it elsewhere for the duration of the campaign and insist that your agent provides adequate staff to cover the whole house (or hire your own discreet security).

A crowd is always good, so invite all the neighbours for a stickybeak, have big, bright 'Open for Inspection' flags fluttering outside, and do everything you can to make it an event. While all you need is one person to fall in love with your property to get a sale, or two people to get an auction going, a crowd at an open always makes people think that the property is sought after.

4. Presentation is Everything

It is a competitive market. Presenting your property at anything less than its best won't work. Even if that best is not a brand spanking new renovation, people like to think that the previous owner at least cared.

Personally I cannot buy deceased estates. I have been through many where the family have been too uninterested or sad to empty the house beforehand, and walking through a person's possessions, left almost exactly as when they lived is just far too eerie and sad for me. All the relatives had to do was clear the previous owner's very personal belongings from the house and I would have been fine. I suspect there are other people out there like me, so the vendors of those properties were cutting out some proportion of their market by not presenting the property this way.

Give the property a thorough clean and, if necessary, the once-over with a paintbrush. Fix leaking taps, oil creaking doors and repair obvious things that might put off potential buyers. And if you have kids, six weeks of strictly enforced discipline will not destroy their free spirits! Toys need to be away, bedrooms clean and walls free of whatever horrible band your teenager is into at the moment. It's also best not to have too many of your treasured photos all over the place — it makes it hard for people to imagine themselves in your house.

Do the dishes and have bathrooms and kitchen sparkling clean. A busy life is no excuse. Put it on hold for the weeks of the campaign. If you can afford to, get in cleaners before every open-for-inspection. Give the garden a tidy up and always mow the lawn and at inspection time keep the dog, the cat and the kids outside or preferably away from the house altogether.

Try not to sell a property while it is tenanted. It's hard to get it looking its best. If you have tenants, it's worth spending the extra money to have professional cleaners come in each week before the open-for-inspections and pay for removalists to pack up and store any surplus items to de-clutter.

Buy the tenants flowers and thank them profusely for every minor indulgence — now is the time you want them 'on board'!

These tips may seem obvious, but the number of places I have inspected over the years that don't even begin to conform to these simple rules is uncountable and the owners are costing themselves money. Most people simply can not see beyond the mess into their dream home or investment and walk away.

5. Fill an Empty Property

If you are selling a property that you don't live in, it's a good idea to put in some basic, but very modern furniture.

At the height of my 'buy, renovate, sell' period, I even bought furniture specifically for that purpose, but you don't need to go that far — there are companies that specialise in hiring furniture to people selling properties and the best of them also offer a free design service to make the place look fabulous.

You don't need the property to be completely full; in fact it works better if it is not. Some hire places even have slightly undersized furniture so the property looks more spacious. If nothing else, put a designer couch in the loungeroom, some nicely framed mirrors on the walls, a bed in the main bedroom with designer bed covers, and some well-placed accessories through the house.

6. Smell Sells

And I don't mean the four-week-old laundry piled up waiting to be done. Buy yourself some oil burners and light them well before the open-for-inspection: lemon in all the bathrooms, lavender in all the bedrooms. My preferred smell in kitchens is cookies. Bake them so they are ready just before the inspection time so the agent can serve them to potential buyers. Some people brew coffee, but only coffee lovers love coffee — personally, I find the smell of freshly brewed coffee irritating.

7. Music Makes the World Go Round

... And the buyers buy. Silence is not golden when it comes to real estate — silence just makes people nervous. If you don't have a house-wide system, play the same CD in every major room of the house, just loud enough to be heard in that room, but not loud enough to interfere with the music in the other rooms.

Light classical is best. Heavy classical makes people nervous. The radio has ads, modern music may not be to everybody's taste, and resist 'whale, dolphin, and rainforest' music. Some people think it is only for nutcases; it sounds just a little too 'guesthouse' for my tastes.

8. Advertise Everywhere

The right advertising can make or break a selling campaign. Avoid the 'three bedrooms, good-sized loungeroom, and a twin garage' style of advertising. Be descriptive and emotive. I wrote this ad for a friend who was having trouble selling. Her property had been listed for seven weeks with only one ridiculous offer. She placed this ad and had it sold within a week:

Highgate Hill — The Views Go on Forever!

Be the first to live in this freshly renovated 2-bedroom apartment in a newly renovated block.

From top to toe this fantastic apartment has been given a make-over that will suit your lifestyle and aspirations.

New designer kitchen with stainless-steel appliances and sparkling new bathroom. Designer fittings and colours abound so you can settle right in and make a real lifestyle statement.

Sitting on top of a hill and facing NE, this top-floor apartment gets magnificant views including front-row city and suburb scapes that are fantastic at any time of day but come alive at night. This position also captures fresh breezes to keep you cool on summer nights. Huge bedrooms with built-ins, separate loungeroom with private entryway leading to a balcony where you can sip a quiet beer or a cocktail if the mood takes you.

Your car is tucked away in a lock-up garage and there's heaps of street parking if you need that too. An internal laundry helps keep everything at your reach.

Close to everything — train and bus are an easy walk, funky cafes and shops 5 minutes away and it's just a hop, skip and a jump to the city.

All this for a pre-renovation price of just $270,000. Call [agent] now on [number]. Hurry, at this price and this location, this amazing apartment will NOT last.

Ensure your advertising campaign covers all the mediums that people buying houses look in and don't forget local suburban publications.

Professionally taken colour photos always ad impact to an advertisement and I use them wherever possible. One property that I renovated was being considered for a feature in a major design magazine (and it's always great to have the magazine casually open at the right page on a coffee table during the open-for-inspection), but they decided only to do the bathroom. The editor saw photos in the paper of the property for sale, so, he sent back his team and the whole apartment was featured — such is the power of a photo. Placement on a well-used website is a must as well.[15]

Flyers distributed to local mailboxes can help to get a crowd to your open-for-inspections, as will a mailing campaign to people on the agents' lists.

9. Timing is Everything (and Nothing At All)

Some people are paranoid about timing the sale of their property and only ever do it in spring. In my experience spring is crowded and, while it is certainly a busy time in the market, unless my property is a stand-out I rarely want to sell it during the spring season lest it get buried with all the other keen vendors. If you are going to sell in spring be early (to get the worm) or be late (to get all the desperate buyers who have missed out so often they are now prepared to pay the price necessary to get in).

However, as I have mentioned, apart from late December and early January, Easter, school holidays and the depths of winter, I doubt if there is a bad time to be selling property, provided your marketing campaign is comprehensive and targets buyers of your type of property.

If you are trying to time the peak of the market to maximise profit, it is very hard to do, and my best advice is don't wait too long. The saying, 'It's best to leave some profit in the deal for the next person,' is always good. Better to have sold at a good profit than not to have sold at all because you waited too long and property has gone off the boil.

10. Listen to the Market

While I would never interfere with the agent doing their job or pseudo-sell, I like to be present at open-for-inspections to listen to what people have to say about my properties, unsolicited and unedited.

I have a thick skin and do not care about personal and narky comments. I am always listening for a general theme. What do people like, what do they dislike, how can I improve my presentation and selection skills? Their comments guide me in everything from marketing campaigns, furniture selection and presentation of the properties, to the type of properties I buy next.

Attend other open-for-inspections in your area for ideas and listen to people there as well. Keep an open mind —you might just learn something.

Lesson

The capital growth forfeited outweighs the quick profit to be made by selling quality property. If you do have to sell, remember that exposure to the market through advertising and open-for-inspections is crucial in creating demand. A well-presented house will appeal to potential buyers, and getting an enthusiastic, knowledgeable agent is a must.

MILESTONE MAKER

Since May and April 2000 I have achieved the following milestones with starting base property $300,000 and equity $100,000:

1. $1.1 million in property
2. Equity $250,000
3. $49,000 rental income

The next 12 months still looks strong. The property will continue to grow, hence equity will grow. Even if I do nothing for seven years, I will still become a millionaire. The time ahead is to improve my skills, knowledge and experience in the market.

PETER, VIC

CHAPTER 37

The Three Dumbest Things I Ever Did

OK, so this list might not be the dumbest things I have ever done, but they sure are the dumbest things I have done in property ...

1. Sold the Good Ones

Good properties are hard to come by. Inspired by a quick profit I often turned over my properties after my rejuvenations. The good ones sold, the bad ones ended up in my buy-and-hold portfolio. Not a way to successfully and quickly build your wealth. Once I started resisting the temptation of selling, my wealth creation gradually took on a momentum of its own so that today my properties earn far more than I do every year.

I once calculated that if I had kept all the properties I had sold (impossible because of serviceability issues but worth the mental exercise anyway) they would have been worth over $60 million by now. That's a *lot* to give up.

2. Overstretched Myself

A little bit of greed is good — it motivates people. It stirs their desires enough for them to actually do something about their futures. But when greed takes over it leads to overstretching.

When I was developing property, I made a few million dollars over the course of three years doing duplexes and four-packs (blocks of four units). They were easy, fast and profitable. At the same time, every week I drove past a piece of land zoned for 22 apartments and thought what a great opportunity it would be. So I overstretched and started a development six times the size of the ones I had undertaken before that. It was a disaster. Things I never anticipated held up the project and the scope of works was beyond my management ability. Costs soared and I ended up losing everything I had made over the previous three years. I was grateful that was all I lost.

Overstretching can also be borrowing too much — going out to the wire and leaving no buffer in case things go wrong. My rule of thumb is that you should have a minimum of three to six months of earnings in cash or a line of credit that you can draw down if things go wrong. That should give you just enough of a buffer to rearrange your affairs if anything unexpected happens.

3. Believed the Boom Times Would Not Come to an End

So many people have been caught by this belief (and it usually goes hand in hand with mistake number 2).

And while in property this may not kill you — you can always just hold on until things get better — it can certainly slow you down. For the history of humankind, growth has always been there in property over the long term, but we can not rely on anything in the short term.

In my early days I seemed to be always attempting my most audacious and risky projects right at the end of the three-year growth cycle and then having to support them through the down times. Always remember the five-year pattern:

- Years 1 and 2, property flat (and, if you need to sell, it may also go down due to lack of demand).
- Year 3, property starts rising.
- Years 4 and 5, property jumps dramatically.

While never following this pattern precisely, woe betide the person who ignores it completely. Being in property for a number of full cycles has taught me patience and careful practice. I commend you to learn from my mistakes.

Lesson

Three tips to avoid failure:
1. Don't be tempted to sell good-quality property for quick profit.
2. Don't take on more debt, projects or scope than you can manage.
3. Don't believe there won't be downturns in the market.

These tips boil down to one: don't be greedy.

HOLIDAY HOME PROFITS

Before I attended a Peter Spann course I owned two weatherboard cottages in Collingwood, Victoria. Adopting your advice I had the houses revalued when properties around me sold at high prices and obtained a line of credit.

With the money I put a deposit on a refurbished boutique development in Fitzroy, in Nicholson St, right opposite the old Exhibition Building. Trams stop out the front and it is a 10-minute walk into the city. The apartments have a beautiful garden aspect, mine is on the first floor and has balconies off the lounge and bedroom. The rooftop overlooks the parklands and city.

It is only a one-bedroom, which is very popular now. The people in charge of the project were fantastic. It was a three-month settlement and they organised a tenant straight away. The end-of-year financial report included the new valuation which is $12,000 above the original purchase price and the rent is $1100 per month, which partially pays the mortgage.

Before the Fitzory property settled, a friend and I went to Noosa. She was keen to get an investment property with me as we often have holidays together. We found and bought a great place in Sunshine Beach. It is only three years old, the owner was a builder, it has three bedrooms, garage, kitchen, living area — and what I love about it is the back yard. It backs on to the national park. It is just spectacular and no one will be able to build there. We have plans to put a pool in at some stage. It is only 1 kilometre from the surf beach; a great area. We have a full-time tenant so, with the rent, Robyn and I only fork out around $100 per month — a night out!

We haven't had this property 12 months yet and it has increased value by $110,000. Unreal! We are so excited by the area we have now invested in a two-bedroom apartment with two bathrooms, right on the beach, part of a complex of only 24 apartments — pool, sauna, BBQ are all on the premises and just a walk from the back door to the beach. The property is up on a hilltop and the one we purchased is one of only two that enjoy the fantastic ocean views.

This apartment is lovely; however, the kitchen could do with a facelift. We are going up for Christmas to see what refurbishments we can do to make the apartment the deluxe apartment everyone wants to be in and will pay that bit extra for the comforts.

Many thanks to Peter for all his advice given during the course — at the time I was overwhelmed that someone with the secrets to great success was kind enough to pass the information on to average Australians who also want a better quality life — thank you Peter.

JOSEPHINE, NOOSA HEADS, QLD

CHAPTER 38

The Three Smartest Things I Ever Did

Just to be balanced, I had better reveal the three smartest strategies I have used.

1. Shoot the Dogs

Selling good property is dumb. Selling bad property (even if it costs you) is smart. Every few years (it needs to be a few years so you don't get caught on the down part of the cycle), I review my portfolio and look at the bottom 10% in growth and return, as well as cost and heartache. I assess, realistically, if things are likely to change (they rarely do), and if I conclude they are not, I simply 'shoot the dogs' by selling the properties. Sometimes this costs money, but it also frees up funds for me to invest in other quality assets.

2. Didn't Listen to Others

I am lucky that I was (practically) an only child because it made me self-reliant. I have always been uninterested in other people's opinions — unless that person is a genuine, hard-core, learned-through-experience expert.

While most people consult just about everybody on their real-estate decisions, I try to consult only a few people whom I trust and who have extensive experience. The 'expert opinion' I don't rely on includes that most intrusive of all mediums these days, the mass media. The media has its place, but factual reporting is often replaced by ill-informed and sensationalist editorial, written by people who could hardly be considered experts. How often have you read the newspaper and on one page it says 'Property boom about to come to an end!' and three pages later 'Now may be the time to get into property!'?

Many newspapers and broadcast media do employ great journalists who are experts, but they can be few and far between and hard to tell from those who just want to fill pages. Stick to quality papers and read the factual reports while staying away from the hype.

Use the media, the Internet, and your expert friends to conduct your research but in the end you have to stand on your own two feet and make your decisions, enjoy your wins and learn from your mistakes yourself. Nobody else can do it.

3. Bought Whenever I Could

People always ask me, 'When is the best time to buy property?' My answer is always the same: 'Yesterday'.

While I don't like high interest rates (unless they are compensated by high rental returns, which often happens), I am always on the look out for quality property at a reasonable price, and when I find it, if I have the money, I will buy it. Simple as that.

In the year or two at the top of the interest rate cycle (which hits every decade or so), with your interest rates fixed before they get crippling, it may be a good time to have some cash lying around to take advantage of falling prices as those who can no longer hold out start shifting their property at low prices to get a sale.

I made my first million (net profit) in property during an era when property was supposed to be in a downturn and the nation was gripped by recession. Lucky I didn't know the recession was on, otherwise I might not have started in property! Often it is easier to make money when things are not hot because you have less competition and it is easier to buy at reasonable prices.

But the boom times make it easy through natural growth. So buy when you can, buy as soon as you can, and buy as much as you can. It'll make you rich!

Lesson

Three tips for success:

1. Get rid of poorly performing property.
2. Get 'expert' advice only from experienced hands. Best of all become an expert yourself.
3. Buy quality property whenever you can.

THE TIME IS NOW

I attended Peter's seminar around three years ago. Since that time I have bought two investment properties in the inner city of Sydney and my own home in Willoughby.

I am 27 years of age and ordered my first 'Money Magic' video set from a hospital bed when I was ill with pneumonia because I did not want to wait one more week before starting my new *mission*. My whole family thought I was *mad*, as I have always been brought up to believe that you own your own home and if lucky, well you may get a few shares and one investment property, but that did not really seem enough to me.

My sister and father are successful business people but I never had the enthusiasm to apply myself to studying or slogging it out in the workforce. Once I realised 'life is easy' and 'money is free', I am more determined than ever.

Today I have already searched the property market to see what bargains are out there and no matter what the time of day is, the time to buy is *now*.

MELISSA, WILLOUGHBY, NSW

CHAPTER 39

Maximum Return, Maximum Profit

At last, after all that preparation, it was time to get stuck into my new house. It's unbelievable what you can do when you are determined and have no money!

To minimise cost, I decided to do as much of the work as I could myself. Amazingly the roof and the walls were fixed by replacing just one stump that had mysteriously gone missing from under the house.

My Beautiful Friend was an artist, so she was responsible for paint and colour selection and for creating amazing blue-sky ceilings for the bathroom and a special bright yellow and blue kitchen. I rented a ute and removed the rubbish and cut the lawn. I discovered I had a knack for destruction and happily removed the fibro from the veranda. The lino came up and the floors were polished. Some new taps for the bathroom and a stove from a second-hand shop for the kitchen and we were just about done.

Well, that blew my $4,000 renovation budget anyway. By the time work was finished, my purchase, costs and renovation came to $32,000.

The funniest thing about all this was that I was really enjoying myself. Never one to do manual labour in the past I was having a ball. Drills and hammers and, most fun of all, the floor sander were all new to me and I loved it. Paint was splattered on clothes, cuts and bumps kissed better and that weary exhaustion that comes over you after a hard day of manual labour was savoured.

Every day the neighbours would pop in and comment on the latest task completed. They were genuinely interested and happy that somebody was finally doing something about the rundown shack that was a blight on their neighbourhood.

Selling that house and getting the profit in the bank was one of the most exciting days of my life. All of a sudden I truly 'got' it. This skill would pave the way to financial freedom forever. It could make me rich and it did. Today, I no longer have to confine my searches to properties less than $30,000, but the principles my Wealthy Friend taught me are the ones I still use.

Maximum return will come from a property when it is at its 'highest and best use'. Highest and best use is when a block of land is being utilised to the maximum potential allowed by its zoning with consideration of the demographics of the area. If a block of land is zoned to allow for a duplex (twin townhouses), its maximum return will come when those two townhouses are built on it in a manner that suits the people who want to reside in the area.

This concept, while simple, is always the best guide to making maximum profit from adding value. Maximum profit will come when you take a block of land that is not at its highest and best use and develop it to that point.

Imagine a block that had a house built on it, but could be split into two blocks. This is very common in the 'newer' cities of Australia such as Brisbane, Adelaide and Perth. When those cities were built, large block size was common. As city councils struggle to keep up with the need for ever expanding infrastructure, they have encouraged increased density by making the minimum block size smaller and smaller. When I first started in property, the smallest residential block size in Brisbane was about 800 square metres. Now, it's less than 400 square metres.

If you buy a block large enough, and the original house is in the right spot on the block, it is possible to make considerable profit by splitting the block and either selling one or all parts or bringing that block to its highest and best use.

For some time, I enjoyed buying big Brisbane blocks with rundown Queenslanders on them, shifting the house to the back of the block and trucking in another Queenslander to put on the front of the block. I would then renovate both of them, maintaining the streetscape and adding considerable value.

Here's an example of one I worked on in Ashgrove, Brisbane:

Loan for original block with house	$220,000
Purchasing costs (including interest)	$18,000
Cost to move house 1	$40,000
Cost to buy and move house 2	$80,000
Cost to renovate both houses	$80,000
Total cost	$438,000
Value of renovated properties	$550,000
Profit	$112,000
Cost of ownership	$30,470 p.a.
New rent	$28,600 p.a.
Weekly cost	Just $36 p.w.

In another project in Windsor, Brisbane, I built two new townhouses at the back of a lovely little cottage:

Loan for original block with cottage	$335,000
Purchasing costs (including interest)	$26,000
Cost to build 2 x townhouses	$260,000
Cost to renovate cottage	$30,000
Total cost	$651,000
Value of renovated properties	$950,000
Profit	$299,000
Cost of ownership	$45,315 p.a.
New rent	$49,400 p.a.
Weekly income	$79

Subdividing land where it is possible to do so can often be one of the most profitable ways of adding value. Smaller blocks are more affordable and together command higher prices than the whole. On the other hand, remembering the Cycle of Life, people often spend a fortune consolidating blocks later to gain one big parcel of land, and it is possible to make money by consolidating blocks of land next to each other. For example, many city or suburban house blocks cannot have apartments built on them, but if you were to buy two, three or four blocks next to each other a rezoning might be possible. Once you have the rezoning in place it is not necessary to actually build the apartments yourself. Often developers will pay a premium for blocks of this nature.

Rezoning is also a good way to make profits. While this is not always a precise science and can at best be called speculative, getting a parcel of land rezoned from single-dwelling residential to multi-dwelling residential, or rural to residential, or residential to commercial, industrial to commercial or residential, and so on almost guarantees that good profits can be made. The variable and the risk always comes from the local authorities' desire, speed (or lack thereof), or assessment of political advantage and disadvantage in allowing the rezoning. Many people have waited years, sometimes decades, for that mythical rezoning to come through, only to waste any profits they could have made on holding costs.

Having said that, I am aware of a colleague who purchased three farms for about $400,000, had them rezoned to multi-dwelling residential and commercial and resold the block for a $16 million profit!

Bringing a block to its highest and best use does not always involve rezoning or using the zoning to its fullest capacity. Sometimes an underdeveloped house can be extended or added to in order to bring it in line with other higher value properties in the area. This is the 'buy the worst house in the best street' principle.

I have even seen an occasion when 'destruction' can add value. In some cases demolishing a house or clearing an untidy block can bring profits, as it allows people to imagine their own dream home on the block without the obstruction of the old house or overgrown vegetation.

There are many variations on a theme here, but always remember 'highest and best use'.

Lesson

Maximum return comes when a property is put to its highest and best use for its potential renters and buyers. Developing, subdividing and applying for rezoning might pay handsome dividends if they are appropriate to an area.

HIGHEST AND BEST USE

Three-bed house in Brisbane, purchased 10/99 for $173,000. First rented out at $210 p.w. Bathroom and laundry renovated and internal paint done around $3,200.

New rent $260 p.w. but also includes gardening and mowing in the new lease (cost approx. $16 p.w.) so still a good deal; importantly it was easier to rent once 'done up'. Current cost to me for the property is $1,500 p.a. after tax. Next go is a kitchen reno. Real exciting stuff is that the block is OK to build another house on.

Cost approximately $140,000 for three-bed replica Queenslander plus $10,000 fit-out and $15,000–$25,000 costs. I understand that I don't have to subdivide to build another place on — just use as a multi-unit dwelling! Can subdivide later if ever I want to sell.

Total extra investment $140,000 + $10,000 + $20,000 = $170,000 to provide a house (once subdivided) worth $275,000. Interestingly, the original house is worth $230,000 and will only lose $10,000–$20,000 from the loss of the 'wasted' land. So net worth increase is $275,000 – $170,000 – $20,000 = $85,000 and the new place will rent for $275 p.w. and provide a positive after-tax cash flow of around $2,500 p.a. from year two!

And guess what I can use the $85,000 for? To borrow another $400,000 for another property!

So the combined properties will be worth $475,000 (with $375,000 borrowed) and provide $1,000 p.a. after-tax positive cash. A great deal if the council OKs!

We currently have three investment properties worth $960,000 fully geared, with our own house worth $1 million with $500,000 equity (i.e. $200,000 mortgage and $300,000 as loans for the investment properties etc.).

CRAIG, QLD

CHAPTER 40

Looking Back and Looking Forward

It's been almost 15 years since I started in property by buying that little rundown cottage and selling it. There have been good times and bad times, challenges and triumphs, but it's all been worth it.

I have used every strategy in this book. I started generating income by buying properties I could afford in areas where there was demand, and rejuvenating them. I didn't spend a lot on them and made the odd mistake — remember these were the days when there wasn't a renovation show on TV every night so I had to learn as I went. It may be hard to believe (given what is available today) but at that time there was literally only one book I could find on investing in property in Australia.

The properties I first acquired were small and there wasn't a lot of profit in them compared to what I would expect today, but then again, $5,000 to $10,000 in profit from one property in just a few months really did seem like a fortune to me then, and so I cut my teeth on simple projects and learned how to make my cheap fittings and finishes look expensive with good old-fashioned elbow grease and a bit of ingenuity.

I knew I was a hopeless builder so never tackled anything that wasn't a 'paint and patch' on my own. I always called in the professionals for building, electrical and plumbing. I knew I could save money if I 'prepped' the job for them, acted as labourer while they were doing it, and cleaned up after them.

I voraciously read anything I could get my hands on, and gradually built up my knowledge bank. I was also building up favour with my financial bank — amazingly a church mezzanine lending fund. I was paying 11% interest when everybody else was paying 7%, but I was happy because that fund gave me the money to get in the market and start making a profit. In fact, I was making so much from my property 'hobby' I was able to give up most of my work at the supermarket.

Over the years I have seen fads come and go (when I first got into property, prawn farms without prawns and land under the high-water mark were the favourite scams). I have seen poor unsuspecting people, who just wanted to get ahead, ripped off and left penniless due to lack of the type of knowledge you now have. I have seen the shonks and sharks hauled off to jail, and too many of them continue to get away with their shady deals. And I've come to know that there will always be the shonks and sharks and it's up to us to arm ourselves well with knowledge, and protect ourselves by eliminating greed from our strategies.

Lucky for me there weren't many of the sharks around in my early days. I was so keen to get ahead I am sure I would have fallen victim to them. Or maybe I was just smart because I learned well from trusted sources — including how to smell a rat. I can certainly understand those of you who want it all now and want it all easily. But it simply doesn't work that way. Being greedy means we act with too little skill and that only ends in disaster.

After perfecting my rejuvenation strategy, I went after bigger fish. By this stage I had changed jobs and had a regular income coming in. Using the concept of 'highest and best use' I observed that there were some very big lots in Brisbane and that, with new council zoning, they were big enough to be cut up into two (sometimes more) blocks. This was long before anybody had coined the term 'splitters' and most agents seemed genuinely concerned that I would have too much mowing to do on such large blocks!

But I persisted, finding corner blocks that I could split into two, keeping the original wooden house on one and moving a cute colonial or Queenslander onto the second block. I would renovate both houses, keep one property and sell the other. Sometimes I would sell both if I needed the money. Back then you could buy a mover house for $20,000 (including restumping), and I was able to make $50,000 from each one I did.

With my job and properties, I was now earning over $200,000 a year (just three years after I had started) and I was finally free of debt, so financing became a bit easier. I was working seven days a week, sometimes up to 20 hours per day, but it all seemed pretty easy at the time.

This was still the early 1990s and the property market was (supposedly) dead, but nobody told me so I pressed on. Property seemed cheap and builders were keen to work at any price, so I turned my hand to small-scale developments. I would find a block of land, build a duplex and sell them both for profit, (still doing the odd paint and patch and splitter for income).

By this time the income was starting to flow really well and, with my newfound friends at the bank, I was actually able to keep more of the properties I rejuvenated. The property market started moving again and with my brief experience as a real-estate 'tycoon', I was well positioned to take advantage of it. Soon I was doing four-packs (blocks of four units), six-packs and larger. I made over $2 million in net profit in two years doing this. But beware: I blew *all* of that $2 million and then some in one development where I overstretched and made mistakes in just about everything imaginable. Fortunately, the properties I had held onto were growing well and already had a couple of million in equity in them so I was doing OK.

Then I moved to Sydney to start my own consulting business. Well, I had never seen anything like the Sydney property market! I remember searching for a house to live in and seeing two-bedroom hovels of apartments selling for more that I had just sold my oceanfront house in Brisbane for. I was amazed. In my Brisbane vernacular I once commented to an agent showing me a property: 'Half a million for a flat? That's ridiculous.'

Offended, she rapidly replied, 'We don't call them flats here darling, they're apartments.' Looked like a flat to me!

But my wealthy friends assured me prices were cheap and I should get in. I saw a rundown block of 12 flats (sorry, apartments) in Darling Point at a mortgagee's auction and in a moment of madness put in a bid. Turned out my bid was the only one on that day and consequently I owned a block of 'apartments'. Luckily there was a 12-week settlement because there was no way I could come up with the money in anything less. I put everything I had in Queensland on the market and, with that state's four-week settlement period and some fast talking at the bank, I was just able to scrape up enough to buy the Darling Point block.

Getting plans for renovations through council was a nightmare but, amazingly, just as I thought the project was becoming a disaster, a boom had started in Sydney and my units were suddenly prime, prime, property. Rents jumped even without the renovation and, after eight months, these units were cash-flow positive.

By the time I was ready to start work on them, prices for apartments in the area had more than doubled. I was able to sell four of the units and make enough to pay back my original loan. I then used my voting power on the body corporate to raise a special levy (I had advised the buyers of this before they signed) and proceeded with the renovation. After selling all the apartments, I tripled my money. I was a multi-millionaire in less than five years, from starting with nothing. (By the way, that single block would be worth over $17 million at the time of writing. If I had kept all the properties, I would have equity of almost $12 million in it now — a valuable lesson in buy and hold).

I looked around Sydney and thought that Elizabeth Bay was perfectly situated for prime property — just minutes from the city and with views of it; and with a good blend of wealthy and hip people living there who had a preference for apartment living. A one-bedder could be bought in this prime position for less than $150,000. As the market was now full tilt into a mini-boom, I leveraged up and I used my profits to buy just about everything that was selling. I remember at one auction I bought everything the agent had. He was flabbergasted. (And by the way, just in case you are getting disheartened with the 'cheap' prices I paid for all this property, I can assure you they *all* seemed expensive to me at the time, none were 'bargains' in that they were fair value at the time. *Every* property you buy will seem cheap in 10 years time!)

I really wanted to buy blocks (to repeat my previous success) but anything that looked like being available was well beyond my financing, so I bought as many individual apartments as I could. I asked a designer to produce a 'palette' (standard design with colours, finishes and fittings) and engaged a builder to supervise the renovations. As each property was finished and rose in value, I used the increased equity to buy another, and so my concept of 'leapfrogging' was born. The bank had given me a huge revolving line of credit and so, as more equity was added at the front, more credit was added at the back. This enabled me to fully take advantage of the boom.

I admit that if things had gone wrong or the boom had ended prematurely I would have had to slow down, but my enthusiasm, the boom and a bit of luck held. My properties were very popular. I kept as many as I could, selling one or two here and there to fund the shortfall between the rents and costs.

I also started investing in shares and commercial property trusts and used their higher yields to fund my cash-flow negative properties. This way I was able to keep even more of the properties.

At one stage, with all my companies and projects I owned 141 individual titles. *And it took me just seven years to pass the magic $10 million mark in property ownership!*

I used the 10th anniversary of buying my first property to add up my wins and losses. After just 10 years and a lot of hard work I had about $12 million in equity from my property portfolio. By using a combination of highest and best use, value adding, leverage, uniqueness, leap-frogging and ingenuity, I had made a fortune from nothing.

I have seen booms and profited from them. I have seen busts and profited from them too. Even though I've been investing for nigh on 15 years, I still consider myself a novice and that, more than anything keeps me interested, humble, active, and ready to learn.

I was already a property multi-millionaire by the time I started teaching others my methods. At first I thought it was very egotistical of me to teach others, and I didn't charge for this at all. Soon my little workshops become so popular I had to hire a venue and so start charging. More and more people came and I began to make money out of the workshops. Soon I had developed another 'hobby' into a successful business. Well before wealth-creation seminars got 'on the nose' in the early 2000s, 70,000 people had been through my seminars. Today I speak to over 10,000 people a year and tell them my 'secrets', which, of course, are not secrets at all now you've read this book.

I have seen friends and clients make a fortune in real estate and their lives change dramatically because of it.

Over those years I have bought and sold countless properties, and amassed a fortune by most people's standards in property. These days I buy whole blocks and renovate them to hold or sell, and I buy land for subdivision. I am always mindful of the possibilities of highest and best use, making hundreds of thousands, or even millions, of dollars in some deals for myself, my clients and investors, and business partners. I think up new ideas, plans and strategies as I go along and hope to emulate the successes of some of my wealthy friends, who have made tens of millions in single property deals. I'll let you know how I go!

While most of my property is leveraged, it is growing in equity by many millions of dollars each year. (In the last five years, no matter how hard I worked, and how successful my company became, my properties still earned more than me!). I have learned the hard way that the easiest way to make money out of property is to get as much of it as you can, as soon as you can, hold onto it and let the market do the rest. Everything else just boosts the kitty.

You don't need a lot of money and you don't need a big income to start. You just need to start, then follow a strategy.

My strategies were and are simple:

- By a quality property whenever you can.
- Add value to it.
- Allow it to grow in equity and income.
- Use increased equity and rent to fund another property.
- Don't overstretch.
- Do it again.
- Enjoy!

It's a simple formula and it works for those who are determined to make it work. And there are ample stories in this book (and literally thousands in my files which you haven't read) that prove it works.

I know of one bedridden client who is rarely able to move out of her house and only then with the assistance of at least two people. She was scared that when her parents died she would be institutionalised because her pension was not enough to employ somebody to look after her. Normally, if I had known, I would have discouraged somebody in her position from attending one of my seminars, because it's hard to justify the fees we charge for somebody in that financial position. But somehow she slipped through the net and bought a home study program consisting of tapes (remember those things), videos (hard to believe they used to exist too) and a manual and workbooks, which she studied from her bed.

She decided that she had just enough to put a deposit on a house (money left over from the meagre compensation she received from the car accident that had left her disabled) and start the leapfrogging strategy. Her parents went out looking at properties each Saturday, bringing home videotapes and Polaroids (yes, there were instant photos before digital cameras kids!) of the apartments they had seen. Just as everybody was about to give up, one was found in the right spot in the right condition at the right price.

She sent her parents to the auction, directed them how to bid down the phone and ended up buying her first investment property. She let her fingers do the walking and hired builders through the phone, determined to do as much as possible from her bed. Finally, the apartment was ready. Before it was tenanted, she was able to manage a field trip to see her brand new, fully renovated investment. She told me that she wept tears of joy.

She soon realised that banks were not the friends of bedridden people on a disability pension and, after reading my book *Wealth Magic*, paying particular attention to the chapter on 'The Law of Universal Convergence', she started a cottage industry buying and selling things through the auction sites on the Internet. She now has a regular income better than most households and doesn't move more than 1 metre most days!

I wish I could report to you that she has made $10 million in property like me but she hasn't. What she has done is to buy five investment properties in six years worth just less than $1.4 million). They are all cash-flow positive. She has about $500,000 in equity in them and she knows that, by the time her parents are ready to retire in 10 years, she will be worth close to $2 million net, with a net income from her properties of about $60,000 a year, indexed and growing for life. With the income from additional properties she plans to acquire, she hopes she will have enough to fund her care for the rest of her life. And you know what? I reckon she'll make it. Whenever I get sooky and think making money out of property is hard, I think of her, give myself a good kick up the bum and get on with it.

So now it's up to you. You can either sit and wait for the Lotto truck to back up your driveway or you can get on with it and make yourself wealthy.

I suggest you go do it! Good luck and have fun!

Lesson

You don't need a lot of money to start getting rich in property. You just need to start. The magic of property is all around us.

$0 TO $9 MILLION IN PROPERTY IN SIX YEARS WITH SEA CHANGE

I think my first course with Peter Spann was in 1999. Back then I was working in the corporate world as a director of a major national retailer. I was earning good money but not necessarily doing what I wanted.

Since then, my life has changed in many ways due to Peter's ideas, and the story I tell here is really only the surface.

In 2003 I retired and I am now investing full-time. I have accumulated about $9 million worth of property, with equity of approximately $3.5 million, and I consider myself financially free.

Peter's knowledge, skill and charisma have made a difference to my life and to the many people I have shared his strategies with. And it is obvious that in his life, the greatest kick he gets is making a difference. Peter should be very proud of his achievements because he really has made a difference.

Thank you, Peter, for your experience, knowledge and generosity.

– MARK, PARK ORCHARDS

Epilogue

I love writing. Some people call me a natural-born storyteller. I prefer the more Australian description — larrikin.

And as a storyteller I'm entitled to a storyteller's licence, which allows me to embellish here and there, change a detail or two, add a character, drop boring incidentals and wrap it up in pretty paper to make it a gem. And I have done that liberally in my anecdotes.

But before you get disillusioned and start questioning the veracity of the book, the principles you have read, the strategies and successes they have produced, and *all* the stories from my clients are 100% true. The strategies have worked for me and they have worked for thousands of people who have listened to me as their own 'Wealthy Friend', taken that wisdom which was passed through me to them, and acted upon it, securing a small piece of whatever property dreams they may have.

My favourite place in Sydney is the (rather tacky, revolving tourist-trap) restaurant at the top of Centre Point Tower. I often take my clients there and explain to them, as we circle around, that it is my favourite spot because from there I can see all the property that I own in Sydney and all the property that I *want* to own!

I hope my love of and enthusiasm for property is obvious in this book and a little or a lot of it has rubbed off on you. No doubt many people who have heard my message or read my books have not done anything. And that is a great tragedy because there is one thing I *have* learned and that is that wealth is within the grasp of everybody using these strategies. I cannot promise you that everything will go smoothly, but I can promise that if you stick at it you will be much, much better off than you are today. Use the wealthy friends that come into your life from time to time — mentors, teachers, successful people, books, seminars, magazine articles, and your own 'higher' self to teach you.

You'll be pleased to know that I still buy property today. No doubt you'll see me at an auction one day and I'll notice you beating me with my own auction techniques! Come up to me, say hello, tell me your story or send it to me in an email. I *love* getting comments.

And finally, everybody wants to know: 'Is Pauline's hair really that perfect?' Oh yes, I've *never* seen a strand out of place, and she is still one of Sydney's best, most successful and gracious real-estate agents. It's always been a pleasure to do business with her.

You all have my very best wishes on your journey to wealth and happiness.

Recommended Reading

It is hard to believe that when I started there was, to my knowledge, just one book on investing in property in Australia written by an Australian author (Jan Somers). I can assure you that if the quantity of books that are available today were available to me when I started, I would have made fewer mistakes and would have been far more profitable.

The problem today, it seems, is not lack of quantity, but rather discerning quality. I may not agree with everything the authors of the following books say, but I know that I can definitely stand behind my recommendation to you of the quality of the information in these books, especially the 'must-haves' and 'highly recommended'. The others I have provided because they add more depth to your understanding of a topic or provide a counter view to some of my points that may be valid in some circumstances.

Whatever happens, expanding your mind and making use of the knowledge of these people can only expand the 'wealthy friends' you have in your life. Enjoy!

* Highly recommended
** A must-have

Graham J. Airey, *Buying and Selling Property in a Nutshell*, Wrightbooks, Brighton, Vic., 2001.

* Graham J. Airey, *The Property Investor's Handbook*, Wrightbooks, Brighton, Vic., 1998.

** Wayne Berry, *How to Get the Be$t Deal Every Time: Without Rubbing People the Wrong Way!*, Information Australia, Melbourne, 2000.

* Wayne Berry, *Negotiating in the Age of Integrity*, Wrightbooks, North Brighton, Vic., 1995.

* Mark Bouris, *Wealth Wizard*, Hardie Grant, South Yarra, Vic., 2002.

Peter Cerexhe, *Smarter Property Improvements: Ways to Maximise Returns by Transforming Your Property*, Allen & Unwin, Crows Nest, NSW, 2004.

* Deepak Chopra, *The Seven Spiritual Laws of Success: A Practical Guide to the Fulfillment of Your Dreams*, Bantam, Sydney, 1996.

** George S. Clason, *The Richest Man in Babylon* (first published in 1926), Penguin, Ringwood, Vic., 1991.

James W. Coghlan, *Capital Gains Tax: An Australian Investor's Guide to Wealth Maintenance*, Wrightbooks, Elsternwick, Vic., 2000.

Tony Compton, *Rental Property and Taxation: An Investor's Guide*, Wrightbooks, Brighton, Vic., 2001.

* Stephen R. Covey, *The Seven Habits of Highly Effective People: Restoring the Character Ethic*, Business Library, Melbourne, 1990.

* Martin S. Fridson, *How to Be a Billionaire: Proven Strategies from the Titans of Wealth*, Wiley, New York, 2000.

* Mchael Gilding, *Secrets of the Super Rich*, HarperCollins, Pymble, NSW, 2002.

Paul Hanna, *You Can Do It!*, Penguin, Ringwood, Vic., 1997.

** Napoleon Hill, *Think and Grow Rich: The Famous Andrew Carnegie Formula for Money-Making* (first published in 1937), Wilshire Book Co, California, 1999.

Tim Hewat, *Super Safe Investing with Syndicates and Listed Property Trusts*, Wrightbooks, Brighton, Vic.

Vivienne James, *The Woman's Money Book*, Anne O'Donovan, Melbourne, 2000.

Neil Jenman, *Don't Sign Anything!*, Simon & Schuster.

Neil Jenman, *Real Estate Mistakes*, Rowley Publications, 2000.

Robert T. Kiyosaki, *Rich Dad, Poor Dad*, Tech Press Inc, Arizona, 1997.

** John McGrath, *Most Valuable Lesson I have Learned: Over 100 Success Concepts to Change Your Life*, HarperCollins, Pymble, NSW, 2002.

** John McGrath, *You Inc.: How to Attract Amazing Success in Your Life and Business*, HarperCollins, Pymble, NSW, 2003.

** John McGrath, *You Don't Have to be Born Brilliant: How to Design a Magnificent Life*, Hodder Headline, Sydney, 2000.

Jim McKnight, *Ordinary Millionaires*, Freehold Press, Oatley, NSW, 2002.

Edward Mundie, *The Beginner Renovator: A Guide to the Repair and Alteration of Houses*, Hyland House, South Yarra, Vic., 1987.

Richard Reed, *Reverse Mortgages: Unlocking the Potential of Your Home*, Wrightbooks, Milton, Qld, 2004.

* N. E. Renton, *Negative Gearing: A Plain English Guide to Leverage for Share and Property Investors*, Wrightbooks, Brighton, Vic., 1998.

E. James Rohn, *The Five Major Pieces to the Life Puzzle*, Brolga Publishing, Ringwood, Vic., 1991.

* E. James Rohn, *The Seasons of Life*, Brolga Publishing, Ringwood, Vic., 1994.

* Jim Rohn, *Seven Strategies for Wealth and Happiness: Power Ideas from America's Foremost Business Philosopher*, Prima, New York, 1996.

Martin Roth and Chris Lang, *How Investing in Commercial Property Really Works*, John Wiley & Sons, Camberwell, Vic., 2003.

* Terry Ryder, *Confessions of a Real Estate Agent*, Wrightbooks, Elsternwick, Vic., 2001.

Terry Ryder, *Property Smart: Learn the Rules of the Real Estate Game*, Wrightbooks, Elsternwick, Vic., 2002.

Barbara Sher, *I Could Do Anything If I Only Knew What It Was: Discover What You Really Want, and How to Get It*, Hodder & Stoughton, Sydney, 1995.

* Jan Somers, *Building Wealth in Changing Times*, Somerset Financial Services, Cleveland, Qld, 1994.

* Jan Somers, *Building Wealth: Story by Story*, Somerset Financial Services, Cleveland, Qld, 1998.

 ** Jan Somers, *Building Wealth Through Investment Property*, Somerset Financial Services, Cleveland, Qld, 1992.

Richard Spencer, *Private Lending Made Public*, Wrightbooks, Elsternwick, Vic., 1999.

Allan Staines, *The Australian Renovator's Manual*, Pinedale Press, Caloundra, Qld, 1996.

Sam Vannutini, *Renovate For Profit*, self-published, www.renovateforprofit.com

Denis Waitley, *Seeds of Greatness: The Best-Kept Secrets of Total Success*, Pocket Books, New York, 1986.

Monique Wakelin & Richard Wakelin, *Streets Ahead: How to Make Money From Residential Property*, Hodder, Sydney, 2002.

Peter Waxman, *Investing in Residential Property: Understanding the Australian Market*, John Wiley & Sons, Camberwell, Vic., 2004.

Mark Wehse, *Home Loans — A No-nonsense Guide*, Wrightbooks, 2001.

** Noel Whittaker, *Golden Rules of Wealth*, Simon & Schuster, Sydney, 1999.

* Noel Whittaker, *Making Money Made Simple*, Simon & Schuster, East Roseville, NSW, 2000.

* Noel Whittaker, *More Money with Noel Whittaker*, Simon & Schuster, East Roseville, NSW, 1992.

Acknowledgements

I have found, over my life, that whenever I acknowledge those who helped me on my journey more success flows into my life. And yet, even with such a philosophy, it still amazes me how few times I stop to simply say thank you. These pages are a small step in remedying that. Thank you …

To those of you who contributed success stories (included or not) for this book — faxes, emails, letters and happy sheets over the years documenting the extraordinary achievements you have made using my strategies and others to build your wealth. It is little known that during my darkest hours one of my favourite 'pick-me-ups' is to go to our archives, which contain literally thousands of your stories, and read them to renew my spirit. I truly hope that you find all the success you so richly deserve.

To my best friend, Leisl Baker, who has been there for the whole story and more; who has helped me to transcend my own weaknesses and ego to realise it is more important to enjoy what you do than to have every material thing in the world. (I still have an ego the size of the whole outdoors but with a little help I can keep it in check.)

To my mum and dad, whose lessons in life I am only just starting to appreciate.

To Shona Mackin, who provided me with the love, care, attention, (food) and space to write this text, and for being the most pleasant of company during those moments in between.

To Philippa (Pip) Bond, who serves as my greatest mentor and teacher by her wisdom, knowledge and deeds.

To Patti Baker, my very first property joint-venture partner, who, without any evidence or track record on my part, put her property on the line for my first development.

To Ben Doyle, who shared with me a dream that we could build a property company that could mix it with the best, create value for our investors and buyers, and go about things in a new and exciting way. Thank you for your enthusiasm and excitement at building that dream, and may your REINSW (Real Estate Institute of New South Wales) 'Rookie of the Year' award be one of only many great acknowledgements and accomplishments along your journey to success.

To Wayne 'Top Gun' Berry, Ian 'Sparky the Wonder Dog' Low, and Paul 'Funny' Dunn, who taught me how to negotiate, sell, and buy.

To John McGrath, who sets a new standard for customer service and sales success for real-estate agents in Australia, and who, apart from being the best in the game, has stood to remind me that it is possible to find honesty, integrity and vision in a game that is often played by shonks, sharks and schemers.

To the true professionals in the real-estate game that I have had the pleasure to do business with — including Pauline Goodyer, Gary Sands, Robert Freeman, and Josephine Johnston-Rowell — may your own personal love of real estate and unwavering standards of ethics and customer service always keep you at the top of the game.

To my publisher, Helen Littleton, editor, Mary Rennie and all the wonderful folk at HarperCollins Australia, who make a work like this appear on the bookshelves; and, just as importantly, all those of you who bought my first book and made it a bestseller — this one certainly would not have happened without your support.

To Fletcher Potanin, Sooz Blythin, Sue McGary, Donna Anderson, Terry Steer, Ross and Claire Bennett, Rob Jamieson, Sean Cowan, Margit Jeppeson, David Leviston, Jane Milton, Karen Booth, Tim Murray and Kaaren Peterson, who took the time to read and critique my first draft of this work.

To all those agents, vendors, buyers, bidders, builders and tradies whose antics over the last 15 years could have filled 10 of these books; who have helped and hindered me in my path to property success; and without whom I would have nothing to write about.

To the authors, teachers, presenters, mentors, and others who have acted as my Wealthy Friends across the years.

To most of my competitors in the seminar field, who — through their antics, schemes tricks and scams, which have sunk what used to be a noble profession to the levels of snake oil salesmen — have helped in making me, my seminars, and my company look fabulous; and to those few out there with integrity, quality strategy and good intentions, for being good enough to keep me at my best.

To those critics who, without care, bundled the good in with the bad, and made many afraid to seek knowledge, for the strength and courage you have fired in me to stick to my convictions, and for the improvements I have made to my strategies and my company because you were there.

To the authorities and agencies who have protected the consumer from the more voracious of the above, I thank you for your vigilance. May we others always stand above that criticism by the strength and quality of our words and actions.

To all my seminar and workshop graduates for your wonderful support, both from a business perspective and also a personal perspective. It is not always easy being a teacher, and harder still when you are pushing the envelope — thank you for listening, implementing and being so successful. You are all my best defence against those who want to criticise.

To my fabulous clients, who trust me every day to manage their money and manage it well. As a financial adviser, I understand the enormous responsibility of this and I promise I will continue to do my very best to bring you wealth.

To my syndicate partners, investors and participants, who have shown the utmost faith in me by handing over their hard-earned cash to ventures and developments on the basis of a dream and unbridled enthusiasm. May we continue to work together for many years.

To my amazing team at Freeman Fox and the other companies I own, for being an inspiration in good times and in bad. May we all continue to share the dream of bringing ethical, high-performance investment techniques to everyday people.

And to all of you who believe in dreams — may they come true in the best of ways for all of you.

Endnotes

1   The Key to Wealth, the Key to Success and the Secrets of Money Magnetism
    are explained in detail in my first book, *Wealth Magic: From Broke to Multi-*
    Millionaire in Just 7 Years, HarperCollins*Publishers*, Sydney 2001.
2   For example, the company Australian Property Monitors, www.apm.com.au
3   Luckily you don't have to do this by hand these days. Due to the wonder of
    the Internet these reports are now available as electronic data with inbuilt
    report generators, or you can simply plot them into any spreadsheet and create
    the report you like.
4   Australian Property Monitors (www.apm.com.au) is an ideal source.
5   At time of writing these cost $150 to $200.
6   I wish I had bought it — an unrenovated three-bedroom unit in that building
    recently sold for $670,000 just eight years later!
7   Little did we both know that he was indeed way ahead of his time and many
    years later there would be dozens of TV shows dedicated to renovating, and
    even a whole lifestyle channel. Back then the whole idea of renovating for
    profit was revolutionary. Today books like this, magazines, and even TV
    shows should be enough to convince you that anybody can do it — you can
    do it — and profit too.
8   This is covered in tax ruling TR 97/23 Income Tax: Deductions for Repairs,
    released 3 December 1997. My simplistic interpretation of the tax ruling is as
    follows:
        A renovation/rejuvenation of the type mentioned in this strategy would
    normally comprise of some expenses which would be classified as repairs and
    some which would be classified as capital.
        If the work is carried out immediately after the purchase of the property
    and before the commencement of income-producing activity then the repair
    expense is likely to be treated as a capital expenditure and therefore not
    deductible at all but added to the cost base of the property and therefore
    deductible upon the sale of the property. The capital expenditure will be
    depreciable from the time the income-producing activity commences, i.e. once
    the property is rented out.
        On the other hand if the renovation/rejuvenation is carried out after a
    'reasonable period' of the commencement of the income-producing activity
    then the repair expenditure would be fully deductible and the capital
    expenditure would be depreciable. What is considered a 'reasonable period' is
    not clear and will vary depending on each individual circumstance. In any
    event, it is handy for your property to have brought in some income prior to

you carrying out any refurbishment, as this will maximise your opportunities in claiming costs.

The capital component of the renovation is depreciable but investors must be advised to obtain a quantity surveyor's tax report to support their claim for depreciation.

Be aware that the tax office is constantly changing the rules on all forms of investing, so before you rely on anything in this book or any other guide, ensure you are fully up to date with the law by consulting your tax professional or accountant.

Depreciation is available to any property irrespective of age. Plant and equipment can be revalued based on the purchase price of the property. For Residential property built between July 1985 and September 1987, a deduction of 4% per annum is available on the Division 43 component of a property (Division 43 = structural component of property, e.g., bricks and mortar).

9   The tax office recognises only certain professionals within the construction industry as having the relevant qualifications to estimate the cost of building components for tax depreciation. Quantity surveyors are recognised by the ATO as having expert qualifications and experience to produce depreciation schedules. A quantity surveyor can be engaged prior to renovation to revalue existing plant and again after renovation to take maximum advantage of the depreciation available on the property. The fee for the preparation of the tax depreciation schedule is tax deductible.

The Australian Tax office allows up to four previous years to be amended where the maximum depreciation hasn't been claimed. Your quantity surveyor should structure your reports to facilitate the back claiming of previous years tax returns.

Kitchen cupboards, bathroom vanities and built-in wardrobes are not depreciable as plant & equipment. They form part of the structural component of the property, thus Division 43 — depreciable at 2.5% pa. All plant items with a cost of $1,000 or less can be depreciated at 37.5% pa. Plant items that form part of a set with a total set cost of less than $300 can be written off at 100% in the year of acquisition. For example, smoke alarms: 2 x $145 = $290, thus 100% deduction in first year.

10 The form is currently called an 'Application For Variation of Amounts Required to be Withheld Under PAYG Income Tax Withholding', or form 1515.

11 Negative gearing is more effective for individuals unless the individuals are in business, and it is effective for the business assets to be held in a company or a trust. In any event you should never hold assets in the name of the business you are trading in. Always use a separate entity.

Generally for PAYE earners, once the negative gearing benefits 'run out' there may be an advantage to purchasing property in a company or trust. Losses cannot be distributed from a trust, and so the company/trust must be able to earn some form of income in order to claim the tax deductions. Seek the advice of your accountant.

12 Try www.cannex.com.au

13 This used to be called the CRAA — the Credit Reference Association of Australia. It is now called Baycorp Advantage.

14 When you read my next book on the share market, you'll realise your share investments could be an ideal source of income while your properties continue to provide you with tax benefits, but that's a whole 'nother book.

15 Try www.realestate.com.au or www.property.com.au

About Peter Spann

Peter Spann started out with nothing and set out to learn everything he could about wealth-creation and success. Through investing and running successful businesses he turned that knowledge into wealth that runs into many millions.

In the process, he has accumulated a wealth of experience. Through trial and error, he has learned what works and what doesn't. And it's this practical experience that he will shares with you in everything he does.

And unlike many others...

Peter Spann made his wealth through *investing*. In 1994, encouraged by friends to teach them his techniques he presented his first seminar. Since then, he has presented seminars to more than 250,000 people.

Peter Spann continues to stand out as a uniquely successful, independent source of quality investment strategies.

It is his amazingly practical and simple approach to wealth creation that makes his approach so successful. He breaks down all the complex processes into simple-to-understand, easy-to-implement strategies that are so compellingly simple you practically can't help but do them and become wealthier.

Those strategies enabled him to go from 'broke to multimillionaire' in only seven years and, as his 'Success Stories' (get a free copy by phoning 1800 000 369) prove, these strategies are having a profound impact on many more people.

Entrepreneur, Businessman, Investor, Developer, Trader, International Speaker and Philanthropist

Peter owns a number of successful companies whose primary activities include property development, portfolio management, pharmacy and health care, importing and information technology.

He is a highly successful property developer, options trader and share investor and uses the income from these pursuits to fund his leisure activities which include flying, yachting and motor racing and extensive travel.

Today, along with his own wealth, he manages many millions of his clients funds as well.

He is renowned for his generosity and particularly favours children's charities.

He has been featured in magazine and newspaper articles and on TV.

Peter's overwhelming message is clear: "If I can do it, so can you!"

To join the growing list of people making millions using Peter's strategies call his company Freeman Fox on **1800 000 369** for more information.

High Performance Investment Techniques from Multi-Millionaire Financial Adviser and Educator - Peter Spann

If you're interested in creating an income stream that will free you from working forever – and if you're interested in creating this income stream fast – then the Wealth Magic series of seminars could be the most intensely challenging and valuable experience you may ever have the opportunity to be a part of.

Peter Spann's company Freeman Fox's presents the Wealth Magic seminars which provide independent investors with an unbiased, quality source of information on property, shares and superannuation to assist them in planning a wealthy future.

The seminars achieve this through a coordinated and graduated program that introduces people to investment strategies that are researched, compiled and devised by multi-millionaire investor, trader and educator, Peter Spann. Since he began educating people about their wealth prospects in 1994, Peter has built a reputation of integrity and innovation in wealth creation.

Plan for the future

Freeman Fox's Wealth Magic seminars are designed to teach you how to invest, how to plan for your future and how to increase the returns and profits from your investments.

They use a combination of strategies that vary from conservative to high leverage. Not only are the strategies fully explained, but so are the risks, allowing you to devise an investment strategy that protects your assets while at the same time increases your returns.

Intelligent Investments

Freeman Fox's Wealth Magic seminars provide their graduates with clear, simple, and highly effective investment and trading strategies that can be easily implemented by the average investor.

The strategies presented at Wealth Magic have been comprehensively tested and refined, originally by Peter Spann himself, then by Freeman Fox's panel of experts in their fields and since by literally thousands of graduates who have successfully implemented them.

You benefit by gaining access to expertly devised strategies at a fraction of the cost it would take to hire them yourself.

Freeman Fox's Wealth Magic seminars package a number of little-known strategies, used and implemented by professional investors and traders, into a format that can be used and understood by ordinary people.

Call 1800 000 369 or go to www.freemanfox.com.au for more information.

The 3 Cornerstones of Wealth Magic's Successful Investment Approach

1.   Build Assets

The wealthy know that quality assets held for the long term are the key to wealth. The Wealth Magic strategy allows for the building of a strong and comprehensive portfolio of quality property and shares.

Held for the long term, these assets build up equity and provide for a stable future for you as an investor. They can later be used to generate an income.

2.   Generate Income

At some stage you may want to stop working or supplement your income from your investments. The Wealth Magic strategy uses income generated through commercial property trusts, share investment and leverage through basic options strategies to generate income.

3.   Protect

All investment strategies carry risk. The higher the return, the higher the risk, so *all* investment strategies need risk management.

The Wealth Magic strategy presents you with various levels of risk, leverage and the risk management strategies you need to protect your investments. The Wealth Magic strategy also allows for share investments to be protected from downturn by various means, including using options to hedge your portfolio.

The Wealth Magic strategy alerts you to appropriate insurances and other methodologies of providing for debt repayment and a legacy.

The Wealth Magic Approach to Building Wealth and Boosting Income

The wealthy know that they have to take some calculated risks to ensure maximum growth, but also that they need quality risk management strategies to ensure their assets are protected.

Our professional financial advisers can devise an investment strategy suitable to your needs based on the wealth strategies of Peter Spann.

Or you can choose to invest in one of our Managed Investments that use Peter Spann's high performance investing methodologies.

To discover more about this unique investment philosophy contact:

FREEMAN FOX

WEALTH STRATEGIES FOR INDEPENDENT INVESTORS

FREECALL:
1800 000 369

WWW.FREEMANFOX.COM.AU